Matt Preston
COOK
BOOK

For Caroline and Donna – good friends and inspiring women – thank you for starting me off on this amazing food road.

Matt Preston

COOK BOOK

187 RECIPES

that will make you

INCREDIBLY POPULAR

plum.   Pan Macmillan Australia

DIRTY DOUBLE
CENTREFOLD!
*Lurking somewhere
around page 176*

Contents

FOREWORD
by Andrew Valentine Kirwan
of the Middle Temple, Esq.*

There is no want of cookery books in the principal languages of Europe and least of all in the English language, in which even in our own generation several hundreds have been compiled and published.

Cookery books are, for the most part, copies of each other; and the first cookery book is only the most original because we cannot trace the plagiarism beyond the period when printing was invented. The plagiarism may be tracked, as a wounded man by his blood, from 1470 to 1863.

The compilers of any new cookery book should lay no claim to originality. They should avail themselves though never servilely, of the labours of nearly all their predecessors and by collation, comparison, addition, experience and discoveries endeavour to improve on works already in print.

It is desireable that we should learn much from our neighbours. In any new cookery book, there should be given within a reasonable compass a short system of French, and a compendium of foreign, cookery. Neither the Spanish, the Portuguese, the Russian nor the Polish cookery are deserving of general commendation but a few national dishes and soups are worthy of attention and adoption. It would also be advisable to introduce a chapter in any coming cookery book on Anglo-Indian cookery. Mulligatawney soup, and curries and pillaus are exceedingly wholesome. From the Turkish and Indian cookery we may adopt more than for the Russian, the pillau and kabobs of Turkey are very relishing and so are the fish and vegetable curries of India – the pish poshes, pepperpots and cutcharees and country captains.

This volume – a household book on the subject of dinners, desserts, and on foods in general – is the result of reading, observation, and a great deal of experience in foreign countries. During a life now nearly prolonged to threescore years, the author has been a diner out of some magnitude, and, as far as means allowed, a giver of dinners. The work presented is in certain parts historical, anecdotical, gossiping and somewhat discursive; but the main object of the author has been to introduce well-informed and sensible people to adopt all that is good in the excellent cookery of our neighbours without abandoning the best of our customs, or the simplicity of our simple food.

Anthony Valentine Kirwan of the Middle Temple, Esq., 1864

* Author's note: A V Kirwan is my distant cousin. He is the author of *Host and Guest* (1864), a rather fine tome on food, drink and the art of entertaining. The above was lifted directly from *Host and Guest*, and while I don't share his views on Spanish, Portugese, Russian and Polish cookery, I do think many of his observations from 150 years ago ring remarkably true today.

INTRODUCTION

Why, thank you, Cousin Andrew … and even though you wrote these words for the Foreword 150 years ago, it's clear that certain food truths remain self-evident no matter what else may have changed around them.

I first came across A V Kirwan's little-known book on cooking and entertaining, *Host and Guest* (1864), in my grandfather's library. (OK, it was just a bookcase at the top of the stairs but 'library' sounds so much more Lemony Snicket-y and therefore much betterer.) It freaked me out to discover that this long-gone relative had trod the same rare and unusual path as me of a gentleman food writer. It could have been much worse. Dueling and sheep-stealing were the other loves passed down in the Kirwan genetic code.

Yet, what was even more amazing was how insightful and relevant his writing remained. Here was a man advising readers to roast their coffee fresh every day; describing cookery as 'an experimental and practical art', a phrase that would please the likes of Heston Blumenthal and Massimo Bottura; and advising that the secret to good cooking was to taste everything a lot to ensure the correct balance of flavour. His borrowed line 'the finger of a good cook should alternate perpetually between the stew pan and his mouth' is a personal favourite, although I baulk at the associated idea of purging your cook regularly to ensure their palate stays fresh!

As this book is published on the sesquicentenary – that's the 150th anniversary – of the publication of *Host and Guest*, I've given my book an equally simple and obvious title: *Cook Book*. It is, after all, a book written by a cook for other cooks. There is no hyperbole in the title because I don't believe that you'll need to be a gifted cook, or even a passable cook, to have success with the simple recipes that follow.

It also seemed fitting not only to litter this book with A V Kirwan's wit and wisdom, but also to start by offering my thoughts on how to be a better host and guest.

BEING A GUEST – OR, WHAT I KNOW ABOUT MANNERS

Manners are the rent we pay for our little space on this planet. Manners form a sort of contract between us all that sets the rules for acceptable forms of behaviour in a number of social situations – especially when visiting others or at the table. The aim is to ensure that we don't stab each other in a flurry of imagined insults and bad fork etiquette.

I really don't care how you hold your soup spoon or whether you tilt the soup bowl towards or away from you; for me, manners are about fitting in and, more importantly, about respect. They are not about providing reasons for people to look down on others.

While manners are always a bit of a minefield, here's a selection of the 24 things I reckon we should expect of each other when eating together or eating out:

- You can put one of your elbows on the table assuming a) you don't slouch and b) two elbows never rest there simultaneously. This makes you look surly and brooding, which is not a good look unless you are Channing Tatum.

- Never whistle at the waiter, your staff, or your mum when you want something – unless you are a bluebird, in which case it is allowed.

- Always wash your hands before a meal and use your right hand to eat with if you are in India, the Middle East or the USA.

- Don't start eating until the person who cooked the meal sits down – unless they rudely take a telephone call from their friend halfway through serving (please take note certain mothers-in-law, everywhere!).

- Electrical Equipment. None to be used at the table, whether it's a tablet, phone, game or mini TV – no matter how important you think you are. Reading is not allowed unless it is a newspaper AND it is breakfast AND your partner doesn't need help making the school lunches, finding that library book, or wrestling the littlest one into their school uniform.

- Don't talk with your mouth full or chew with your mouth open.

- Moderate your tone. No one really wants to hear about your latest pay rise or the graphic details of Aunt Selma's recent operation. And it sounds so much more conspiratorial and fascinatingly salacious when things like this are discussed in hushed tones.

- Any form of expulsion of air that isn't a word, a laugh, a giggle, or a sigh is not acceptable at the table. So no burping unless you are dead sure that this is the part of India/China/the Middle East/Taiwan where this really is a sign of appreciation of a great feed.
- Don't wave your cutlery around no matter how much more dramatic this conducting makes your story. Following this rule is an easy way to avoid stabbing your neighbours in the nose with your fork.
- Use the cutlery provided – even if you think the original Neapolitan way of eating spaghetti by lifting it high with your right hand and then dangling it into your mouth seems so much more authentic, and easier than curling it on a fork.
- Don't play with your food, or with your cutlery.
- Don't season your food until AFTER you've tasted it.
- Eat with small bites, slowly and, above all, quietly. Occasional small and involuntary grunts of pleasure are allowed if the food is especially good. You can slurp noodles or soup if you are Korean or Japanese.
- Don't double dip.
- Use bread to wipe your plate but not your knife, fingers or tongue. You can only eat off your knife if you are a rebellious top chef who doesn't care what others think.
- When we eat we give our host visual clues to what we want to happen next. That's why you should close your menus when you are ready to order at a restaurant and why putting your knife and fork together (blade facing inwards) is important, as it lets everyone know you are finished. Placing them at 6.30, 5.25 or 4.20 are all acceptable.
- When eating with people you don't know, ask them as many questions as they ask you, but never pry. You must also listen to their answers! Religion, sex and politics are off limits; at least until after dessert.
- Don't eat anything off a dining companion's plate unless invited to. This rule is obviously null and void if eating with siblings, in which case stealing is allowed – assuming you don't get caught doing it.
- Don't ever use your napkin as a handkerchief.
- Drink from the glasses to your right and eat the bread roll on the plate to your left.
- Don't set fire to the table settings unless you are dining with the High Chancellor of Denmark. Then it becomes an amusing anecdote to bore your grandkids with. I speak from experience.
- Don't wear hats or sunglasses at the table unless you a) are a woman at a Melbourne Cup lunch or similar; b) are a balding man who is cripplingly embarrassed by his dreadful hair replacement treatment that makes him look like your Barbie that time you gave her a haircut; c) have a terrible drug problem that your eyes would betray.
- Always say please.
- Always say thank you, please!

All these rules on manners can be reduced down even further, to just two words. For me, manners are about *showing respect*. For your other diners, for the cook, for your elders, for the culture that you are a part of, for the meal, and even for the beast you are eating.

50 RULES FOR HOSTING THE PERFECT DINNER WITH FRIENDS

'We're having a few people over for dinner.' It sounds so simple and by rights it is. Just pick an interesting mob of people and ply with them with food and alcohol to get the conversation going around the table. But, as is so often the way, even the calmest waters can hide dangerous reefs on which your dreams of a fun night can run aground.

The Six General Rules

1. This dinner you are having is all about your guests. You aren't a restaurant, they aren't critics. The only similarity is that you must do everything in your power to make them feel at home and help everyone have a good time – including yourself! Basically, don't show off unless you can nail it.

2. While it's great to catch up with a couple of friends over a bowl of carbonara, if I am going to the trouble of organising a proper dinner then I want between eight and a dozen guests. The main questions to ask yourself are how many guests do you have chairs for and how big is the table? Also, if you've only got eight good glasses and eight sets of cutlery then don't invite 10 people. Oh, and don't do a soup and a dessert if you've only got 10 bowls! It's such a bore to have to wash up mid-party.

3. Include a single person. We all have friends who are single, post-divorce, or who are sensibly unwilling to go out with a substandard mate. I'm not afraid of odd numbers. In fact, I think it can mix things up nicely.

4. A dinner is really about showing your guests respect. You do this by showing that you've made an effort for them – even if that's just by serving them spag bol and making the effort to clean the dunny!

5. Don't call it a dinner party. 'Having friends round' has far less pretentious connotations. Dinner parties are something that happened in the eighties, with the hostess in a long, flowing chiffon number – and with the hostess actually calling herself a 'hostess'.

6. Always imagine your guests are coming an hour early. This leaves you time for a bath, a drinkie and a chance to kiss your partner and tell them they look gorgeous. Remember, you set the mood of the party. You are the mortar that holds it all together. So you want to feel relaxed, positive and in control. PS. If it takes you an hour to get ready, imagine your guests are arriving 90 minutes early!

The 23 Rules About the Food

1. It's not about the money you spend, it's about the care you take. I've had friends round and spent $10 on food and it's been a rip-roaring success. I've spent $100 and it's been a disaster. You just need to do something special like taking the time to bake a dessert or pick a recipe that uses cheaper cuts of meat cleverly.

2. It's not about the food. I'll happily sit down to a table with toast and pots of baked beans done three ways – curried, smoky BBQ and classic – if the company is good.

3. Once again: Don't Show Off! Plan your menu so that you're only motoring in third gear. That way, if problems occur you can sort them, and you'll have time to make the table look gorgeous – and then yourself!

4. Make three lists: what you need to buy, what you need to do in the kitchen and what you need to do in the house. Having a shopping list, a prep list and a chore list makes it far easier to delegate tasks to partners who otherwise struggle to make themselves useful.

5. Don't forget to put BBQ gas, booze and other drinks, too much ice, and toilet paper on that shopping list.

6. Don't try something new. Do a crowd-pleasing classic or a recipe you know you can nail and your guests will love. This is important, this one. Remember, a good burger is always better than a bad fillet steak.

7. When you are planning the menu, serve as many things as possible that can be prepped ahead. You want to spend time with your guests not alone in the kitchen. Think desserts like chocolate mousse, panna cotta or trifle – or huge bowls of crunchy salads (just remember to dress them at the table).

8. I love using braises, tagines or stews because they'll hold in the oven until I need them. Resting big hunks of grilled or roasted meat can also buy you a good 15 minutes to half an hour with guests.

9. Family-style platters are easier than plating up individual dishes and give good theatre to the table.

10. Organise your fridge so you have loads of spare space for those platters and other stuff. This might mean putting beer, wine and champagne into a bucket or sink with some of that extra ice I told you to get. There is nothing worse than trying to cram things into an over-full fridge.

11. Think seasonal – it's cheaper and less needs to be done to produce that is perfectly ripe.

12. Some of your guests will have dietary requirements or may just be fussy. Ask them that when you invite them over and factor this into your planning. If you've got veggos in the mix then a selection of salads and grilled meat is an easier option to customise to them than a casserole.

13. Don't dress stuff like salads before sitting down, no matter how tempting. Always dress at the table (unless it's potato salad).

14. Think of a balanced menu. If it's hot, temper the amount of heavy sauces, carbs and red meat you serve in favour of crisp salads and seafood. And remember that serving size is just as important. A full serve of

chocolate pudding is perfect for winter, but reducing it by a third and serving with some fresh raspberries and ice cream means it will work for summer too. (OK, so this is self-serving as well as self-saucing. I'm trying to ensure that people will think to serve self-saucing chocolate pudding to me over the next four months of summer. Sorry!)

15. Think about presentation and garnishes that provide contrast in flavour and texture. That boring old vegetable soup can start looking (and tasting) rather fancy dressed with a dollop of herby pesto, a blizzard of finely chopped herbs and flecks of lemon zest, or a swoosh of good olive oil.

16. Put simple things in fancy bowls and dishes to make them look classy. Nuts, rum balls or a dip all look so much fancier in small, old-fashioned glass bowls. If you don't have any, nip down to your local op shop and pick some up for a couple of bucks. Just make sure you wash them before use. Dead people might have touched them.

17. Remember to warm plates, platters and bowls before placing any warm food on them. Warm your plates in the bottom of the oven or in hot very water before serving hot food. Dry them. Careful – they are hot!

18. Always serve sauce on the side; it'll hold its heat better. Always warm the gravy boat or jug before filling.

19. Clean up as you cook and prep. You want to try and keep the kitchen clean and tidy.

20. Note that self-assembly food – like tacos or pulled pork buns – is great for starting conversations, as people ask for the elements to be passed around and discuss their own spin on their taco or bun.

21. Always serve dessert but feel free to take shortcuts if pressed for time. I'll usually make a tart or a cake, but remember that a shop-bought one can be easily spruced up with fruit, edible flowers or a rich sauce to look homemade; chocolate chip cookies can be turned into sexy ice cream sandwiches; and no one complains if big bowls of cherries and dark chocolate, hulled strawberries, or grapes, nuts and cheese finish the meal.

22. Just like you'll lay out everything you'll need on the dining table – cutlery, salt, pepper, etc. – also lay out everything you'll need for serving in the kitchen. The plates, the implements and any of the garnishes (or cheese for the end of the meal) that need to be at room temperature.

23. OK, so the hour leeway you gave yourself has been eaten into by the usual last-minute disaster but you should still now have half an hour to give the kitchen a final clean and get yourself into the shower.

The Eight Rules About the Drinks

1. Start with a cocktail. Spirits and mixers are cheaper these days than half-decent wine, while cheap sparkling can be elegantly disguised with a few drops of angostura bitters and a sugar lump! Or just pick a signature cocktail or punch that you'll give everyone on arrival. Sangria, Cosmopolitans, Pimms, mulled wine and martinis can all be prepared for arrival and then just finished for each guest as they arrive. The choice of a green olive or a twist of lemon zest for the martinis, for example. Remember to offer a non-alcoholic drink as well so the designated drivers feel just as special. Those bitters can be your secret weapon here too!

2. Delegate. Give someone the role of being in charge of the bar, whether it is your partner or a responsible early-arriver, as guests are often reticent to help themselves. Or worse, they will open that 20-year-old bottle of port you were saving for your son's twenty-first because they 'thought it was a McLaren Vale shiraz but it was horrid and sweet'. I have no problem with asking for help – in fact, if you are planning a bigger party, hiring a bartender is always a brilliant idea as they'll keep the glasses full, your guests feeling loved and the party rolling.

3. If it is warm, ice everything, including all the soft drinks, well in advance. Running out of ice is one of the biggest disasters to befall any party so that's why I suggest you buy double the amount you need.

4. Remember to have lots of iced water on hand in jugs. Throw in ice with clean sprigs of mint or rough slices of lime, lemon or even orange to make it look pretty.

5. Decant the red wine you are serving; it'll stop people carrying on about it and encourage them to just drink it. I have three different decanters and claret jugs that I have picked up over the years from op shops for the princely sum of about $18. They tend to make bottles of ordinary wine look about $20 more expensive each time I use them! There is a neurological reason for this, as Dr Charles Spence will tell you.

6. Introduce people to each other. Try and do this by pointing out a link between them. Remember, dinner is about your guests. 'Well, Ratface, you're a member of the Mongols motorcycle gang, and Tarquin, you're a Coffin Cheater; do you prefer ape hangers or drag bars on your hogs/have you ever been to Perth/how do you both feel about Campbell Newman?'

7. I do like the idea of serving salty appetisers or snacks with drinks, even if it's as simple as cheese straws fresh from the oven, a little shop-bought pâté, or just some good nuts or warmed olives. The main thing is not to stress about these, as your focus in the kitchen should be all on the meal itself.

8. Think about serving drinks in a different space to where you'll be eating … whether that's a sitting room, the garden, or the park across the road. This means your guests then get the 'oooh, errr, wow!' *MKR* moment when they come in and see the dining table.

The 10 Rules About the Table

1. We are in a family home, not Buckingham Palace, so whether it's the drinks or the table, the rule is the same: keep it casual and don't be fussy.

2. Casual doesn't preclude you from ironing the napkins and tablecloth – ideally on the table so the cloth loses its ridges. This is a simple way of making things look so smart – and leaving a terrible burn on your heirloom mahogany drop-leaf table if you don't take care or use an undercloth.

3. Unless it's hot, I like to sit people close together (10 on a table for 8) as it encourages intimacy and conversation. Also, if you have the choice, pick a narrow table as this will further help intimacy.

4. I do like a little something to dress the table; more than just the glassware, place settings and condiments. Flowers are great but nothing too high; eye contact is vital across the table. I've used everything from bowls of apples or clusters of lemons to branches of blossom or herbs cut from the garden. Cabbages, however, look silly. Oh, and keep the theme contained and constrained. That's why that bowl of lemons looks so good!

5. I do think it's important to think about the seating plan, and with a small table of 12 or less I think it's ideal to split up couples. Get the kids to do double-sided name cards so everyone knows where to sit (and your guests can remind themselves that they are sitting opposite Charlee and the name-blind like me can see that it is Carly sitting at the other end of the table).

6. When working out who to put where, think about what your guests might have in common, split up any alpha males and pop the biggest personality at the middle of the table so they can work both ends. Avoid putting shy people at the end of the table, as they can get isolated down there.

7. If you are cooking, sit yourself in the seat nearest the kitchen.

8. Lighting is crucial. I love candles in any form – the way that their light dances over the glasses and glints on the cutlery. In fact, I reckon you can never have too many candles – unless it's 40°C, in which case plant a few tea lights in a long mound of ice! Freezing candles can stop them dripping and slow down the melting process. Oh, and always avoid scented candles.

9. If you aren't going for candles then think of looking for pink or salmon-coloured light globes. This light is even more flattering than candlelight.

10. Music is equally crucial to setting the mood and covering up any awkward silences. Nothing too fast and maybe just a little jazzy is my rule. So leave your 2 Chainz collection until after dinner.

Final Tips and Chores

- Put flowers or a bunch of herbs from the garden in the dunny. And light that scented candle you were given as a Kris Kringle. Clean the dunny and replenish the toilet paper.
- Ask for help, whether it's clearing the table or getting someone else to bring a cheese board. Failing that, just pay for help. We're happy to pay for a babysitter, so why not pay someone to wash the dishes while you're all enjoying ancient cognac and fine Cuban cigars in the mahogany-panelled billiard room.
- And one final rule – again. Remember that dinner is all about your guests. There is no need to show off!

'A MORNING'S MEAL IS NO UNIMPORTANT THING ... OUR MENTAL ENERGIES, IN A GREAT DEGREE, DEPEND ON OUR PHYSICAL CONDITION AND WELL-BEING AND THE PHYSICAL CONDITION OF THAT MAN WHO HAS HAD AN INDIFFERENT BREAKFAST CANNOT BE GOOD.'

Andrew Valentine Kirwan, 1864

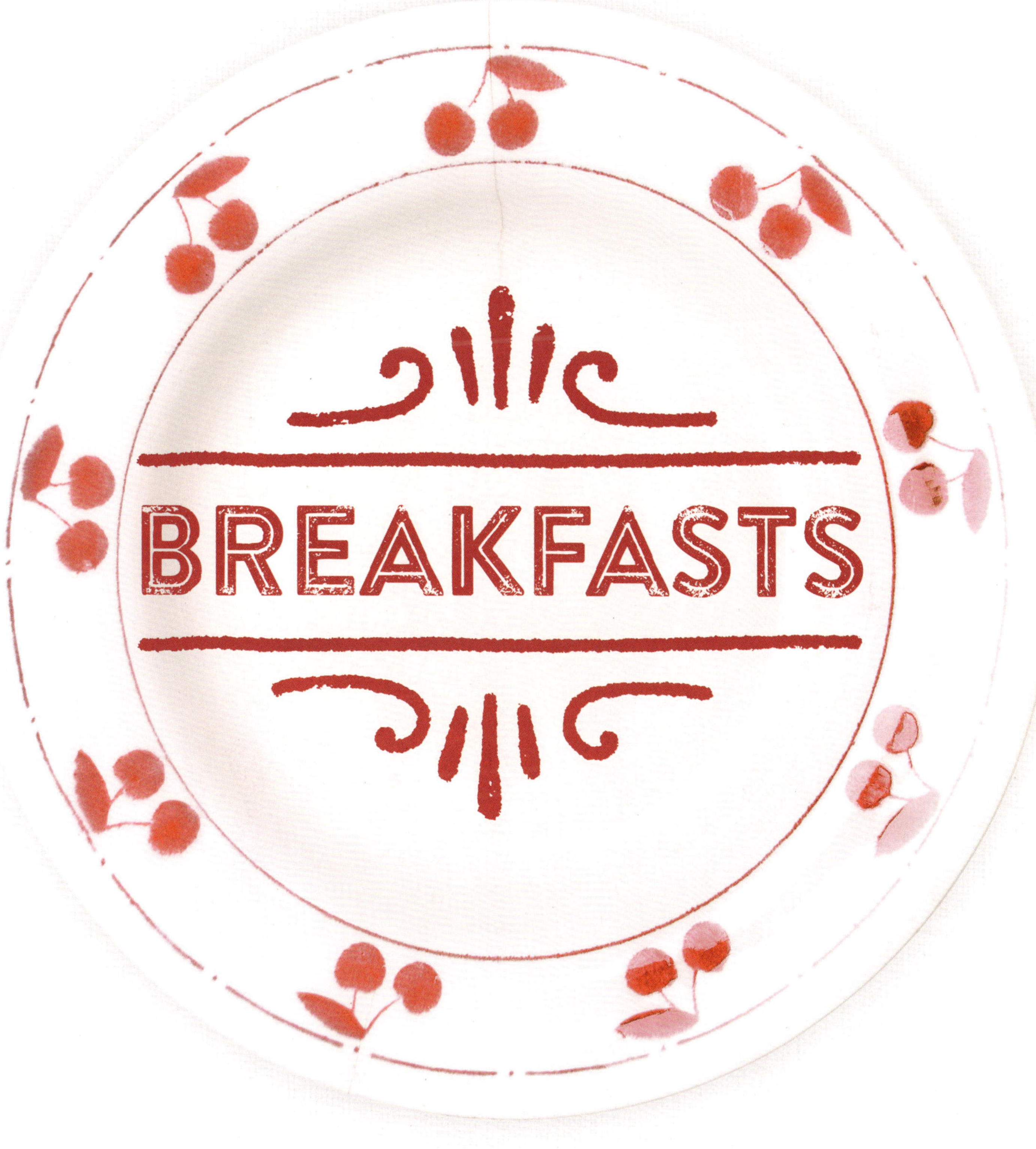

BREAKFASTS

DAD'S MARMALADE
and SAUSAGE SANDWICHES

Economy airline meals are usually lacking in any redeeming features but it was on a long haul that I first paired snags with one of those little plastic tubs of marmalade, trying to turn the inedible into something a little tastier. The result was about the best thing on a flight since seat-back entertainment screens, or the note that woman in seat 54J sent me. Bizarrely, at the other end I went for brunch at Gabrielle Hamilton's Prune in New York and the same thing was on the menu. Weird!

2 pork breakfast sausages

**2 slices of soft-centered,
    country-style white bread**

butter, for toast

1 tablespoon orange marmalade

Cook the sausages in a frying pan over medium heat until done.

Slice them into longish pieces on the angle.

Toast the bread, butter while it is still hot and slather one buttered piece generously with marmalade. Lay the sausage on the marmalade, top with the other piece of buttered toast and eat straight away with a nice strong mug of builder's tea.

SERVES 1

Brûléed Pancakes

OK, so this is about the best idea in this whole book and it is so simple. How come no one that I know has ever before sprinkled sugar on one side of their pancakes to give them the same crunchy, melty burnt sugar top that is so prized on a crème brûlée? And all without the hassle of a blow torch…

125 g (1 cup) self-raising flour
pinch of salt flakes
1 egg
375 ml (1½) cups milk
50 g butter, almost melted
2 ruby red grapefruit
115 g (½ cup) caster sugar

Whisk together the flour, salt, egg and milk to make a smooth batter.

Pour in the melted butter and stir through – it's fine if there are still a few globs of softened butter amongst the melted golden stuff.

Leave the mixture to stand while you peel and segment one of the grapefruit and juice the other.

Heat a – and this is important – non-stick frying pan and pour the batter in to form as many pancakes as will fit with some space around them.

As the top starts to bubble, sprinkle 1 teaspoon of caster sugar over the upturned face of each pancake. Leave for a minute and flip the pancake over. You do this so the sugar adheres to the pancake. Cook on a high heat until the sugar melts and burns a little. You want it to have a sizzly burnt sugar crust.

Serve the pancakes in twos or threes, burnt-sugar-side up, with some of the segments of pink grapefruit and some juice drizzled over the top.

SERVES 4

TIP

See page 66 for how to expertly segment citrus.

JAMIE'S POST-SURF ONE-PAN WONDER

Charlie don't surf, but Jamie does. This recipe is from an occasional member of my fab food team. When I said I was looking for a cracking good egg dish that wasn't just a Middle Eastern baked egg or *shakshooka*, Jamie pulled a picture of this off his phone. It's inspired by early mornings in the summer surf down at Torquay. It's also super-quick, super-tasty and – more importantly – all cooked and served in one pan, because – let's face it – a group of starving boys aren't going to help with the dishes. And it's a great way of using up all the odds and ends in the fridge. This means it is never likely to be the same dish twice. So here's a good base to get you started and then use whatever else you have around.

Heat your frying pan over medium to high heat, add a glug of olive oil and your rashers of bacon and fry to your liking (crispy, of course), rendering out all the tasty bacon fat. Remove the bacon to a plate, keeping all the lovely fat in the pan.

Add your garlic, onion, spring onion and 1 tablespoon of oregano and fry until fragrant, about 2–3 minutes.

Add the paprika, fresh tomato and drained beans and fry until your beans are nice and toasty.

Add your salsa from last night's taco fiesta and the canned tomatoes, season well, toss about, lower the heat a little and simmer until nice and saucy. This should take about 5 minutes.

Re-introduce your bacon and nestle it evenly around the pan.

Make indentations in the middle and around the pan for your eggs. Crack the eggs in and season lightly again, cover with a lid or another pan and let them poach away in their smoky bean bath for 3–4 minutes, until the whites are done but the yolks are still runny.

Remove from the heat and liberally grate over some parmesan, then spoon over your avocado in chunks, sprinkle with the remaining oregano and, if you like it spicy, throw on some pickled jalapeños for good measure.

To add your last little bit of flair, pierce the egg yolks to show how perfectly cooked they are, then place the pan on a board to serve, with a sprinkle of mint leaves (or any other herb), something bready and your favourite hot sauce, and refuel.

SERVES 4

TIP

Other known culprits to appear in this concoction are pulled pork, leftover roast chicken or meats, chorizo, all manner of half-used veg and BBQ'd bits, to name a few. Sour cream or yoghurt, lemon zest or chopped herbs can be employed as a garnish.

---

good-quality olive oil

4 rashers good, fatty bacon

2 garlic cloves, chopped

1 onion, sliced (use those leftover onion halves in your fridge)

1 spring onion, sliced

2 tablespoons roughly chopped oregano leaves

1 teaspoon good-quality smoked paprika

1 tomato, roughly chopped

1 × 400 g can black beans (or mixed beans or whatever darned beans you've got in the pantry), drained and rinsed

½ cup leftover fire-roasted tomato salsa (if you are a celeb TV chef), passata (if you are Italian) or the end of the can/tube of tomato paste (if you are me)

1 × 400 g can whole peeled tomatoes

flake salt and freshly ground black pepper

6 large eggs

Parmigiano Reggiano (or that nuggety dry end of the tasty cheese)

½ avocado (that one in your fridge you swear you'll use up)

1 tablespoon pickled jalapeños, sliced

fresh mint leaves (or any damn herb you please), to serve

lovely toast, warm corn tortillas or, better yet, the cheat's flatbread on page 120 and your favourite hot sauce, to serve

WAFFLE HASH BROWNS

HACK

It might not be wise, and might even void the warranty, but I do like to use different appliances for tasks not usually illustrated on the pack – like reheating pizza or cooking fish fingers in a toaster. Don't try this at home unless you've been initiated into the secret knowledge required to do this safely! However, making hash browns in a waffle iron is far easier and actually rather delicious – and dear old cousin A V Kirwan would appreciate these potato *gaufres*, as waffles were called in his day.

8 rashers bacon
3 potatoes, well scrubbed
¼ cup olive oil

Cook your bacon in the waffle maker first, on medium heat, and wonder at how the ridges let the fat effortlessly drain away from the meat. Do remember to save the fat that's rendered off the bacon to grease the saucepan next time you are popping corn. Delicious!

Turn the waffle maker up to high.

While the bacon is cooking, grate your potatoes into a large bowl of salted water. Leave to stand for 3 minutes.

Drain and squeeze out as much liquid as you can by placing the grated potato between double thickness sheets of kitchen towel and pressing down. The drier the better, when it comes to crispness.

Grease the waffle maker's plates with some of the olive oil. Layer on enough grated potato to cover the bottom plate. That should be about a quarter of the grated potato. Press down the top plate and cook for 12 minutes. You might want to flip the waffle over after about 8 minutes to ensure that it cooks evenly. Grease and repeat with the remaining potato.

Serve with bacon. Fried eggs are good too.

SERVES 4

TIP

For a pescetarian version, dump the bacon, grease the waffle maker's plates with melted butter and serve the hash browns with smoked salmon and a dollop of sour cream cut with grated horseradish and dill.

SAM'S BREAKFAST SMOOTHIE

Bored with Weet-Bix and rising to the challenge of no processed sugars for a week, my young friend Sam, son of my marginally older – not that she looks it (shoot, nearly got myself in trouble there) – friend Marnie, created this smoothie. It has become his regular go-to breakfast on school days. The only thing that sweetens this is the dates and the love of his mum. This is the world's shortest recipe – but also the most sucky-uppiest.

250 ml (1 cup) soy, almond, rice or cow's milk

2–3 dried dates, pitted

1 tablespoon oat bran

1 tablespoon blanched, slivered or flaked almonds

¼ teaspoon vanilla extract or essence

¼ teaspoon cinnamon

4–6 ice cubes

Blitz it all up in the blender and drink immediately.

SERVES 1

TIP

Other suggested additions include: 1 teaspoon chia seeds, psyllium husks, lecithin, 1 raw egg, or maybe some yoghurt.

SAVOURY MINCE THAT ISN'T GREY

In Queensland they call it 'savoury mince on toast' and this retro throwback is now the coolest of café breakfasts there. In Mumbai, they call it *kheema pav* and also eat it for breakfast, while *rou jia mo*, from China's Shaanxi Province, consists of stewed pork, beef or lamb on a steamed bun. You see, savoury mince is a bit of a thing worldwide. In the US South they call it 'sloppy joes' (aka the 'manwich'). According to legend, a cook named Joe at Floyd Angell's café in Sioux City, Iowa, added tomato sauce to his 'loose meat' sandwiches and the sloppy joe sandwich was born. Loads of peas, feta and parsley in this version banish the haunting memories of old, grey school minces of the past.

Fry the bacon and sugar with a touch of the oil until the bacon is browned and cooked. Add the parsley stalks, stir and set aside in a bowl.

Add a little more oil (about a tablespoonful) to the same pan, then add the onion and garlic and cook for a couple of minutes until the onion has softened.

Add the mince to the pan and fry until browned, breaking up any lumpy bits with a wooden spoon as it cooks.

Add the bacon back to the pan. Stir in the stock, tomato paste, Worcestershire sauce and the sherry vinegar, scraping any yummy browny bits on the pan back into the sauce.

Bring to the boil and immediately reduce to a simmer, cover and cook for about 10 minutes.

Remove the lid and continue to cook for a further 10–15 minutes to reduce the liquid and allow the flavours to intensify.

Blanch the peas and throw most of the peas and parsley leaves in with the mince at the end of cooking, saving a scatter of both for the top.

Serve on hot toast, with the remaining peas and some feta crumbled on top. I like a heavy multigrain as the toasty raft for this breakfast!

SERVES 4

3 rashers bacon, finely diced

2 teaspoons brown sugar

60 ml (3 tablespoons) extra-virgin olive oil

1 tablespoon chopped flat-leaf parsley stalks, 2 tablespoons finely chopped leaves, saved for later

1 brown onion, finely chopped

1 garlic clove, finely chopped

500 g beef mince

250 ml (1 cup) salt-reduced beef stock

1 tablespoon tomato paste

½ tablespoon Worcestershire sauce

½ tablespoon sherry vinegar

155 g (1 cup) frozen peas

4 slices of heavy multigrain bread, toasted

feta, to crumble on top

Middle Eastern Rice Pudding

Rice pudding is one of those rather venerable inventions that leaps from being baked as an English school-dinner classic or cut with lemon zest as an elegant Spanish breakfast to a Greek chocolate bar or an Italian ice cream. Here it gets a rather tasty sheikh-up that would be equally at home in a Mughal court or a Damascus palace; as a breakfast or a dinner party dessert!

165 g (¾ cup) arborio rice

750 ml (3 cups) milk

250 ml (1 cup) cream

220 g (¾ cup) sugar

2–3 cardamom pods, gently split

1 vanilla pod, split and scraped

1 cinnamon stick

pinch of salt flakes

TOPPING

1½ tablespoons crushed pistachios

½ cup raspberries, fresh or frozen and thawed

1 teaspoon rosewater (optional)

pinch of ground cinnamon, to dust

scatter of dried rose petals, for fun

Put the rice, milk, cream, sugar, cardamom pods, vanilla pod and seeds, cinnamon stick and salt into a saucepan.

Bring to a gentle boil while stirring, then reduce immediately to a low heat and allow to simmer for 45–50 minutes. You will need to stir the rice regularly and then constantly but gently towards the end to ensure it doesn't catch.

When the rice is cooked, remove the vanilla pod, cinnamon stick and cardamom pods and discard.

Spoon the rice pudding into bowls and finish with whatever you like. I like to sprinkle over crushed pistachio nuts, some tart raspberries that have been doused in rosewater, the barest dusting of cinnamon and for a special, but by no means essential, touch: a few rose petals.

SERVES 4

TIP

Instead of raspberries you could use any berries, pomegranate seeds, chopped quince paste, an exotic jam – like Turkish rose or English gooseberry – or any nuts of your choice.

BOTSWANA BREAKFAST

Peanut butter on toast would have to be one of my breakfasts of choice, along with porridge, so imagine my delight when I was in Botswana (as one is! That's what happens when you slavishly follow your sat nav without thinking – who'd have thought there was a Church Street in Gabarone as well as in Brighton?) and discovered that almost everyone there got a little dreamy over the idea of their local mealy pap porridge dolloped with peanut butter.

Sounds totally weird, but it tastes equally as good eaten at a suburban Australian breakfast table as it does while checking out the tracks of the elephants, baboons and hippos that have nimbly cruised between your fragile tents the night before.

What's also fascinating about this recipe is that the use of maize meal (or, in this recipe, the easier-to-find semolina) to make the porridge echoes the US Southern breakfast of grits served with eggs and steak or the softer, sweet 'cream of wheat' puddings. Peanut butter is big in America, too, and if we are going to get all historical here, as I am wont to do, one can see a link between the tragic enforced 'migration' of so many Africans and the transfer of food traditions west from one continent to another.

As maize meal is hard to find here, I suggest making this recipe with semolina that's readily available in most supermarkets. You'll have to find your own troop of baboons to leave their footprints through the kitchen, though – luckily I already have one of them!

1 litre (4 cups) milk, plus more milk to serve

200 g (1 cup) coarse semolina

½ teaspoon of salt flakes

1 × 375 g jar crunchy peanut butter

220 g (1 cup) demerara sugar

jam or marmalade, to serve (optional)

Heat the milk until it starts to froth and reach the boil. Whisk in the semolina in a steady stream like rain. Season with salt. Reduce the heat and simmer until it has thickened and the tiny grains of wheat have swollen to their full voluptuousness.

Serve hot in wide bowls with chilled milk poured around the edge. Dollop a dessertspoon of peanut butter into the middle and sprinkle over the crystals of sugary crunch to taste. It's not traditional but this dish is equally delicious with a dollop of marmalade or jam, as in our picture.

I like to eat the semolina from the edge, each hot mouthful with a little cool milk and a scrape of the peanut butter. Or eat it the African way, which is to mix in the peanut butter so that it marbles the semolina.

SERVES 6

▶ FAMILY SECRET ◀

My not-very-good-at-cooking grandmother served semolina as a dessert, especially chocolate semolina. This nursery favourite is as simple as stirring cocoa powder and caster sugar into your cooked semolina until it is sweet and chocolatey enough. Try it hot or set into a sort of thick mousse – always with runny cream.

SCRAMBLED EGGS *with* CREAMED LEEKS

I do occasionally have moments of extreme air-headedness, which I fear is probably a sign of early-onset Alzheimer's. This is marginally more palatable than believing that I've always been a wee bit stupid, which is probably closer to the mark. Anyway, if I wasn't, I would never have been sitting in a Sydney café called The Grounds, reading the menu while waiting for friends who were actually waiting for me in a Malaysian coffee house three suburbs away. The long and the short of it was that I had to rush off before having breakfast, but the idea on the menu of serving creamy leek scrambled eggs stuck with me. I have no idea how they actually do it but this is what worked for me when I got back home two days later, still craving that brekkie combination. I suppose I ought to go back and actually try their version to see if mine bears any resemblance at all! If you get there first, let me know on Twitter at @mattscravat.

Using all the stealth of a bush tracker, sneak up on your stove and turn the heat up to medium. Place your favourite and most trusted frying pan over the heat and casually throw in the butter to the rapidly warming heart of the pan. Melt.

Add the leeks and water, season with a touch of salt and pepper, cover, and reduce heat to low, cooking for about 10 minutes, or until the leeks are soft.

Take the lid off and allow the leeks to colour a bit. Stir in the cream and parmesan. Keep warm until you're ready to serve.

For the scrambled eggs, crack the eggs into a bowl, add the cream and whisk until frothy.

Add the butter to a non-stick frying pan over low heat. Pour in the egg mix and cook slowly. Slow cooking is the secret to creamy scrambled eggs. With this in mind you can cook the leeks and the eggs simultaneously – just make sure you moderate the heat on the eggs to ensure they don't overcook.

As the egg is just starting to catch on the bottom of the pan, very gently scrape the bottom of the pan with a non-abrasive, flat implement to form soft folds in the egg. Remove from the heat when just cooked.

Place the toast on individual plates, spoon over the soft scrambled egg and top with creamed leeks. Season with salt and pepper and, if you like, scatter over some fresh herbs of your choice – chives, parsley, basil, chervil, tarragon and dill all go well.

SERVES 4

CREAMED LEEKS

30 g unsalted butter

3 large leeks, washed, thinly sliced into 0.5 cm-thick rounds

40 ml (2 tablespoons) water

salt flakes and freshly ground black pepper

40 ml (2 tablespoons) cream

½–1 tablespoon good-quality, finely grated parmesan

SCRAMBLED EGGS

8 eggs

40 ml (2 tablespoons) cream

20 g butter

toast, to serve

fresh herbs, such as chives, thyme, parsley or tarragon, to serve (optional)

Spiced Honey 2 Ways

The sourness of yoghurt loves sweetness the way reality TV loves tears. It doesn't matter whether you are in Sri Lanka swathing silky curds in molassesy kitul palm syrup or sitting at a rickety table in some dusty Cycladean café, with your tin spoon dragging local honey the colour of true liquid amber through the milky goodness drawn from the udders of a local goat. These two breakfast recipes, however, nod to slightly garbled memories of Turkey and India.

1. TURKISH BREAKFAST

200 g (1⅓ cups) pine nuts
200 g (1½ cups) slivered almonds
1 litre Greek yoghurt
150 g of the fruitiest, plumpest Kalamata olives
   you can find

SPICED HONEY

1 thick slice of lemon
6 whole cloves
1 cinnamon stick
350 g (1 cup) honey

First, make your spiced honey. Stud the lemon slice with cloves.

Place the lemon slice, cinnamon and honey in a small pan and bring to a gentle boil. Remove from the heat and leave to stand to cool a little, and allow the flavours to infuse.

Toast the pine nuts and slivered almonds in a pan until well golden. Spread out on a baking tray to cool. That way they will stay crunchy if you store leftovers in an airtight container once cooled.

Plate the creamy Greek yoghurt, drizzle it with the spiced honey and place a pile of the black olives on the side to add salt and fruitiness. Finish with a scattering of nuts.

SERVES 4

TIP

Call me an Aussie bogan but this spiced honey is equally as good softened in the microwave and drizzled over your Weet-Bix.

2. INDIAN SPICED HONEY WITH 'CURDS'

350 g (1 cup) honey
6 cardamom pods, lightly crushed
3 blades of star anise
1 cinnamon stick
6 cloves
1 × 1 kg tub pot-set, low-fat plain yoghurt
155 g (1 cup) roasted, salted cashews

Slowly bring the honey and the spices to a gentle boil in a saucepan. Reduce the heat and simmer for a minute or so. Remove from the heat and leave to cool. Leave the spices to steep in the honey as it cools, then remove to serve.

When cooled, serve this spiced honey drizzled over a good mound of the low-fat yoghurt, which has a similar consistency to Indian sour curds. Dot the combo with some cashews for the occasional salty crunch.

SERVES 4

Espresso Martini and a Hot Bloke

There wasn't going to be a breakfast section in this book but it began to seem logical when we were sitting round as a team discussing what recipes this book needed. It seemed like a good idea to include recipes for each of our favourite breakfasts. I won't blight the name of the team member who instantly said her dream breakfast was 'an espresso martini and a hot bloke' because I fear it rings a bell for many!

This recipe requires pre-meditation. But at least when you invite someone up for 'coffee', for once you won't be lying. They'll just get to drink it cold the next morning.

Stir the sugar into your hot espresso coffee until dissolved. Chill the espresso in the refrigerator.

Once the espresso is chilled, add all ingredients to a shaker along with the ice. Shake well and strain into chilled glasses.

SERVES 2

15 g sugar

60 ml espresso coffee – chilled

120 ml vodka

60 ml Kahlua

a bunch of ice (about 8 cubes)

a hot bloke – you may or may not be able to get this at your local supermarket

'FAR BETTER TO HAVE ONE FIRST-RATE SOUP AND ONE GOOD FISH THAN A MULTIPLICITY OF DISHES – UNLESS YOU HAVE GOOD COOKS AND A RETINUE OF SERVANTS.'

Andrew Valentine Kirwan, 1864

SOUPS

EMMA'S LIGHTEST CHICKEN AND VEGETABLE SOUP

This soup is very clean, very bright and very virtuous – a bit like the woman I love, whose recipe it is. I am sure that just eating it makes you a better person. Let me know after you've made a batch if your partner stops bagging footy umpires, your kids stop bickering or you get nominated for that sainthood you so justly deserve.

1 brown onion, peeled and roughly chopped

1 fresh bay leaf, crushed

1 bunch thyme

12 black peppercorns

1 × 1.5 kg chicken

olive oil, for frying

2 carrots, diced

3 celery stalks, diced

¼ head white cabbage, cut into 1 cm-wide ribbons

2 leeks, halved lengthways and sliced into half-moons

2 potatoes, peeled and cubed

1 × 400 g can borlotti beans, drained and rinsed

salt flakes and freshly ground black pepper, to taste

8 slices of toast, to serve

Bring 3 litres of water to the boil in a large stockpot or saucepan with the onion, bay leaf, a sprig of thyme and the peppercorns.

Carefully lower your chook into the pot, breast-side down. Remove from the heat immediately, cover and leave for 75 minutes, or at least 1 hour, or whenever you remember it's there.

Remove the chook, cover it and place in the fridge to cool. Keep the poaching water.

When cool, strip off the meat and use the best of the meat for salads or chicken sandwiches for lunchboxes. Keep back about a quarter of it to eventually add to the soup.

Throw the bones, skin and carcass in the poaching water and simmer for 30 minutes.

Strain, reserving the stock.

When you want to eat the soup, bring the stock back to the boil and simmer happily for 5 minutes.

While this is happening, splash a little oil into a big pot and place on medium heat.

Throw in the remaining veggies except the potatoes. Toss and cook until the leek starts to soften. Throw in the potatoes and pour over the stock. Cook, uncovered, for 20–30 minutes or until the potatoes are soft. Don't let the soup boil.

Now add the borlotti beans and throw in any of the shredded chook meat you have left. Remember not to let the soup boil!

Season to taste and serve poured over a slice of lightly toasted bread.

SERVES 8

ROASTED CARROT SOUP *with* CRUNCHY BONE MARROW CROQUETTES

The US and Australia had vaudeville. The English had music hall, which seemed strangely obsessed with food, whether it's 'a lovely bunch of coconuts', 'a little bit of cucumber' or 'boiled beef and carrots'.

This last top tune from 1909 rather nobly extols the virtue of a carnivorous diet with the immortal line, 'Don't live like vegetarians on food they give to parrots / Blow out your kite, from morn 'til night on boiled beef and carrots.'

While that tenement stew might be cheap, I reckon this here take on a classic combination of ingredients shows off both to greater advantage. Far better to roast the carrots to intensify their sweetness and make this hearty meal-in-a-bowl with them instead! I also love that this is a soup that cries out to be made the day before (when you start soaking your bone marrow). The bone marrow is a brilliant idea taught to me by Buenos Aires punk chef Alejandro Digilio. It is the perfect example of turning something cheap into something totally exquisite. And it'll certainly blow out your kite – or fill your belly, to translate the ancient slang.

1.25 kg carrots, peeled and gnarly ends chopped off

olive oil

salt flakes

125 g (about 5–6) golden shallots (eschallots), peeled and sliced

50 g butter

750 ml (3 cups) light stock, such as chicken or vegetable

freshly ground black pepper

2 teaspoons honey

1 bunch watercress, trimmed and separated into strands

fried shallots

CRUNCHY BONE MARROW

12 × 5 cm lengths of bone marrow removed from the bone. Ask your butcher to do this. Note that you'll need to soak this before using.

lots of cornflour or plain flour, for dusting

40 g butter

TIP

Not a fan of bone marrow? Try crème fraîche with picked thyme and chervil leaves instead of the bone marrow and watercress, or candied pecans with maple syrup–fried bacon shards.

To prep the marrow, you'll need to soak it in cold, slightly salty water for 24 hours before using. If you want the soup today then plump for one of the alternative garnishes listed in the Tip below, but note that bone marrow is cheap, and to my mind, it is like our foie gras but without nearly the same level of cruelty. When you fry it, you will find it goes deliciously gooey and works wonderfully with the carrots.

Leave the bone marrow covered in the fridge for 24 hours. Change the water three times in that period for fresh, cold, salted water.

Preheat the oven to 180°C.

If the carrots are brutes slice them in half lengthways. Divide between 2 baking trays in a single layer and toss with plenty of olive oil. Sprinkle with salt. Bang them in the oven, turning them over after 30 minutes. They should be softening. Turn the heat down to 130°C and give them another hour or so, but watch them. We want the carrots to get a little golden at the edges and start to look a little shrivelled. When cooked, remove the carrots from the oven.

Slowly fry the shallots in the butter for 3–5 minutes until golden.

Blend the roasted carrots with the shallots while both are still warm, using a little of the stock to moisten. Now season with salt, black pepper and honey as required.

Keep adding stock until the carrots are the consistency of thick soup. Pour into a saucepan. Add more honey and salt to season. Reheat when needed and make the crunchy bone marrow, just before serving.

Remove the bone marrow from its water bath and pat dry. Now pour the cornflour or plain flour into a cereal bowl and roll each finger of bone marrow in the flour. Make sure you coat all sides and each end.

Gently heat the butter in a small frying pan. When the butter is starting to get foamy, slip 4 pieces of the bone marrow into the pan and fry it over medium heat until the flour gets all crunchy. Gently turn the marrow to ensure all floured sides go crunchy. This will take a few minutes and you'll need to watch to make sure the flour doesn't burn. When crunchy all over, remove the pan from the heat. Season.

Pour the soup into preheated bowls and garnish each with a nest of torn watercress and fried shallots. Gently lift the crunchy bone marrow explosions into each nest and serve. Warn your guests that the marrow with be deliciously hot!

SERVES 4

SUNDAY NIGHT CHICKEN NOODLE SOUP

Every family I know seems to have had a cheap Sunday night dinner routine. Maybe it was baked bean jaffles, fried eggy bread or, in my case, chicken noodle soup from a packet. It was, I suppose, pretty close to eating two-minute noodles but with little short twigs of vermicelli that tradition insisted had to be saved until last. While I still love that packet soup, this is a far more elegant take on the classic, that comes with about the best chicken broth you can find!

Preheat the oven to 90°C.

First of all, make your stock. Place a large roasting pan on the stovetop over a high heat. Add a little oil and, when it is hot, throw in the chicken wings and cook until they start to brown.

Move them around a bit and then throw in the onions and sprinkle over the skimmed milk powder.

When the wings are well browned, remove the pan from the heat, take out the wings and drain the fat.

Deglaze the pan with a little water, replace the wings and onions and pour in enough hot water to cover the wings. Cover the pan with foil and place in your preheated oven for about 3 hours.

After 2½ hours, remove the roasting pan from the oven, remove the foil, throw in the chopped vegetables, peppercorns and half of the parsley and bake for another 30 minutes.

Remove the stock from the oven and drain though a fine sieve lined with muslin into a clean bowl. Cover and place in the refrigerator until completely cold and jellified.

When you are ready to use, scrape the fat from the top of the jellified stock and discard. Use as much of the stock as you desire for your soup and bring to the boil in a saucepan.

Season as you like, add as much of the vermicelli as required, about 35 g per person, and turn off the heat. Allow to stand for about 3 minutes for the noodles to become tender.

Chop the remaining parsley to garnish and serve while still hot.

SERVES 6–8

•NOTE

That skimmed milk powder is a Heston Blumenthal trick for adding a burnt-butter, roasty richness to the stock.

oil, for roasting

2 kg chicken wings, chopped into pieces

2 large brown onions, quartered, skins left on

50 g skimmed milk powder

2 litres (8 cups) water

2 carrots, chopped

2 celery stalks, chopped

5 black peppercorns

1 bunch flat-leaf parsley

250 g rice vermicelli noodles

CAULIFLOWER SOUP
with WALDORF GARNISH

I love soup. What could be simpler than roasting, steaming or simmering your favourite veggies until they are cooked, then blending them with hot stock or milk? That's the basic peasant soup. But how easy it is to elevate the bowl to peerage quality by what you add. This cauliflower soup is a case in point. Playing with the flavours of the classic Waldorf Salad, as this recipe does, is one way to add contrast, texture and sophistication, but there are so many more.

You could always blend 200 g of blue cheese into the soup to add a sharper flavour and then garnish with a swirl of cream. You could play with the flavour of cauliflower cheese and add loads of grated parmesan. Some batons of crispy fried bacon and finely shredded cos lettuce would be the perfect garnish for either of these variations. Or how about frying the cauliflower in a little oil and butter along with 1 teaspoon of cumin seeds to give a nuttier taste and darker colour to the soup, as well as adding the slight smokiness of the spice that will conjure up images of the Middle East, especially if you garnish with pine nuts and currants. Or you could just make the recipe below.

800 g cauliflower, stalk trimmed and head thinly sliced

1 brown onion, diced

200 ml water

1 litre chicken stock

salt flakes and freshly ground black pepper

125 ml (½ cup) cream

GARNISH

1 green apple, cut into batons

zest and juice of 1 lemon

5 rosemary leaves

1 teaspoon salt

1 stalk celery

50 g walnut pieces

100 g blue cheese (something creamy and made of cow's milk), crumbled

olive oil, to drizzle

Place the cauliflower in a large stockpot or saucepan with the onion, water and stock. Bring to the boil and then reduce to a simmer, uncovered.

Cook for about 40 minutes, until the cauliflower is softened.

Blitz the cauliflower with your stick blender while still warm. Season with salt and pepper, and then stir in the cream to finish. If the soup is too thick, add some milk until your preferred consistency is reached. Keep gently warm.

DANGER, DANGER, WARNING: If you decide to blend in a liquidiser or other enclosed unit, remember that blending hot vegetables and stock will release steam. Allow some way for it to escape to ensure that the lid doesn't blow off your liquidiser and the soup splatter you and your kitchen ceiling! Either allow the soup to cool before blending or, if you have to, seal the blender, remove the central access stopper, cover it with a tea towel and hold it in place. The towel will allow the steam to escape.

For the garnish, toss the apple batons in lemon juice.

Put the rosemary and salt in a mortar and pound until the rosemary is finely ground. Pick out any large pieces then set aside. (You could use cumin or thyme instead if the mood takes you – or just omit altogether! There are no rules here.)

Remove any stringy bits from the celery stalk and cut the stalk into 3 mm dice.

Pour the soup into warm bowls. Arrange a pile of the apple batons in the middle of the soup with walnuts, some blue cheese and celery. Grate over a little lemon zest and a sprinkle of the rosemary salt. Drizzle over some olive oil and serve.

SERVES 6–8

•NOTE

I love using celery leaves as part of this garnish, if there are any on that random heart of celery everyone has in the crisper.

Pork Hock and Cabbage Soup

'Russian cabbage soup may suit a people who love train oil but surely it would be rejected by any civilised Englishman,' or so wrote Andrew Valentine Kirwan 150 years ago. In this case I fear he is wrong. I like this soup as I think the gelatinous stock from the hocks, the blushing pink smoked pork that falls from them, and the silky strands of wilted cabbage are a brilliant combination. I suspect this means you'd better call me Boris or a barbarian.

1 large pork hock

2 bay leaves

8 black peppercorns

½ tablespoon fennel seeds

8 sprigs thyme

3 celery stalks

2 garlic cloves, smashed

1 brown onion, peeled and halved

1 carrot, peeled

¼ bunch flat-leaf parsley stalks

1.5 litres (6 cups) chicken stock

1 litre (4 cups) water

1–2 tablespoons extra-virgin olive oil

20 g butter, plus extra if flash-frying pork at the end

2 leeks, cut into 10 cm pieces then into long strips

½ small savoy or drumhead cabbage, sliced into 1 cm ribbons

salt flakes and freshly ground black pepper

Place the hock, bay leaves, peppercorns, fennel seeds, thyme, celery, garlic, brown onion, carrot, parsley, stock and water in a large stockpot or saucepan. Bring to the boil, reduce the heat and then simmer uncovered for 30 minutes.

Remove the hock from the pot and set aside until cool enough to pull off all the pink rosy meat. Discard the skin.

Strain the stock through a colander into a bowl and then return the liquid to the same pot.

In a large frying pan heat the olive oil and butter over medium heat. Add the leeks. Sauté for a couple of minutes before adding the cabbage. Toss the cabbage for about 5–6 minutes until it wilts just a little.

Shred the pork hock meat and return to the stock. (Alternatively, you could flash-fry the shredded meat in butter and pour it sizzling into the soup as you serve it.) Add the cabbage and leeks to the stock and bring to the boil. Reduce the heat to a simmer and cook for a further 15 minutes.

Season to taste.

SERVES 6–8

TIP

In winter, when cabbage is in season, ribbons of drumhead or savoy cabbage make every vegetable soup seem heartier and deliver both a luxurious satin texture and a bit of bite. Fry it in butter first if you want to be decadent.

THAI PUMPKIN SOUP

Pumpkin soup is Australia's favourite soup and Thai is the restaurant takeaway tucker that we do better than any other country (well other than Thailand, natch). So it's obviously delicious and crowd-pleasingly popular to combine the two in one soup – a bit like the Republican Party finding a presidential candidate who is both a soap star and a churchgoing war hero.

Place the onion, garlic, ginger, lemongrass, coriander root and chilli (if using) into a large pot with the oil and cook over low to medium heat for 3–5 minutes.

Add the kaffir lime leaves and sugar and sauté for a couple of minutes until the fragrance starts to permeate the kitchen.

Add the pumpkin to the pot and stir for a couple of minutes to coat, then add the stock and water. Bring to the boil.

Once boiling, reduce the heat and allow to simmer, uncovered, until the pumpkin is soft. This will take about 20 minutes, depending on how small your pumpkin pieces are.

Remove the kaffir lime leaves and blend with a stick blender or in a processor until smooth.

Add half the coconut milk and taste. If you think it needs more, add it a little at a time until it is just as you like it. Season with salt and pepper to taste.

Pour the soup into bowls and garnish with sprigs of fresh coriander, a little pile of fried shallots and some slivers of chilli.

SERVES 8

1½ brown onions, diced

2 garlic cloves, diced

2 teaspoons freshly minced ginger

1 tablespoon finely chopped lemongrass

4 coriander roots, scraped and chopped

1 red chilli, finely diced (optional)

1½ tablespoons coconut oil, or peanut or vegetable oil

2 kaffir lime leaves, torn

30 g palm sugar or 1 tablespoon sugar

1 kg peeled pumpkin, cut into small chunks

1 litre chicken or vegetable stock

250 ml (1 cup) water

125 ml (½ cup) coconut milk

salt flakes and freshly ground black pepper, to taste

GARNISH

coriander sprigs

1 tablespoon fried shallots

½ red chilli, finely sliced

'TO MAKE A PERFECT SALAD, THERE SHOULD BE A MISER FOR OIL, A SPENDTHRIFT FOR VINEGAR, A WISE MAN FOR SALT, AND A MADCAP TO STIR THE INGREDIENTS UP AND MIX THEM WELL TOGETHER.'

Andrew Valentine Kirwan, 1864

SALADS
and vegetables

JUST A SIMPLE TOMATO SALAD

This salad is simply French. It is all about the quality and the ripeness of the tomatoes and the restrained elegance of the dressing.

7–8 medium-sized ripe tomatoes or 800 g mixed tomatoes

2 small French shallots, finely sliced

DRESSING

½ teaspoon salt flakes

1 tablespoon red wine vinegar

3 tablespoons vegetable oil

⅛ teaspoon ground white pepper

Pour the salt and vinegar into a bowl to dissolve, then add the oil and pepper and mix with a fork.

If the tomatoes are small cut them into quarters or halves, and thickly slice any larger tomatoes.

Mix the shallots and tomatoes and steep in the dressing for a couple of minutes before serving.

To be a true Francophile, serve alongside a crusty French baguette and a chunk of gooey French brie. Mop up the tomato juices with some of the baguette.

SERVES 4–6

WHAT, THIS OLD THING?
Watermelon, feta and pepita salad that still gets admiring glances

Northern Greece claims this salad combo as their own but I ate my first version of it at one of Geoff Lindsay's places. He's a top chef so his had green olives and a decadently loose tomato-water jelly. I'm a daggy home cook so mine's simpler, adding a couple of handfuls of un-toasted nuts for creaminess and crunch. It's not too bad either.

One tip: this is best thrown together just before you eat. It goes really well on its own or with slow-cooked lamb shoulder. Oops, that was two tips. Sorry!

1 small bunch mint, leaves picked

juice of 1 lime

about 1 kg watermelon, skin off (sweet, ripe and with the seeds 'cos it is better that way)

1 Lebanese cucumber

100 g feta, broken into chunks (something creamy but firm like Dodoni)

2 tablespoons pepitas

2 tablespoons sunflower seeds

Add the mint leaves to the lime juice.

Slice the watermelon into 1 cm-thick slices, and then break the slices into chunks.

Peel half the cucumber, slice the whole thing into 2 cm lengths and then cut these into quarters. (Peeling half the cucumber is optional, but it looks pretty.)

Toss the cucumber pieces with the watermelon and spread them over a platter.

Scatter the feta on top.

Pour the lime juice with the mint over the top and garnish with a sprinkling of pepitas and sunflower seeds.

SERVES 6–8

Leaf Salad with Special Dressing

In his *A Discourse on Sallets* (1699), John Evelyn writes extensively about the refreshing role of the 'sallet' and of the 35 different herbs and other flavourings that can be added, from simple coriander leaf and chervil to pickled capers and samphire. This salad pays tribute to his simple and rather stolid belief that this was what a vegetarian Adam and Eve ate in the Garden of Eden.

A great salad is also all about the dressing, something that Evelyn's countrymen were going to become obsessed with 100 years later when, fleeing the French Revolution, London welcomed two Frenchmen who became celebrated for their skill at dressing salads.

Aristocratic homes would pay the princely sum of a guinea for one of these gentlemen to call at their home to dress the salad for their finest dinners. The average wage at the time was only 10 pounds a year, so getting paid a pound and a shilling for each salad was a fine fee indeed!

One of these salad dressers, named D'Albignac, would arrive with the flair of a modern celebrity chef, in a fine coach with a liveried servant, carrying a mahogany case filled with perfumed vinegars and oils flavoured with fruit, soy, caviar, truffles, anchovies or ketchup gravy. As well as dressing salads he also sold copies of his mahogany case like modern celeb chefs sell their pots and pans! D'Albignac retired back to France with a small fortune of 80,000 francs in his keeping.

Ideally use this dressing fresh but it will keep in a clean, sealed screw-top jar or plastic tub for a few days. Be generous but timely with your application to the leaves.

Whisk the mustard and the egg yolk in a large mixing bowl.

Slowly drizzle in the oil in a steady stream, incorporating it as you go.

Add the vinegar, salt and a twist or two of freshly ground pepper. It will resemble a mayonnaise in consistency.

In a processor or by hand, finely chop all the herbs and add to the dressing. Add a tablespoon or two of water to thin the dressing, but not too much.

This is a thick dressing – very herbaceous. It's perfect to dress plain, soft green leaves such as butter lettuce, but never oak, which is the devil's lettuce. If you don't know what oak is, it's that gross stuff that always goes soggy and uneaten in your mixed lettuce bag.

SERVES 4–6

Soft, green salad leaves (butter lettuce is best but gem, cos or iceberg will also welcome this dressing)

DRESSING

1½ tablespoons Dijon mustard

1 egg yolk

600 ml vegetable oil

60 ml (3 tablespoons) white wine vinegar

1 teaspoon salt flakes

freshly ground black pepper

½ bunch chervil (optional)

¼ bunch tarragon leaves, stripped off stalks

½ bunch basil

½ bunch flat-leaf parsley

1–2 tablespoons water

(makes 2½ cups)

A RED CABBAGE SALAD *of* STOLEN FLAVOURS

With all the colour and shimmer of an eighties disco, this salad dances to the beat set by the surprising compatibility that red cabbage has with seeded mustard. If you don't believe me, try serving your next pork chop on a bed of butter-fried red cabbage dressed with a dollop of popping wholegrain mustard. Or this salad!

about 270 g (2 cups) frozen edamame beans in pods (130 g podded beans)

100 g thickly sliced pancetta or bacon, cut into batons

½ small red cabbage (about 500–600 g), finely shredded

¼ bunch flat-leaf parsley, torn or roughly chopped

DRESSING

1½ tablespoons balsamic vinegar

1½ tablespoons wholegrain seeded mustard

1½ tablespoons soft brown sugar

3 tablespoons extra-virgin olive oil

pinch of salt flakes

freshly ground black pepper

juice of ½ orange

Blanch the edamame beans in boiling water for 45 seconds, refresh under cold water and then pod.

Cook the pancetta in a pan over medium heat until dark and crunchy, then drain on paper towel.

Mix the dressing in a jar or with a whisk.

In a large bowl, toss the shredded cabbage, half the edamame, half the pancetta and most of the parsley with half the dressing. If you think it needs more dressing add a bit at a time – you don't want to overdress.

Tumble the remaining ingredients over the top, and serve.

SERVES 4–6

TIP

If you don't have any edamame, use fresh or frozen podded broad beans instead.

AMBIVALENT ASIAN SALAD *with* CHARRED CHICKEN THIGHS

I love a strong woman. My friend Georgina is one of these; a fine cook who is quite capable of disregarding orders if she thinks she can do things better. This was the salad she and her offsider, Glenbie, worked up for the Jeep Marquee at the Portsea Polo (if you don't mind). It was better than the prawn one that I'd suggested we do – mainly because of the sourness of the green mango and how well the quite severely bitter char on the BBQ thighs goes with that sourness and with the sweetness of the dressing. That's why it's here. I should note that if you have a mandoline this salad takes about half the time to make and, as I suspect you'll want to make this salad again and again, you might want to invest in one. Georgina would.

THE THIGHS

cleaned roots and stems of 1 bunch coriander

2 garlic cloves

1 tablespoon peanut oil

juice and zest of 1 lime

4 chicken thighs (about 600 g), skin off

THE SALAD

1 bunch red radishes, topped and tailed

1 large daikon radish, topped and tailed

2 small (or 1 large) green mangoes, or 1 crisp green apple

1 long (telegraph) cucumber, peeled and deseeded

1 bunch coriander, leaves picked

1 bunch mint, leaves picked

1 bunch Thai basil, leaves picked (optional)

THE DRESSING

2 tablespoons fish sauce

juice of 4 limes

1 red chilli, finely diced

60 g palm sugar

THE THIGHS

Blend the coriander, garlic, oil and lime together until they become a paste. Spoon the paste into a large ziplock bag with the chicken thighs. Seal the bag and massage it until the thighs are well coated. Leave for at least 30 minutes to infuse.

Heat your BBQ. You want it hot!

Sear the chicken on the grill for 10 minutes. Now drop the heat or, if your BBQ has a lid, move the chook off the direct heat and close the lid of your BBQ. Cook the thighs gently like this for 20 minutes. Now crank up the heat again and get some good charry bar markings on the meat. Remove when just cooked through and rest (the chicken thighs, not you!).

While the chicken thighs are cooking make the salad.

THE SALAD

Cut the red radishes into quarters or eighths depending on their size. Place in a bowl with cold water and a good handful of ice cubes to firm up.

Finely julienne the daikon and green mango (or apple) and the cucumber. Place in the salad bowl.

Add the herb leaves to the salad bowl.

Drain and add the radishes and the sliced grilled thighs. Dress with ... um ... err ... the dressing.

THE DRESSING

Mix the fish sauce, lime juice and chilli. Add a little sugar at a time to balance the saltiness of the fish sauce and the sourness of the lime juice. You may not need it all. Sweet, sour, salty is the mix we are looking for, in that order of prominence.

SERVES 4

NOT A DAMN PASTA SALAD ... A SOBA NOODLE SALAD

I have a few rules guiding the three cookbooks that I've written. 1) The recipes must be simple; 2) the ingredients in the vast majority must be readily available from a local supermarket; 3) there can never be a pasta salad in the book. This soba noodle one seems to have snuck through in part because the dressing is so darned delicious it distracted me from its true nature. Also, it has to be said, there is something wonderfully cooling about the Japanese love of cold noodles that's perfect for a hot summer's night. And soba's not pasta really, is it?

Cook the noodles as per packet instructions, then refresh in cold water so they don't overcook.

In a large mixing bowl combine the ponzu sauce, soy sauce, caster sugar, ginger and sesame oil.

Add the shallots and mushrooms and leave them to soften in the dressing before adding the noodles, edamame and coriander leaves to the bowl.

Gently toss to combine the ingredients and coat everything with the dressing.

Plate up and top with fried garlic chips, black sesame seeds, chilli slices (if using) and a few coriander sprigs.

SERVES 4–6

TIP

You can use podded broad beans instead of edamame but, quite frankly, if you are heading to the Asian grocer for the fried garlic, black sesame seeds, soba noodles and the ponzu sauce you might as well grab some frozen edamame as well!

1 × 270 g packet soba noodles

2 tablespoons ponzu sauce

2 tablespoons light soy sauce

1 teaspoon caster sugar

the slightest grate of fresh ginger

½ teaspoon sesame oil

4 red Asian shallots, peeled and sliced super fine

8 oyster mushrooms, cut finely in long strips

270 g (2 cups) frozen edamame beans, podded

¼ bunch coriander and a few sprigs to garnish

2 tablespoons fried garlic chips (from your Asian grocer)

black or white sesame seeds

red chilli, finely sliced (optional)

AGRIDULCE SALADO VALENCIA

Admission time. I used to love peanut butter and apricot jam sandwiches, but this obsession has turned into another love – peanut butter with honey and salt flakes. Any aficionado will know that the best peanut butter is both savoury and sweet and these additions hypercharge the PBS to a special level.

Having said that, there is something special about honey and salt on their own and I wanted to knock up a dish that highlighted this combo. Then along comes a hot night, a cool rooftop bar called Bomba and Jesse Gerner's take on a Valencian salad that sets this flavour contrast against cos lettuce hearts and slivers of orange flesh. I've moved it along by adding walnuts and goat's cheese – both of which love honey like sharks love blood – and by adding some protein to take this from a refreshing side dish to a light meal. Happy days ... especially as goat's cheese loves honey in a very special way indeed!

100 g sugar

100 g (1 cup) walnut pieces

3 oranges

2 tablespoons good olive oil

2 teaspoons white wine vinegar

1 tablespoon runny honey, warmed, plus extra for drizzling

leaves from 2 small cos lettuce heads

salt flakes

150 g soft goat's cheese

Melt the sugar in a small pan. Let it bubble and turn into a brown caramel. Toss the walnuts into the pan and stir to cover in caramel. Spread them out onto a baking tray lined with baking paper to dry.

Now, to segment the oranges, slice the peel off, removing all the pith. Then hold each orange over a bowl (to catch any juice) and, using a very sharp knife, slice between the membranes to remove the flesh of each segment. Reserve the flesh.

Make the dressing by roughly mixing the oil and vinegar with the honey. The honey will firm up into little nuggets of sweetness between the oil and vinegar. Nice!

Assemble the orange and lettuce and pour over the dressing. Add a couple of good pinches of salt flakes. The salt interacting with the sweet honey is the key to this salad! Toss.

Tear up the goat's cheese over the salad. Drizzle a little extra honey over the goat's cheese. Throw over the candied walnuts and serve with more salt flakes so your guests can tweak the sweet, sour, salty flavour to their liking.

SERVES 4–6

TIPS

1. This salad can be simplified with the omission of the walnuts and the goat's cheese. This is great with BBQ'd chicken or steaks or with meaty fish like tuna.

2. If you want to go another way, think of these additions: green or black olives or thin slices of red onion pickled in sherry vinegar. Or dump the goat's cheese and walnuts in favour of pan-fried slices of chorizo mixed with chunks of warmed Manchego and crushed, salted almonds.

Crying Tiger Beef

Pomegranate molasses and lamb; pineapple juice and pork; teriyaki and chicken. These are some very simple ways of adding flavour to what you want to grill using just the contents of a bottle. In this recipe, marinating the beef in sweet Malaysian or Indonesian soy sauce (kecap manis) gives a little oomph to the surface of the meat that helps a good crust form – a lovely contrast to the stridently rare interior. Accordingly, buy a smaller piece of better beef and fill up on rice and a simple Asian coleslaw.

1 x 300 g piece of good-quality, thick-cut porterhouse or rump steak, excess fat cut off

100 ml (5 tablespoons) kecap manis

oil, for frying

fresh chilli, to serve (optional)

fried shallots, to serve (optional)

DIPPING SAUCE

60 ml (3 tablespoons) lime juice (about 1½–2 limes)

40 ml (2 tablespoons) fish sauce

15 g palm sugar or 1 teaspoon caster sugar

2 smallish shallots, super-finely sliced

⅛ teaspoon chilli powder or ground chilli flakes

1½ tablespoons finely sliced Thai (or normal) coriander, plus extra to serve

Marinate the whole steak in the kecap manis for at least a couple of hours. Remove from the marinade and pat dry.

Heat a heavy-based frying pan with a touch of oil over medium heat. Sear the steak on both sides and cook it the way you like it. Take care not to burn it – the sugars from the marinade will burn quickly. I think it's best a little rare on the inside. Remove from the pan and leave it to rest, covered, for 5–10 minutes.

Combine all the dipping sauce ingredients in a bowl and stir until the sugar has dissolved.

Slice the meat thinly and lay it on a serving plate. Scatter over the coriander, as well as the fresh chilli and fried shallots, if using. Serve with the dipping sauce on the side.

SERVES 2

TOFU WITH PONZU AND FRIED GARLIC

Here's another use for the black sesame seeds, ponzu sauce and kecap manis (Indonesian or Malaysian) you bought for the Crying Tiger and Soba Noodle salads (pages 68 and 65). While tofu is almost the emblem of the vegetarian movement, this dish has enough tang, sweetness and textural interest to have even the most hardcore carnivores contemplating booking into an ashram.

Cut the tofu into small cubes, about 2 cm square. Divide the tofu among small bowls or pile into one bigger bowl. Toss the tofu in the ponzu and leave to marinate whilst you get the other ingredients ready.

Gently toss through the spring onions, coriander and ginger. Drizzle over the kecap manis and top with the fried garlic chips and sesame seasoning.

SERVES 2–3 AS A STARTER

•NOTE

You can buy fried garlic chips and black sesame seeds from Asian supermarkets and even some regular supermarkets these days. You can usually find black sesame seeds in health food stores too.

about 400 g medium (as opposed to firm or silken) tofu

3 tablespoons ponzu sauce

2 spring onions, super-finely sliced

6 sprigs coriander

1 tablespoon pickled ginger, torn (optional)

2 tablespoons kecap manis

2 tablespoons fried garlic chips

Japanese sesame and vegetable seasoning (or black sesame seeds)

NIÇOISE FARRO SALAD

There is something rather wonderful about how the chewy nuttiness of these traditional dried grains of wheat goes with the sunny flavours of the Mediterranean veg here. As for the crispy fried chickpeas, these are a wee bit addictive so keep them hidden while you are prepping the salad or else they'll be largely snaffled by marauders passing through the kitchen before you've plated up. Leave the tuna out if you are feeding vegetarians. It's still a great salad.

230 g (1 cup) farro

500 ml (2 cups) vegetable stock

olive oil, for frying

20 green beans, trimmed

2 zucchini, quartered lengthways and chopped into chunks

1 red capsicum, cored, deseeded and cut into 2 cm tiles

3 garlic cloves, very finely diced

1 × 425 g can tuna in brine

1 × 400 g can chickpeas, drained, rinsed and left to dry in a colander

1 teaspoon ground coriander

salt flakes

½ cup halved and pitted green olives (black are fine too)

1 × 250 g punnet cherry tomatoes, cut lengthways

1 bunch flat-leaf parsley, chopped, to serve

juice and zest of ½ lemon, to serve

DRESSING
3 tablespoons good olive oil

2 tablespoons red wine vinegar

Cook the farro according to the packet instructions (depending on the type of farro it can take from 15 to 40 minutes) but using the stock and a little extra water if required. Drain and leave to cool.

Splash a little olive oil into a frying pan. When hot, fry the beans gently until a little softened.

Increase the heat, add the zucchini and the tiles of red capsicum and fry for a few minutes until the faces of the zucchini are tanned and the capsicum has softened.

Add the garlic and the tuna. Toss some more until fragrant. Remove and reserve.

Add a little more oil to the pan and leave on the heat.

Throw the rinsed and drained chickpeas into the pan. Turn the heat up to high and toss. When the chickpeas start to brown a little, toss in the ground coriander. Cook for another few minutes until the chickpeas start to get a little crispy on the surface but stop before anything starts to burn! Sprinkle in some salt flakes.

Make the dressing by pouring 3 tablespoons of good olive oil and 1½ tablespoons of red wine vinegar into a bowl. DON'T mix!

Just before eating fork up the farro so it is fluffy. Fold in the capsicum, zucchini, bean and tuna mix along with the olives. Arrange as a mound in the middle of a platter. Pour the dressing around the edge of the salad.

Cover the mound with the halved tomatoes and a good drift of chopped parsley. Squeeze over the juice of ½ a lemon, but no seeds please. Garnish with the pan-fried chickpeas and a little lemon zest if you like.

SERVES 4–6

NAM JIM, GRAPEFRUIT, CUCUMBER *and* MINT SALAD

Some confusion revolves around the differences between *nam jim* and its slightly thicker, more complex Thai sauce brother, *nam prik*. Which that last sentence should have cleared up! The sweet, sour, salty and hot dressing that is *nam jim* is perfect with the cooling calm of the cucumbers and the juicy pop of those pink grapefruit carpels.

Eat this salad on its own or served with anything from BBQ'd chook thighs or deep-fried chicken to grilled salmon or pork chops. Feel free to add prawns or rice vermicelli to bulk things out, or even substitute chunks of pomelo flesh or ripe mango for the grapefruit.

If you leave the dressing on the salad for a while before eating, it will weave its magic on the cucumber and the salad will slowly morph into a nam jim *taengkwa* as the cucumber starts to pickle. This is perfection with satay.

4 Lebanese cucumbers, sliced into ribbons with a peeler

1 pink grapefruit, segmented, each segment cut in half lengthways

¼ bunch mint, leaves picked

NAM JIM

40 g palm sugar

2 garlic cloves

2 long red chillies

1 bullet chilli (optional)

3 coriander roots, scraped and well washed

2 tablespoons lime juice

1½ tablespoons fish sauce

½ teaspoon salt flakes

To make the nam jim, pound the palm sugar, garlic, chillies and coriander roots using a mortar and pestle, blitz them in a processor or cut finely by hand.

Add the lime juice and fish sauce. Season with salt to taste.

When you are ready to plate up, toss the cucumber ribbons in a large bowl with a few tablespoons of nam jim.

Lay the wavy ribbons of cucumber on a serving plate, place the grapefruit segments on top and scatter over the mint.

Serve with the remaining nam jim on the side.

SERVES 4–6

TIP

Too often when recipes call for coriander they just use the leaves. The roots and stems have delicious flavour and can be saved by mincing and freezing for later use. Or by making this salad!

TUNA SASHIMI *and* SPICY AVOCADO SALAD THAT IMPRESSED THE BOSSES

Raw fish? It's not everyone's cup of miso, you know. Burly blokes who will happily ask for their steak 'bloody' will blanch at the prospect of trying kingfish carpaccio, go a strange shade of green at the approach of an oyster and ask for their salmon to be cooked way past pink, until the fish's flesh is as splintery dry as balsa wood.

Of course there are good reasons why the Japanese do not share these common taboos about eating raw fish. Fish is central to the Japanese way of life because Japan is a system of islands and from the late 7th century, Japanese rulers were inspired by Buddhist principles that banned the eating of cattle, horses, dogs, chickens and monkeys. There is also a commonly held Japanese attitude about food which states that the freshest fish should be eaten raw, slightly less fresh fish should be grilled and older fish should be braised.

Interestingly, while raw fish might form one of the stronger European taboos – alongside not eating insects or animals that might be pets – the US has seen a movement called 'raw foodism' growing over the last 20 years. The core principle of this movement is to eat nothing that has been heated above 46°C, based on a belief that cooking food impacts negatively on its nutritional worth. Nuts, seeds, sprouted seeds and veg, both pickled and raw, all form part of the diet.

While many raw foodies are vegan or vegetarian, there are also wings of the movement that espouse a fully carnivorous approach to raw food, such as the Primal Diet championed by Aajonus Vonderplanitz, who has eaten an all-raw diet for 38 years (please note his surname is not to be pronounced 'Underpants' but 'WonderPlanets') and the Paleolithic Diet. This very Californian affair is based on the belief that we should all eat a diet like our ancient ancestors did in the age before agriculture. That means lots of raw meat and fish, but usually no grains, dairy or oils.

In order to keep happy both Paleo and Japanese readers, I present this simple recipe that requires no cooking and pays homage to the Japanese culinary art of *namasu*, which was the way the Japanese ate raw fish before sushi became popular in the 17th century. With *namasu*, fish was just dipped into a vinegar dipping sauce.

I am working on the principle that, if we can accept that we always eat raw things in salads, then maybe this salad-like creation will con people into eating raw fish. You can also claim that the use of sauce and citrus on the fish is actually curing it a little so it has become more like ceviche or gravalax!

Inspiration for this recipe comes from the sashimi cubes that Glenn Bowman used to serve at Alegria in Sunshine Beach in Queensland, the bigeye tuna David Rayner used to make at Noosaville's River House, the crazy mix of miso and avocado with nori served at the Ichi Ni Izakaya in St Kilda in Melbourne – and Poh.

Combine the avocado cubes with a squeeze of lime and wasabi to taste. It should be a little hot but not scalding. Alternatively, mix until you have a smooth purée.

To make the dressing, squeeze 80 ml lime juice – that will be about 2 limes – into a bowl. Slowly add up to 40 ml soy sauce or 2 tablespoons, tasting as you go. You want it to be mainly citrusy and not too salty or vegemite-y from the soy.

Trim the seaweed into credit card–sized pieces.

Take all the components to the table ready to assemble as you go; you should have the avocado, dressing, seaweed, tuna and ginger.

Dress the tuna at the table, tossing it in just enough dressing to make it glisten. Serve the rest of the dressing in a bowl alongside the ginger, extra wasabi, avocado, seaweed and ½ a lime cut into wedges.

To eat, pile a little tuna on a tile of seaweed, dot with a spoonful of hot avocado and ginger and eat immediately.

SERVES 4 AS A SMALL STARTER

3 ripe avocadoes, cut into cubes

3 limes

fresh wasabi root or wasabi powder or paste, to taste

40 ml soy sauce (a Japanese one is best)

1 × 100 g packet pickled ginger

1 × 36 g packet crispy seaweed sushi sheets, available from the Asian grocer or Asian section of some supermarkets. These are dried toasted seaweed, sometimes flavoured with chilli or wasabi.

400 g sashimi grade tuna (yellow fin or bigeye), cut into 1.5 cm cubes

BITTER? SWEET? WHO, ME?
Witlof, Date and Green Olive Salad

'Chicoree or endive is in season at the end of Autumn and it is not usual to add any *herbe de fourniture* to that salad.' Cousin Andrew's declaration on chicoree is hardly the most effusive. I love it somewhat more, whether it is sliced into crescents to toss through salads or grains for wet crunch and earthy bitterness, or sprinkled with sugar and pan-roasted into a soft, sweet, charry mess. As a salad leaf you have two options: partner it with something aggressively salty like parmesan or blue cheese, or pair it with something sweet like a balsamic or honey dressing instead. I like both together! Here, the olives bring the salt and the dates give us the perception of a sweet dressing.

2 whole witlof

8 large, pitted green olives or Sicilian olives, roughly chopped

5 dates, chopped into small pieces

fennel fronds from 1 small fennel bulb, or dill (optional)

1 orange, segmented and juice reserved (see page 66 for how to expertly segment citrus)

a drizzle of extra-virgin olive oil

freshly ground black pepper

Gently peel the leaves from both witlof, doing your best to keep them intact. Arrange them on a serving plate.

Toss the olives and dates in a small bowl with lots of fennel fronds (if using).

Spoon a little into each witlof leaf then pile any left over in the middle.

Place an orange segment on top of each fennel leaf.

Drizzle over a little orange juice (not too much) and finish with a scatter of fennel fronds, a drizzle of oil and a few grinds of black pepper. This is perfect for eating with your hands.

SERVES 6

TIP

Instead of oranges you could use blood oranges, when they're in season, or mandarins.

SWEET? SALTY? WHO, ME?
Roasted Beetroot Salad with Mint, Orange and Oregano

This salad is as much about how you assemble it (to ensure the elements remain separate until the very last moment before they are eaten) as it is about the sure-fire combination of flavours and textures, from the fresh creaminess of the yoghurt base to the sweet, soft beets, the fragrant orange zest, the crunch of the pistachios and the honest freshness of the oregano.

500 g thick Greek yoghurt

salt flakes

½ bunch mint, leaves picked and finely chopped

1 garlic clove, minced

juice and zest of ½ lemon

about 3 tablespoons extra-virgin olive oil

3 beetroots, ends trimmed

1 tablespoon red wine vinegar

½ bunch fresh oregano, leaves picked

½ cup pistachios, roughly chopped and tossed in a little oil

zest of ½ an orange

freshly ground black pepper

Preheat the oven to 200°C.

Line a strainer with muslin or a clean Chux cloth, spoon in the yoghurt and stir in a generous pinch of salt.

Fold the fabric over the top. Suspend the strainer over a bowl, place in the fridge and allow the yoghurt to drain for at least an hour. Liquid will leach out of the yoghurt leaving a super-thick yoghurt/labna.

After an hour or so, tip the labna into a bowl, add the mint, the garlic, lemon zest and juice and a touch of salt. Set aside in the fridge for the flavours to infuse.

Drizzle a little olive oil over the beetroots and wrap them individually in foil. Bake in the preheated oven for about 45–60 minutes.

Allow the beetroot to cool off a bit before putting on gloves and peeling them. But note that it's easier to peel or rub off the skin while they are still warm. Cut each beetroot into small cubes, about 1.5–2 cm. Toss them in a bowl with the red wine vinegar and 1 tablespoon of oil.

To serve, spread the labna over the bottom of a large serving plate, then scatter over the oregano leaves. Pile the beetroot on top, tumble over the pistachios and orange zest and season with a touch more salt and freshly ground pepper.

SERVES 6–8

THE RED SALAD

Botswana … a country of beef-lovers … too many elephants … lessons on how to spit impala poo … lions that want to eat you … the nicest people with a wonderful pride in their independence … an all-red salad that can go with either the best roo fillet or beef.

Rub the sugar and salt into the red onion slices. Leave for a minute. Splash over the red wine vinegar and toss so it coats all the onion.

Trim the meat of any fat. Pat dry and brush with the macadamia (or grapeseed) oil.

Heat your BBQ flat grill or heaviest frying pan until it's savagely hot.

Keep the heat up and cook the meat for a couple of minutes, or until the surface is charred in places.

Flip the steaks over onto another hot part of the pan and sear the other side.

Sear the edges. Don't overcook – you want the meat rare and red.

Remove. Rest and slice thinly – about 4 mm should do it. Season with salt flakes.

Drain the red onions, which are now tangy.

Arrange the red kidney beans in a line down the middle of a platter.

Organise the meat, capsicum and radishes over the beans.

Drape over the slices of red onions.

Dress with a simple vinaigrette made by pouring over the macadamia (or grapeseed) oil then 1 full tablespoon of red wine vinegar.

Finally sprinkle over some salt flakes.

SERVES 4

¼ teaspoon caster sugar

¼ teaspoon pink salt flakes

½ red onion, very thinly sliced

1 teaspoon red wine vinegar, plus more for dressing

400 g very lean red meat (young roo or beef fillet like porterhouse)

salt flakes

1½ tablespoons macadamia or grapeseed oil, plus more for dressing

1 × 240 g can kidney beans, rinsed and dried

150 g (about ½) red capsicum, deseeded and cut into 1 cm tiles

75 g (about 8 or a small bunch) radishes, topped, tailed, cut into quarters, then halved into chunks

3 ways with
JERUSALEM ARTICHOKES

1. THE CALM JERUSALEM ARTICHOKE SALAD

1 tablespoon lemon juice

1 teaspoon finely grated lemon zest

2 tablespoons extra-virgin olive oil

2 pinches of salt flakes

freshly ground black pepper

4 anchovies, roughly chopped

½ cup Sicilian olives, pitted and halved

2 baby gem lettuce

150 g Jerusalem artichokes

¼ cup shaved Parmigiano Reggiano

Place the lemon juice, zest and oil in a medium-sized bowl and give it a quick toss. Add the salt, pepper and anchovies and toss to combine. Add the pitted olives.

Cut the lettuce into quarters. Carefully pull off the outer leaves, trimming the base to release the leaves as you go. Add the leaves to the bowl. Peel the Jerusalem artichokes and slice very finely using a mandoline or food processor. Add them to the bowl and toss with the dressing. Top with the shaved parmesan and serve.

SERVES 4

2. ROASTED JERUSALEM ARTICHOKE CHIPS

extra-virgin olive oil

50 g butter

500 g Jerusalem artichokes, halved lengthways

juice of 1 lemon

1 bunch thyme, leaves picked

salt flakes and freshly ground black pepper

Preheat the oven to 180°C.

Cover the bottom of a roasting dish with oil. Put it on your gas burner and heat it, then add the butter. When the butter begins to froth add the artichokes cut-side down, then leave them be for a few minutes while they lightly colour. Shake them about in the pan.

Add the lemon juice to the pan. Scatter over the thyme leaves, season with salt and pepper, and place in the hot oven for about an hour. Depending on the size of the artichokes, they will be ready when they are golden brown on the cut side and tender enough to squash with a fork.

Toss through salads or serve with roast chook.

SERVES 4–6

3. JERUSALEM ARTICHOKE GRATIN

1.5 kg large Jerusalem artichokes, peeled and cut into 5 mm slices

1½ tablespoons unsalted butter, cut into small pieces

2 garlic cloves, chopped

2 tablespoons chopped flat-leaf parsley

salt flakes and freshly ground black pepper

300 ml double cream

Bring a saucepan of salted water to the boil. Add the artichokes to the water and cook until just tender when pierced with a fork, about 15 minutes.

Preheat the oven to 200°C.

Butter a gratin dish and cover the bottom of the dish with a layer of Jerusalem artichoke slices, overlapping them slightly. Dot with some of the butter and add a sprinkle of the garlic and parsley, then season with salt and pepper. Repeat the layering until you have used up all the ingredients. Pour about 200 ml of the cream evenly over the surface.

Bake for about 30–35 minutes, until the top is crusty and the cream has become custard-like. Remove from the oven, add the remaining cream and return to the oven. Raise the oven temperature to 220°C and continue to bake until the surface of the gratin is golden brown, about 15 minutes. Serve immediately with anything roasted or BBQ'd.

SERVES 6

2.

1.

3.

3 ways with KALE

1. GREEN SMOOTHIE

One great way to harness all of the nutrients in kale is to use it in your morning smoothie or juice. The secret here is to find ways to mask the bitterness of the kale juice by adding frozen raspberries, over-ripe bananas, green apples, beetroot, fresh ginger or ripe mango to the mix. You'll find this type of smoothie is a great place to hide a dose of protein powder as well. Yes, the on-trend aspiring supermodels among you can add coconut water too.

1 bunch kale

1 bunch flat-leaf parsley

2 Lebanese cucumbers or ½ continental cucumber

2–3 sweet apples, such as Golden Delicious

½ bunch mint

juice of ½ lime

Bung everything but the lime through an electric juicer – stalks, stems, skin, leaves and all – and what comes out is a wonderfully verdant 600 ml of goodness.

Squeeze in the lime juice, give it a stir and enjoy!

SERVES 2

2. KALE CHIPS – HONESTLY!

This is probably one of my favourite ways of eating kale. And these chips are so simple to make that it's hardly fair to call this a recipe!

1 bunch kale, washed, stems removed and leaves cut into 5 cm lengths

2 tablespoons olive oil

1 garlic clove, minced (optional)

salt flakes and freshly ground black pepper

1 teaspoon chilli flakes

splash of red wine vinegar

pinch of vinegar powder

pinch of *shichimi togarashi* or *gomashio*

Preheat the oven to 175°C. Line a tray with baking paper.

Dry your washed kale really well, so the oil will cling to the leaves. Then just toss the leaves in the olive oil (you can add some minced garlic to this if you like), salt and freshly ground black pepper and lay them on the lined baking tray.

Bake in the oven for about 15 minutes or until the kale leaves feel crackly.

Eat them hot, sprinkled with a little flaked chilli, red wine vinegar, vinegar powder, the Japanese seven-spice seasoning *shichimi togarashi* or *gomashio*. The latter is a very trendy mix of salt, dried seaweed and unhulled black or brown sesame seeds that's easy to make at home (assuming you can get the ingredients from a health food store or Japanese grocery nearby).

SERVES 2

3. KALE PESTO

Bored of basil and pine nut pesto, or even coriander and cashew pesto? Then here's your solution – a pesto made with kale and walnuts in which the saltiness of the parmesan helps cut through the bitterness of the other two ingredients. I like to stir a generous spoonful of this pesto through al dente angel hair pasta, spread it on flatbread under BBQ'd chicken thighs, or even dollop it in soups and stews.

100 g kale, well washed, hard stalks cut out

50 g (½ cup) walnut pieces

80 g parmesan or other hard cheese, grated

100 ml (¼ cup) olive oil

40 ml (2 tablespoons) lemon juice

1 garlic clove

1 small red chilli

pinch of salt flakes

Blanch the kale in boiling water for a few seconds then refresh in cold water immediately and leave to dry.

Preheat the oven to 170°C.

Pop the walnuts on an oven tray and toast them until just golden. This will only take a few minutes.

Now place all of the ingredients into a food processor and blitz to your preferred texture. I love a little texture and crunch, but remember that processing those walnuts will bring a delicious creaminess. Maybe save a few walnuts to drop in for crunch to the finished pesto.

MAKES 1½ CUPS

1.

2.

3.

'SALADS ARE NOW COMPOSED OF CERTAIN POT HERBS, WHICH GREATLY ADD TO THE ZEST OF THE MIXTURE … NAMELY GARDEN CRESS, WATERCRESS, CHERVIL, CHIVES, SCALLIONS OR GREEN ONIONS, TARRAGON, PIMPERNEL OR BURNET, PARSLEY PERT, HARTSHORN, SWEET BASIL, PURSALIN, FENNEL AND YOUNG BALSAM. THERE ARE TOO HOTCH-POTCH SALADS MADE EN MACEDOINE, WITH A VARIETY OF ROOTS AND VEGETABLES … THERE ARE ALSO SALADS OF MEAT, FISH AND GAME. THERE ARE ALSO SALADS OF LEMONS, ORANGES, POMEGRANATES, PEARS, APPLES, &C.'

Andrew Valentine Kirwan, 1864

UBERSALADS

SMOKED CHICKEN *with* GRAPES, LEMON APPLE, ICEBERG, TARRAGON *and a* BLUE CHEESE DRESSING

Smoked chicken is one of those criminally underrated ingredients – but not here, not now! Here it is the milky-fleshed, film-noir femme fatale in a smoke-filled room dallying between the crisp innocence of the salad and the loose, rich decadence of the dressing. Saucy!

1 Granny Smith (or other crisp green) apple

juice of 1 lemon

½ iceberg lettuce

200 g seedless grapes (ideally red), halved

400 g (about 2) smoked chicken breasts, skin removed, then sliced

1 bunch tarragon, leaves only

DRESSING

200 g sour cream

80 g mild blue cheese (or 60 g of a stronger blue cheese)

1–2 pinches of caster sugar

2 teaspoons white wine vinegar

Make the dressing by mixing the sour cream and blue cheese roughly together with a fork.

Mix in a little sugar and half the vinegar, adding more vinegar until the salty aggression of the blue cheese and the richness of the cream recedes a little.

Cut the apple into matchsticks and douse with the juice of the lemon. Reserve in the juice.

Arrange the iceberg and red seedless grapes in a large salad bowl (or you could use a long serving platter).

Sprinkle over the apple batons and lay on the slices of smoked chook.

Dollop the dressing over the salad and sprinkle over the tarragon leaves.

SERVES 4

A BARLEY CORN SALAD, JOHN

A trip to Kentucky – and the triple discoveries that bourbon 1) could be enjoyed without cola; 2) did not always immediately make you want to 'hoon'; and 3) was made from a mash of corn and a little barley in charred oak barrels – inspired this dish. The corn with turmeric and mustard seeds is something Maharashtrian that I think I saw in Mumbai. I have no idea how the smoked yoghurt got in there but, like kids in a multicultural kindergarten, they all seem to play nicely together! In fact, I'd go as far as to say that this is one of my five favourite recipes in the book. This might have something to do with the combination of a couple of drops of liquid smoke (which you can buy from most BBQ stores and big foodie stores), yoghurt and maple syrup. I am rather in love with that combo of sweet, creamy, smoky, salty.

220 g (1 cup) barley

1 litre chicken stock

4 sweet potatoes (about 2.4 kg), scrubbed

20 g butter

2 tablespoons olive oil

500 g frozen corn kernels, or fresh kernels cut from 6 boiled corn cobs

1 cup Greek yoghurt

1 teaspoon salt flakes

1 teaspoon liquid smoke

GARNISH
2 fresh serrano or jalapeño green chillies

olive oil

2 teaspoons mustard seeds

2 teaspoons ground turmeric

¼ cup (3 tablespoons) bourbon

2 teaspoons cider vinegar

2 tablespoons maple syrup

80 ml (4 tablespoons) mild olive oil

salt flakes, to serve

TIPS

1. To make this veggo recipe go further, mix a finely shredded head of cos or iceberg lettuce through the salad. Or, stir a cup of cubed Gouda, Gruyère, Edam or Fontina cheese into the corn and barley mix just before serving and keep it warm.

2. To make this recipe non-veggo, fry 6 rashers of smoky bacon then cook the corn in the rendered pork fat. Sigh.

Preheat the oven to 180°C.

Simmer the barley in the chicken stock until cooked. This will take about 35 minutes. Test it after 30 minutes. If the barley is looking dry, add another half a cup of stock. If it is cooked, drain it and return to the pot, off the heat.

While the barley is cooking, pop the sweet potatoes onto a greased baking tray and roast for 50 minutes or so.

Heat the butter and oil in a frying pan and fry the corn kernels until burnished at the edges. When the corn is cooked, pop it in the pot with the drained barley.

Mix the yoghurt with a teaspoon of salt and between half and a full teaspoon of liquid smoke, depending on how smoky you like things. Cover and place in the fridge to firm.

Now for the garnish. Use a small knife and, working from the stem end, devein and deseed the green chillies. Then slice them thinly into rings. Splash a little more oil in the corn pan, place over medium heat and flash-fry the chilli rings until they start to shrivel. Remove the chillies to a plate.

Turn up the heat. Throw in another splash of oil. When it's sizzling stir in the mustard seeds. Cover the pan and shake. When the mustard seeds start to pop, throw in the ground turmeric and immediately remove from the heat. Scrape the seeds and turmeric onto the green chilli.

Check the sweet potatoes. They are ready when their middles are fudgy, their skins go papery and they leach out a little stickiness. Slice the potatoes in half lengthways.

Now for the dressing. Deglaze the pan with the bourbon and cider vinegar. Add the maple syrup to sweeten and stir to combine. Remove the pan from the heat and pour in the 80 ml of mild olive oil.

To serve, make a long skid of the smoked yoghurt across the bottom of the serving platter. Pour over the mixed corn and barley mixture. Sprinkle over the mustard seeds and green chillis. Splash the dressing over the salad so it pools around the edge of the mound and the smoked yoghurt. Serve with a bowl of the sliced roast sweet potatoes, sprinkled with salt flakes.

SERVES 8–10

Black Quinoa with Roasted Cauliflower, Pistachio Tarator and Mint AKA Marnie's Salad

Not to be mistaken for the tzatziki-like Bulgarian soup of the same name, the tarator in this recipe is more of the Turkish or Middle Eastern style, where pounded nuts meet oil and sometimes tahini. This style of tarator isn't just for this salad, it can also be served on everything from whole baked fish, roast chicken or lamb chops to battered mussels or fried calamari. You should also try it splashed across slices of oven-roasted pumpkin, spears of well-grilled broccolini or brown rice salad loaded with plump sultanas, lemon-soused apple batons and pine nuts. I find the presence of lots of lemon juice essential to stop the sauce being too claggy!

1 cauliflower, cut into small florets

2 tablespoons extra-virgin olive oil

2 heaped tablespoons panch phoron

1 teaspoon salt flakes

freshly ground black pepper

zest and juice of ½ lemon

1 teaspoon tea leaves

½ cup golden or normal sultanas

1½ cups black (or any colour) quinoa, cooked as per packet instructions

½ bunch mint, leaves picked, to serve

a few pistachio kernels, to serve

TARATOR

140 g (1 cup) pistachio kernels

1 teaspoon ground cumin

60 ml (3 tablespoons) lemon juice

80 ml (4 tablespoons) warm water

2 tablespoons extra-virgin olive oil

1¼ tablespoons tahini

2 garlic cloves, chopped

1 teaspoon salt flakes

2 tablespoons chopped fresh coriander

½ teaspoon dried chilli flakes

Preheat the oven to 200°C.

Put the cauliflower in a low-sided baking tray and toss with the oil, panch phoron, salt, some pepper, the lemon zest and juice. Bake until it's golden brown and cooked through, about 25–30 minutes. Remove from the oven when cooked.

Steep the tea leaves in about 1 cup of boiling water for a few minutes and strain. Then add the sultanas to the tea, leave to soak for 10 minutes, then drain. The sultanas should be plump after the soaking. If you are really slack, you can soak the sultanas in water with a tea bag in it at the same time.

Reduce the oven to 180°C.

To make the tarator, spread the pistachios over a lined baking tray. Bake for 4–5 minutes or until golden. Sprinkle over the cumin. Cool.

Process the pistachios, lemon juice, water, oil, tahini, garlic and sea salt in a food processor until smooth. Place in a bowl and stir in the coriander and chilli.

In a large bowl combine the cooked quinoa and roasted cauliflower with the panch phoron, the soaked sultanas and half the mint leaves. Season with some extra salt and freshly ground pepper to taste.

In a serving bowl, spread the tarator on the bottom, pile the quinoa on top and finish with a scatter of mint leaves and a few extra pistachios.

SERVES 6–8

• NOTE

Panch phoron is a five-spice blend used in Bangladeshi and East Indian cuisine. You can buy it at Indian supermarkets and some ordinary supermarkets, or try making it yourself. Simply mix together equal quantities of cumin seeds, fennel seeds, nigella seeds, fenugreek seeds and brown mustard seeds, and store in an airtight jar.

WARM MIDDLE EASTERN HERB SALAD
with ZUCCHINI, PEPITAS, CRISPY CHICKPEAS *and a* LEMON TZATZIKI DRESSING

This is the perfect salad for the beach or BBQ as it's one of those dishes where the elements get better if they are left alone for a while before combining. So start it first and then head off halfway to grill your lamb chops, spank that backyard cricket ball, or chase your terrified kids around the garden demanding a cuddle.

First make the lemon tzatziki so the flavours can develop. Add the lemon zest to the yoghurt and stir to combine.

Toss the cucumber in a little salt and the lemon juice. Leave for 10 minutes.

Drain the cucumber, reserving the liquid. Mix the cucumber into the yoghurt. Taste and add more lemon zest or a few drop of the reserved salty lemon and cucumber juice to taste. Crumble over the feta in a smallish rubble. Cover with plastic wrap and leave in the fridge until ready to serve.

Heat 1 tablespoon of olive oil in a frying pan, then add the zucchini chunks and the chickpeas. Fry them until the pan side of the zucchini is browned. Flip over the zucchini and keep frying; jiggle the pan. When everything starts to look brown and gnarly, stir in the garlic.

Cook for another minute or so and then add the vinegar. It will sizzle and put up an eye-watering steam. Now pour the contents of the frying pan onto a plate to cool to just warm. Now is the time to chase those kids of yours or to grill the lamb.

Using the same pan, fry the pepitas with the remaining 2 tablespoons of olive oil. Add the coriander and cumin seeds. Cook, tossing occasionally, until the pepitas start to turn from green to tannish.

While the pepitas are toasting, bundle the herbs together in your left fist so they look like a compressed green baton and slice them finely. Or you can use scissors to snip the herbs directly onto a generous-sized platter. You'll have a lovely pile of fragrant herbs.

Part the herbs and push them to the sides of the platter, leaving a clear bit in the middle. Now, work quickly so the herbs stay fresh! Pour the cooled but still slightly warm zucchini and chickpeas into that gap in the middle. Pour over the warm, spiced pepitas. Sprinkle with salt flakes and toss.

Serve your salad warm and dolloped with half of the lemon tzatziki, with any remaining tzatziki served on the side.

Some flatbread (see page 120 or 134), pickles, skewers of BBQ lamb and goat's cheese make good additions.

SERVES 4–6

TIP

To sexy up the salad, add ½ cup pine nuts or pistachios and ½ cup currants.

---

3 tablespoons olive oil

2 zucchini, quartered and cut into chunks

1 × 400 g can chickpeas, rinsed and well drained

3 garlic cloves, sliced

2 tablespoons red wine vinegar

70 g (½ cup) pepitas

1 teaspoon coriander seeds, crushed

½ teaspoon cumin seeds, crushed

1 bunch mint

1 bunch flat-leaf parsley

salt flakes

LEMON TZATZIKI

zest and juice of 1 lemon

1 cup Greek yoghurt

1 small Lebanese cucumber, peeled and diced

salt flakes

100 g feta

STICKY PORK BELLY SALAD

For those who are not fans of rabbit food, this is a salad that is loaded with sticky, fatty porky goodness but still allows you to claim, 'But honey, I'm only having a salad for dinner.'

As part of a calorie-controlled diet, this salad could help you lose weight … please note the word 'could' and the fact I don't discuss serving size here or how few other calories you need to restrict yourself to.

Oh well, at least you'll probably lose a few extra calories running from pantry to stove to fridge gathering all those ingredients!

PORK AND MARINADE

100 g palm sugar

425 ml water

1 cinnamon stick

1 star anise

1 thick slice ginger

5 g tamarind concentrate

60 ml (3 tablespoons) soy sauce

20 ml (1 tablespoon) fish sauce

pinch of salt flakes

700 g boned pork belly, scored

125 ml (½ cup) white wine vinegar

COLESLAW

½ small (or ¼ large) red cabbage,
    finely shredded (white cabbage is
    also fine, or a mix of both)

4 spring onions, finely sliced

¼ bunch coriander leaves

DRESSING

1 long red chilli, chopped (optional)

2 garlic cloves, peeled and
    roughly chopped

40 g palm sugar or 1½ heaped
    tablespoons caster sugar

2 coriander roots, scraped, cleaned
    and chopped

2 tablespoons salted, roasted
    peanuts

80–100 ml lime juice, to taste

1 tablespoon fish sauce

TO SERVE

8 sprigs coriander

2 tablespoons fried shallots
    (home-made or bought)

Throw the palm sugar, 300 ml water, cinnamon stick, star anise, ginger and tamarind concentrate together into a saucepan and bring to a gentle boil to dissolve the sugar, stirring occasionally.

Once the sugar has dissolved, remove the pan from the heat and add the soy, fish sauce and salt. Allow the marinade to cool down.

When the marinade is cool, put the pork in a bowl, cover with the liquid and marinate in the fridge for at least 2 hours and preferably overnight.

Preheat the oven to 170°C.

Let the pork return to room temperature before placing it in a baking dish with the remaining 125 ml water and the white wine vinegar. Cover with foil and cook for 45 minutes.

Now make the coleslaw and dressing but don't dress the slaw until the end. Combine the cabbage, spring onion and coriander leaves in a bowl.

To make the dressing, pound or process the chilli, garlic, sugar, coriander roots and peanuts together. Stir in the lime juice and fish sauce. Taste and adjust with more sugar, fish sauce or lime juice, as needed. You want the flavour to be sweet, tangy and funkily salty in that order.

Heat a heavy-based pan on medium to high heat. Cut the whole piece of pork into cubes about 2.5 cm thick, baste each slice with marinade and then pan-fry, searing each side until brown.

Heat the remaining marinade in a saucepan on medium to high heat. Boil for 5 minutes until it is thick and syrupy, then add it to the frying pan and toss with the pork to coat.

Lightly dress the coleslaw and serve as a share plate or as individual serves with the sticky pork. Top with coriander sprigs and fried shallots.

SERVES 4

POTATO SALAD WITH BACON, MAYO AND CRISPY CORN

Here's another salad that's certain to become a guilty pleasure. The joy here isn't just that the mayo is lightened and freshened with dill and yoghurt, or that bacon and corn is a flavour combination as catchy as an Avicii chorus, but that there are few things as addictive as bacon candied with smoked paprika and maple syrup! That smoky sweet marriage is a chart-topper. No wonder it's on heavy rotation in these pages.

2 tablespoons mayonnaise

1 tablespoon thick, plain yoghurt

2 tablespoons finely chopped dill

1 kg new chat potatoes

2 corn cobs

200 g bacon (about 6 rashers), cut into thin batons

1 teaspoon smoky paprika

2 tablespoons maple syrup

3 spring onions, trimmed and finely sliced

Combine the mayonnaise with the yoghurt and dill and set aside.

Place the potatoes in a large saucepan of cold water. Bring to the boil, then lower the heat a little and cook uncovered until done (about 25–40 minutes, depending on the size of your potatoes). Turn off the heat, drain, and immediately return to the hot saucepan to steam dry and cool to near room temperature.

Blanch the corn in boiling water, then strip the kernels from the cob.

Heat a large frying pan over medium heat. Fry the bacon with the paprika until it's near crunchy. Turn down the heat, add the maple syrup and continue to cook to coat the bacon and turn it all sticky and dark. Remove the bacon from the pan.

Using the same pan, add a touch of oil if necessary and toss the corn kernels over medium heat for a few minutes to coat with the flavours. Beware, they can pop in the pan.

Gently mix the potatoes with the mayo dressing, along with half of the bacon, corn and spring onion. Spoon into a serving bowl, pile the remaining bacon, corn and onion on top and serve.

SERVES 6–8

SMOKY SALAD OF FREEKEH, SUGAR SNAPS *and* ALMONDS

If freekeh was any cooler it would have a hipster beard, ride a fixie and know its way around a six-station Slayer. High in fibre, as good for protein as quinoa, and with a lovely nuttiness, it also helps that these berries of green wheat have a slight smoky note from the drying process. Given a choice, go for the wholegrain variety rather than nibbed as I find that the nibbed – aka cut – freekeh berries run a far higher risk of going soggy. The wholegrain is far nuttier. That, along with freekeh's smoky notes, is why the burny edges of the sweet onions and the crunchy smoked almonds work so very well in this salad!

Put the freekeh into a pot with loads of salted water and place on the stove. Follow the packet instructions or bring to the boil, then simmer until it's cooked. That's about 15 minutes for nibbed freekeh, 30 minutes for wholegrain, or longer. It once took me 1 hour to cook, but I feel that freekeh, like a watched pot, hates to be hurried.

Slowly fry the onions in the butter and oil until they are caramelised. This will take about as long as it does to cook as the freekeh, which is jolly convenient.

Organise a bowl of iced water next to the stove and bring a small pan of water to a merry boil. Remove the strings from your sugar snaps by snipping off the stem end and pulling away from the pod.

Now blanch these sugar snaps until they are bright green and still a little squeaky and undercooked. This will take a minute or so.

Remove with a slotted spoon and add the peas to the iced water to halt their cooking.

Now, blanch the broccolini stems in the same water and refresh in the iced water. Finally, blanch the broccolini florets and refresh.

Drain the freekeh, then return it to the pot (off the heat). Pour in the olive oil and vinegar and mix. Tip the freekeh onto a serving platter to cool.

Add the sugar snaps, caramelised onions and broccolini stems to the freekeh.

Top with the broccolini florets, feta, lemon zest and, just before serving, the smoked almonds.

This can also be served as a warm salad.

SERVES 6–8

300 g freekeh

2 red onions, diced

50 g butter

a splash of olive oil

200 g sugar snap peas (or mange touts or, failing that, frozen peas)

2 small bunches broccolini, florets pulled off, stems sliced into coins

70 ml olive oil

50 ml sherry vinegar

200 g feta, crumbled

zest of 1 lemon

200 g smoked almonds, roughly chopped, some left whole

Melon, Prosciutto, Basil and Blue Cheese Salad

Thinking about it, I'd suggest that my somewhat OTT approach to fashion is perhaps also something of an explanation of this dish, and why I think it works. The big question to ask yourself is this: How can too much of a good thing be 'too much of a good thing'? Isn't it really just more of what you love?

100 g (1 cup) pecans

1 tablespoon balsamic vinegar

3 tablespoons olive oil

55 g (¼ cup) brown sugar

freshly ground black pepper

1 ripe cantaloupe, seeded, peeled and cut into small wedges

50 g basil leaves, 10 leaves torn apart

12 wafer-thin slices prosciutto

150 g mild blue cheese (such as Blue Castello)

a splash of hot water

zest and juice of 1 lemon

Grease a baking tray or pull out a silicon mat.

Toast the pecans over medium to high heat in a dry pan for 5 minutes. Don't let them catch – they will burn quickly. Remove the nuts.

Now mix the balsamic, 1 tablespoon of the olive oil, brown sugar and pepper in the pan over the heat. This mix will start to bubble and when it does, throw in your toasted pecans and stir occasionally.

Watching all the time, cook the pecans in this dark, tar-pit hell for 6 minutes, until they are candied.

Take the pecans out of the syrup and spread them on the greased baking tray or mat to cool.

Spread the melon pieces on a platter, grind over some black pepper and then toss on the 10 torn basil leaves. Curl the prosciutto between the melon and the basil. Crumble over the blue cheese in little nuggets. Throw on about a third of the candied pecans. Reserve the rest for 'Ron … Later on!'

Using a stick blender blitz the remaining basil, adding 2 tablespoons of olive oil bit by bit. Continue to blitz and add a little hot water. This will make the basil dressing nicely creamy. Season.

Dress the plate with dollops of this basil ooze. Grate over some lemon zest. Squeeze over a little lemon juice. Serve.

SERVES 6–8

•NOTE

Simply scatter rocket leaves over the melon if you don't want to make the creamy basil purée.

SPELT, MACADAMIAS, PEPITAS, CELERY, BURNY LEEKS, SMOKED MAYO *and* NASTURTIUMS

This is one of the most customisable salads ever. Feel free to leave things out or replace at your whim. Use almonds and pistachios instead of macadamias and pepitas, or trade the pepperiness of the nasturtiums for some easier-to-find rocket. Or how about using chunks of fried smoked speck instead of bacon – or just leaving out any animal altogether to keep your veggo side happy. Fun and games! This can be served as a warm salad, too. All in all, it's more flexible than a seven year old negotiating a later bedtime.

1.5 litres (about 6 cups) chicken stock (you may only need 1 litre)

460 g (2 cups) spelt

50 g butter

4 rashers smoked bacon, diced

2 leeks, sliced into 5 mm coins

125 g (1 cup) pepitas

florets from ½ head of cauliflower

160 g (1 cup) macadamias

½ cup Japanese Kewpie mayo

liquid smoke or 1 chipotle chilli (a smoked and dried jalapeño)

3 celery stalks, cut into 3 mm dice

6 spring onions, cut into coins

¼ cup maple syrup

20 nasturtium leaves or a good handful of rocket

Pour 1 litre of the stock and the spelt into a big pot. Bring to the boil and then simmer until the spelt is cooked – it should have softened but still be nutty. Packet instructions will help but let your palate decide. If the spelt starts looking dry during cooking add more stock. Allow at least half an hour for cooking the spelt.

In a frying pan melt the butter and fry the bacon dice and the leeks on a medium heat until they start to catch and burn at the edges. Leave the bacon out if you are feeding vegetarians, as they tend to get offended by it. The burny leeks will give this grain salad some sweetness and some bitterness. Using butter will make you feel decadent, which is good. Take the leeks and the bacon out and reserve.

Toast the pepitas in the leek pan until they are crunchy, nutty and a few are golden. Watch they don't burn.

Blanch the cauliflower florets by dunking them in boiling water for a minute or so. Reserve.

Smash the macadamias. I use the bottom of my frying pan 'cos I'm a rebel, but you might like to be neat and put them in a ziplock bag and then bash them with a rolling pin. You want chunks of macadamias, not dust, so don't go into a nut-crushing frenzy remembering your last boyfriend.

I like smoking the mayo by mixing it with a few drops of liquid smoke, or even adding a finely chopped and reconstituted chipotle chilli with its intense smoky flavour.

When the spelt is cooked, drain it and place on a large platter. Stir in the celery, leeks, cauliflower, spring onions, pepitas and nuts. Season with salt flakes. Dollop on the mayo in splotches, drip over the maple syrup and place nasturtiums leaves between the splotches. Serve.

SERVES 4–6

TIP

Choose small, soft nasturtium leaves, which are peppery and delicious. The larger ones can be bitter.

SMALL KIPFLER POTATO SALAD *with* HARDBOILED EGGS, SMOKED TROUT *and* DILLED SOUR CREAM

You'll find a bit of a theme if you read more than a couple of the salad recipes in this book. It is my rather predictable obsession with combining the creamy and the smoky with the tart and the salty. So, here we go again!

Place the potatoes in a pan and cover them with cold water. Season with salt. Cover and bring to the boil, then cook until a potato will slowly slip off the blade of a small knife jabbed into its middle. That's about 30–40 minutes. Drain well and place in a salad bowl to cool.

While the potatoes are cooking, carefully remove the flesh from the frame of the trout taking care to leave behind the bones, especially the fine bones in the fillet just behind the head. Tweezer out any fine bones you see. Place the trout flesh in a clean bowl.

Arrange the hardboiled eggs haphazardly on the potatoes. Flake the smoked trout over the potatoes (watching out for bones as you flake it) and between the eggs.

Place the red onion dice into a sieve and pour boiling water over to soften the onion's heat. Sprinkle over the salad.

Cut the best fronds off the top of the bunch of dill. That's about the top quarter. Reserve these for garnish.

Cut the rest of the dill leaves off the bunch (and any bits of clean stalk that come with them). You can be quite cavalier here. Reserve these bits of dilly goodness for the dressing.

Mash the sour cream with a little of the lemon juice, a good pinch of salt and the mustard. You want it to be a loose, dollopable consistency. Chop the dill finely and stir it into the sour cream mixture. This turns the dressing a pretty shade of green.

Dress the egg-and-trout-topped salad with thick stripes of the dressing and then the dill fronds and some of the lemon zest.

SERVES 4–6

1 kg small kipfler potatoes, halved if necessary (you want each potato piece to be two-bite-sized)

salt flakes

1 smoked trout (about 500 g), skin removed

6 hardboiled eggs, cut into quarters

1 red onion, finely diced

1 bunch dill

1 × 250 g tub sour cream

zest and juice of 1 lemon

1 scant teaspoon Dijon mustard

TIP

Any small new potatoes work wonderfully with this salad.

SPECIAL UNFRIED RICE

I'm no fan of a stir-fry, or of the sort of fried rice people usually make at home. This, however, is my attempt at capturing the flavours, supercharging them and avoiding using too much frying. It tastes rather good – half way between a warm salad and a main course, which is, I suppose, the definition of an ubersalad.

600 g (about 3) carrots, peeled and halved lengthways

a little grapeseed oil

2 teaspoons five-spice powder

1 lemon

1 teaspoon salt flakes

1 knob butter

2 tablespoons runny honey (or warmed honey)

2 tablespoons sesame seeds

200 g lap cheong Chinese sausage, sliced on the diagonal, 5 mm thick

200 g brown rice, cooked and kept warm (this will yield about 400 g cooked rice)

2 celery stalks, diced

1 fennel bulb, diced, with maximum fronds reserved

1 teaspoon sesame oil

1 tablespoon soy sauce

4 spring onions, sliced on the diagonal into 1 cm lengths

80 g (½ cup) roasted, salted cashews

Preheat the oven to 180°C.

Rub the carrot halves with oil, arrange in a baking tray, sprinkle with five-spice powder and bake for 40 minutes, or until the carrots are soft.

Remove the zest from the lemon leaving the pith behind. Use a zester or, if you don't have one, use a potato peeler and then cut the zest into 2 mm-wide strips. Place the zest in a tiny container. Sprinkle on the salt. Cover with plastic wrap and shake to coat the zest in the salt. Reserve.

Cook your rice.

When the carrots are cooked turn off the oven, dot the butter over the carrots and drizzle over the honey, sprinkle on the sesame seeds and return the carrot tray to the hot but cooling oven.

Fry the lap cheong slices in a little hot grapeseed oil until cooked and golden on each side.

Rinse and pat dry the salted lemon zest. Drain your rice.

While the lap cheong is cooking, arrange the warm rice on a large warmed platter. Sprinkle over the diced celery and fennel. Lay the carrots on the rice and drizzle over the sticky contents of the baking tray along with any sesame seeds that have fallen off. Splash over the sesame oil.

Arrange the cooked lap cheong between the carrots. Splash over the soy sauce. Sprinkle over the spring onions, the cashews, the salted zest and the chopped fennel fronds. Serve.

SERVES 4–6

ROAST 'N' SMOKY SALAD

OK, OK, OK – so this whole obsession with smoking is getting a little out of control, but at least there is one place where smoking isn't a dirty word, and that's in the kitchen. Here, sweet and golden root vegetables get down with a delicious trio of smoky characters. The result is a salad that bangs more than an eight-armed death-metal drummer – or even an outhouse dunny door in a gale for that matter. It's also not the sort of thing you'll want to share, so save this recipe for a night when everyone else is out.

Preheat the oven to 180°C.

Toss the parsnip chunks and Jerusalem artichokes in grapeseed oil and place on a baking tray.

Toss the cherry tomatoes and garlic cloves in a little oil too, and put them on a separate baking tray.

Place the tomatoes on the top shelf of the oven and the root veg on the second shelf.

After about 15 minutes, or when the garlic cloves and tomatoes have both softened, remove them from the oven.

You'll need to leave the root veg in there for at least another 30 minutes, tossing them occasionally. Basically, remove them when the artichokes feel soft and creamy-centred. Feel free to remove the parsnip pieces first if you think they look like burning. Just reserve them with the tomatoes and the garlic.

Mix the Kewpie mayo with the liquid smoke, adding more smoke to taste if needed.

Pop the garlic cloves out of their papery skins.

Now plate up. Slice the Jerusalem artichokes into chunks slightly bigger than the cooked parsnip. Place both on a platter mixed together.

Carefully, using a teaspoon, place the tomatoes among the root veg where there is a suitable resting place. Be careful – they are very tender and you don't want them to burst. Do the same with the garlic cloves.

Sprinkle over the smoked almonds and the smoked cheddar. Dollop on the mayo around the edge. Marble the mayo with drizzles of maple syrup. Devour without sharing.

SERVES 4 (IF YOU HAVE TO)

500 g (about 4) parsnips, peeled and cut into chunks

300 g Jerusalem artichokes, peeled

a little grapeseed oil

250 g cherry tomatoes, ideally Perino (because they're my favourite!)

1 head of garlic, broken into cloves

¼ cup Japanese Kewpie mayo

2 drops liquid smoke

100 g smoked almonds

100 g smoked cheddar, cut into 5 mm dice

2 tablespoons maple syrup

'THE PIG WHO LIVES IN HIS STY WOULD HAVE SOME EXCUSE BUT IT IS REALLY QUITE SHOCKING TO SEE ANY OTHER ANIMAL OVERPOWERING HIMSELF AT MIDDAY WITH SUCH A MIXTURE AND SUPERABUNDANCE OF FOOD ... THE GENTLEMAN SHOULD PREFER SIMPLICITY AND EXCELLENCE TO VARIETY.'

Andrew Valentine Kirwan, 1864

ZUCCHINI FRITTERS *with* 3 DIFFERENT TOPPINGS

There is strong evidence to suggest that zucchini is Australia's favourite vegetable and there are few better ways to showcase this home veggie garden favourite than to turn them into the fresh green bulk of crunchy golden fritters. Then it's just a matter of how you adorn them!

600 g (4–5) zucchini, coarsely grated

salt flakes

4 spring onions, finely chopped

1 small garlic clove, finely chopped

200 g feta, crumbled

2 tablespoons finely chopped coriander leaves

2 tablespoons finely chopped flat-leaf parsley leaves

2 eggs, well beaten

75 g (½ cup) plain flour, sifted

2 tablespoons rice flour, sifted

2 teaspoons ground coriander

freshly ground black pepper

oil, for frying

Toss the grated zucchini with a little salt and sit in a strainer to drain for 15–20 minutes. You can weight it down with a plate. Rinse quickly then squeeze excess juice out and pat dry. Place it in a large mixing bowl.

Mix the zucchini, spring onion, garlic, feta, herbs and beaten eggs in a large bowl. Add both flours, then season with ground coriander and pepper and stir to combine.

Heat a little oil in a non-stick frying pan over medium heat until sizzling. Drop tablespoons of the batter into the hot oil and flatten them gently. Fry for 2–3 minutes on each side, or until cooked and golden brown. Drain on kitchen paper and serve piping hot.

MAKES 16–18

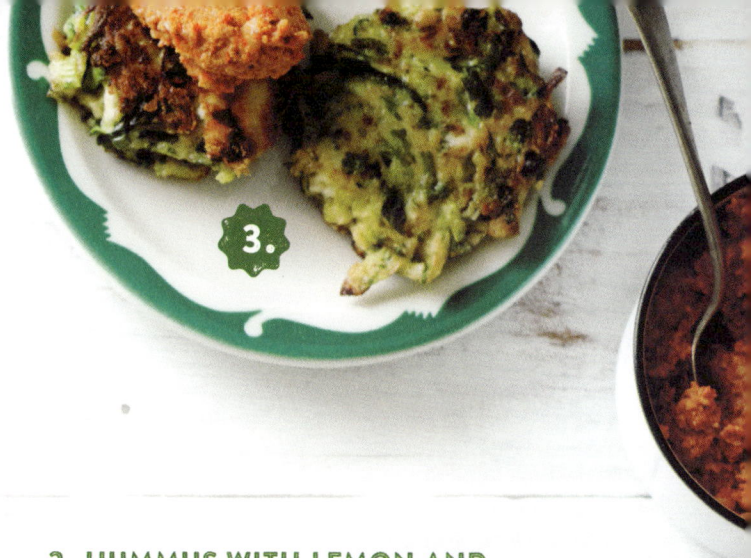

3 Topping Ideas

1. DILL AND MINT LABNA WITH POMEGRANATE MOLASSES

Mix 1 cup of Greek yoghurt with 2 tablespoons chopped mint leaves and 2 tablespoons chopped dill, ½ teaspoon cumin and 1 small crushed clove of garlic. Hang in muslin or a clean Chux cloth for at least an hour. Avoid mess and hang over a bowl to catch the draining whey.

Spoon a little yoghurt on each fritter and drizzle a little pomegranate molasses over the top.

2. HUMMUS WITH LEMON AND TOMATO DICE

Buy a small tub of your favourite hummus. Segment one lemon. Chop segments into a small dice but not a mush. Blanch a tomato, peel and deseed. Chop into a small dice and cover in olive oil. Reserve in a warm place to soften their intensity.

Dollop hummus on each fritter, and place a couple of pieces of tomato and lemon on top. Sprinkle over some sweet paprika or Tabasco, if you like.

3. TURKISH MUHAMMARA

Preheat the oven to 200°C.

Rub a little oil on each capsicum, wrap individually in foil and cook in the oven for 1 hour. Once soft, remove the capsicums from the oven and allow to cool sealed in the foil until you can touch them. Peel and deseed and return the flesh to the base of the oven on a baking tray to dry out. Check every 15 minutes or so. Remove when they're no longer slippery, but are still sticky.

Blend the capsicum with the walnuts and breadcrumbs. Keep the blender going and add ¼ cup of the olive oil. Add the lemon juice, cumin, salt and freshly ground black pepper to taste. Add more of any of the ingredients if you think it needs it.

Add up to another ¼ cup of olive oil to finish. The texture should be somewhere between a paste and a dip.

½–¾ cup mild extra-virgin olive oil
2 red capsicums
100 g (1 cup) walnut pieces
80 g (1 cup) fresh breadcrumbs
juice of ½ lemon
1 teaspoon ground cumin
salt flakes and freshly ground black pepper

ALSATIAN HOT DOGS

OK, so this is more piggery than gastronomy – even if I point out, with the greatest sophistry, that we are basically deconstructing Alsace's 'national' dish of *choucroute garnie* and putting it in a bun – and, as they say, there's nothing wrong with that! Oh, and hot dog bars are just so cool in London at the moment.

24 mini pork frankfurters

¼ cup Dijon mustard

¼ cup tomato ketchup

1 large jar sauerkraut

24 mini hot dog rolls

400 g mature tasty cheese, grated as finely as you can. Use a microplane if you have one

pickled chillies (optional)

Heat the frankfurters – either in the packet or on the BBQ grill.

Mix the mustard and ketchup together so it goes all marbley.

Split the rolls but leave the halves attached. Drain the sauerkraut.

Pop some sauerkraut in each roll. Top with a frankie, a smear of the ketchup mix and then hide the lot under a blizzard of grated cheese.

Some pickled chillies make a fine addition to this dog for their heat and for their piquancy, even if they step away from the bun-shaped homage to Alsace's famous *choucroute* that we are shaping here.

MAKES 24

TIP

For a real Alsatian flavour blitz the following into a powder: 1 bay leaf, 2 juniper berries, a few caraway seeds, 1 tablespoon brown sugar and 1 teaspoon salt flakes. Sprinkle a little pinch or two over your sauerkraut when assembling!

THE SIMPLEST INSTANT DOUGH FOR FLATBREAD, NAANS OR PIZZAS

HACK

I'm always looking for ways to save time in the kitchen or for recipes that will let me add a little homemade pep to a meal without too much hassle. That's why this dough is so cool. The self-raising flour means it doesn't need to prove and the yoghurt brings some rather nice acidity as well as helping the digestibility of the bread. This simple dough can be used for pizza bases, piadina or other flatbreads. It's a real ancient peasant hack and a whole lot easier than the traditional flatbread recipe on page 134!

250 g (1 cup) plain yoghurt

225 g (1½ cups) self-raising flour, plus an extra ½ cup for flouring the kneading surface

Stir the yoghurt into the flour until they are combined.

Dump onto a clean and heavily floured surface. It's a wet dough so it's hard to lift it up and slap it down to develop the gluten. Add more flour until the dough is kneadable. It needs to be a little springy, which shows that the gluten has developed.

Knead until the dough is smooth. This will take at least 5 minutes. A mixer with a dough hook will make this much quicker.

Keep in a bowl covered in plastic wrap until needed (it's good to rest the dough for a bit, but it's not essential).

Use as you want. I reckon it is best served as a flatbread cooked in a very hot pan or pizza oven so it remains soft in the centre but with toasty burnt spots on the surface.

To do this, cut the dough into 8 equal-sized pieces. Roll each bit out into thin discs. The thinner the disc, the crisper the bread. But if you make them thicker, they'll reheat in the toaster. Double hack!!!

This can then be topped for pizza, or cooked in a dry pan to make a simple flatbread to serve with meat or seafood from the BBQ.

Or use the dough to make a simple piadina – cook one side until it puffs and spots with a light golden toastiness. Flip the bread over and load one half of the cooked side with your filling of choice – thinly sliced prosciutto and brie; wilted, garlic-kissed spinach and fontina. Fold the other half of the bread over so the filling is covered and the bread looks like a half-moon in the pan. Leave in the pan to cook the underside, then flip it over to cook the uncooked topside. Simple!

MAKES 8 FLATBREADS

TIP

This recipe contains no salt so the bread works best with salty butter or by adding salt in other ways, such as seasoning any fillings or toppings. I love to serve it with cheap, pink, George-annoying taramasalata, like in our picture. Add a smear of gochujang (Korean garlic and chilli paste) if you want to live on the edge.

Pumpkin, Ricotta and Bacon Frittata

The sweetness of pumpkin, the virtuous bulk of milky ricotta and the salty pep of bacon – what's not to love about this family-friendly frittata that, in terms of flavour, punches well above its weight?

300 g pumpkin, peeled, deseeded and chopped into small bite-sized pieces, about 2 cm long

1 red onion, cut into quarters, then each quarter cut into thirds lengthways

olive oil

85 g (about 3 rashers) streaky bacon, chopped

6 eggs

4 tablespoons cream

¼ teaspoon ground nutmeg

salt flakes and freshly ground black pepper

70 g ricotta (firmer is better)

rosemary sprigs

Preheat the oven to 200°C.

Place the pumpkin and onions in a small baking dish, toss with some olive oil, and bake in the oven for 20 minutes. The pumpkin should be tender when done.

Meanwhile, fry the bacon in a little oil until golden and starting to crisp. Drain on kitchen paper and set aside.

Turn the oven down to 180°C. Beat the eggs with the cream and season with the nutmeg, salt and a sprinkle of freshly ground pepper.

Butter a ceramic pie dish or a small baking or frying pan about 20 cm-wide. Arrange your pumpkin, onion, bacon and ricotta evenly in the dish. Gently pour over the beaten egg mixture and bake in the oven for about 25 minutes, or until the egg is cooked in the middle. Serve hot topped with some sprigs of rosemary and eat cold leftovers the next day.

SERVES 4

4 ways with JAFFLES

1. CRAB & EGG JAFFLE

The egg jaffle is the height of the jaffle maker's skill. The egg needs to be perfectly cooked – this recipe uses scrambled eggs so there's no risk of the jaffle oozing snotty underdone white when you cut into it.

2 eggs
1 tablespoon cream
150 g cooked crabmeat – fresh, packet or canned
1½ tablespoons fried shallots
4 slices of bread
Japanese Kewpie mayonnaise
hoisin sauce, or oyster sauce or kecap manis
coriander sprigs and fresh chilli, to serve

Gently scramble the eggs with cream, leaving them slightly undercooked.

Put the scrambled eggs, the crabmeat and fried shallots in the sandwiches. Toast in a jaffle iron.

Place on a plate and drizzle over the mayo and hoisin sauce in stripy patterns. Serve with coriander and chopped fresh chilli on the side.

2. BAKED BEANS & MAPLE BACON JAFFLE

My favourite sweet and salty bacon treatment lifts my favourite childhood jaffle to 'another level' – as we say in the *MasterChef* world.

3 rashers smoky bacon
1 tablespoon maple syrup
1 × 420 g can baked beans
4 slices of bread
1 diced red chilli, to serve
¼ bunch coriander leaves and stems, chopped, to serve

Fry the bacon. When nearly done, add the maple syrup to the pan and coat the bacon. Pile the beans on 2 slices of bread, top with bacon and close with the other slices of bread. Place in the jaffle iron and cook until golden brown.

Serve with chilli and coriander on the side.

3. TURKEY, BRIE & CRANBERRY JAFFLE

An old-school eighties classic sanger get a jafflicious makeover.

200 g turkey, super-finely sliced
4–6 slices brie
cranberry sauce
4 slices of bread

Pile it all in the sandwich and cook!

4. RICOTTA & FIG JAFFLE

Anything that would go in a calzone pizza is great for a jaffle. Like this combo …

300 g ricotta
½ teaspoon cinnamon
1 tablespoon honey
zest of ½ lemon
pinch of salt flakes
4 slices challah (egg bread), found in Jewish delis or bakeries. Brioche is a good substitute
2 fresh figs, sliced

Mix the ricotta with the cinnamon, honey, lemon zest and salt. Spread the ricotta on the challah to make 2 sandwiches, top with slices of fig, the rest of the bread, and cook in a jaffle iron until golden.

Other combo suggestions

- Canned corn kernels, spring onion and cheese – here's the filling for my favourite empanada in handy jaffle form.

- Creamy mushrooms, finely sliced leeks and Dijon mustard with thyme – this is your classic Frozzie jaffle. A little bit French and whole lot Aussie.

- Miso, tasty cheese, tomato – a ripper, this one. Umami plus!!!

- Wilted spinach, garlic and fontina cheese – serve this with a wedge of lemon for freshness.

1.

4.

2.

3.

SPANAKOPITA FILO TRIANGLES

It seems that every nation has a cheese they like to cook with. The Italians have their parmesan. The Swiss have their gruyère. The English have their cheddar. In Greece, the popularity of feta for cooked dishes is probably only eclipsed by one cheese – *kefalograviera*. Made from ewe's milk, or a combo of that with goat's milk, this is the true cheese for saganaki and great for adding some funky bite to a moussaka. You could also use *kefalotyri* and *graviera*, but note that the *graviera* we get here can often be saltier than *kefalograviera* – well, unless it comes from Crete, where they make *graviera* that's nutty and slightly sweeter/less salty.

OK, enough with this cheese nerdery. Having said all that, these filo triangles are equally as delicious made with any hard cheese – or even a softer mix of feta and ricotta. Don't stress about the cheese!

500 g spinach

50 ml extra-virgin olive oil

1 garlic clove, finely chopped

juice of ½ lemon

200 g feta

150 g ricotta

40 g finely grated hard cheese, parmesan, pecorino or kefalograviera

4 eggs

4 spring onions, chopped

¼ teaspoon ground nutmeg

4 tablespoons dry breadcrumbs

salt flakes and freshly ground black pepper

150 g unsalted butter

375 g fresh (not frozen) filo pastry

sesame seeds

Trim the stems of spinach and soak the leaves a couple of times in cold water, drain and spin. Leave to dry thoroughly.

Heat a large pot with the oil over high heat. Add the garlic then throw in the spinach and toss for about 2–3 minutes until it has just wilted. Squeeze in some lemon juice then tip the spinach immediately into a colander and press out any excess liquid. Chop and set aside.

In a large bowl mash the feta roughly with a fork, then add the ricotta, parmesan (or other hard cheese), eggs, spring onions, nutmeg, breadcrumbs and seasoning. Combine with the spinach.

Melt the butter and brush one sheet of filo, lay another sheet on top and repeat until you have 3 sheets. Cut in half lengthways. Keep the remaining sheets covered with a tea towel to keep them from drying out while you work.

Spoon about 60 g, or ¼ cup, of filling on an angle at the bottom of each strip. Fold the pastry over to enclose the filling to form a triangle. Now turn it upwards to form another triangle, repeat the folding upwards until you reach the end. You should be left with about 2 or 3 cm of pastry, which you can brush with a little butter and fold over to seal the triangle. Brush the tops lightly with butter, sprinkle with sesame seeds and sea salt, and bake for 20–25 minutes or until the pastry is golden brown.

MAKES 16

Not Classic Cheese and Zucchini Quiche Lorraine

Not classic because traditionally quiche Lorraine was made without cheese, just with bacon. And certainly never with zucchini. But I have a rule that you can never have enough zucchini recipes, so we've shoehorned some in here and it adds some lightness to the custard.

Of course the whole idea of a *classic* quiche Lorraine is a misnomer anyway. The archetypical French dish actually originated in Germany, not France, and there's even evidence that the English were doing the same dish in the 1300s.

PASTRY

220 g plain flour

¼ teaspoon salt flakes

100 g cold butter, cut into small pieces

2 egg yolks (reserve the whites)

20 ml (1 tablespoon) iced water

FILLING

about 250 g (2 zucchini) finely grated

½ teaspoon salt flakes

200 g streaky bacon, cut into 3 mm batons

300 ml crème fraîche

2 egg yolks and 3 eggs

freshly ground pepper

pinch of ground nutmeg

40 g gruyère, finely grated

Place the zucchini in a colander, toss with the ½ teaspoon of salt and leave for about 20 minutes. Squeeze as much liquid from the zucchini as you can and set aside.

Fry the bacon for a few minutes in a pan to evaporate any water inside the bacon, then set aside.

To make the pastry, place the flour, salt and butter into a food processor and pulse until the mixture resembles coarse breadcrumbs. Add the egg yolks and pulse again, then add the water and blend again to combine.

Tip the pastry onto a lightly floured surface and quickly shape into a disc. Wrap in plastic wrap and refrigerate for at least 1 hour.

Preheat the oven to 180°C. Butter and lightly flour a 24 cm fluted flan pan.

Roll out your pastry on a floured surface and line the buttered pan. Bake blind (see page 304) for 25 minutes, remove from the oven and, while still hot, use the remaining pastry mixed with a little of the reserved egg white to seal up any cracks. Brush the entire base with the egg white.

Lower the oven temperature to 170°C.

Whisk together the crème fraîche, the 3 whole eggs and 2 extra egg yolks and seasoning until frothy. Place some of the bacon and zucchini in the bottom of the pastry base, scatter over the cheese and pour over the egg mixture, then add the remaining bacon and zucchini.

Bake in the oven for about 30 minutes until the middle of the quiche has cooked through. The top of the quiche should be golden brown. Serve warm with a simple salad of frisée or butter lettuce with a light vinaigrette.

SERVES 6–8

PEKING DUCK SLIDERS

In the shortest amount of time sliders have almost become a cliché. Their appearance on a menu is often the last desperate lunge of the old celebrity chef for 'relevance'; whatever that is. I'm assuming it loosely translates as 'just one last lucrative endorsement deal', but I might be wrong.

If you've seen what I wear, you'll know that being fashionable is not really on my radar. I hate the very notion of the conformity the phrase implies. I suspect that, just like you, I just want to be bright, and sweet, and tasty, and complex, and sharp, and fun. And I'll wear what I like, thank you very much.

Which leads us to these sliders, which are bright, and sweet, and tasty, and complex, and sharp, and fun. They also really don't care what the trend slaves say about the soft, sweet glazed buns they come in. Neither will you when you get your laughing gear around them!

6 soft, glazed buns (any sweet buns, even brioche), cut open and gently warmed in the oven

about 350 g cooked Peking duck (pick up ½ a duck at your local Asian restaurant, or 2 pre-cooked breasts)

2–3 tablespoons hoisin sauce

2 Lebanese cucumbers, sliced into ribbons using a vegetable peeler

2–3 spring onions, finely sliced

¼ bunch coriander

Cut the buns in half and lightly toast them in a low oven for a few minutes only – they shouldn't be crunchy.

Slice or shred the duck meat (if you've bought pre-cooked duck meat allow time to heat in the oven or microwave first).

To assemble, spoon some hoisin in each bun. Lay a couple of slices of duck on top of the sauce, followed by a ribbon of cucumber and a scatter of spring onions and coriander.

SERVES 6

TIP

The ideal buns are available at Asian bakeries.

ICE CREAM BREAD HACK

Australian country cookery is thick with canny little recipes for using melted ice cream in different ways, from a sort of Thousand Island dressing to all manner of baking. I was told about this lurk by an 80-plus-year-old CWA member. This proved one of two things to me: either there is nothing new about hacks, or those CWA women have their finger firmly on the pulse of the latest internet trends. The result is like a suitably crusty soda bread, but sweet. Serve warm with slabs of cold butter or toast it the next day when it becomes almost cakey.

2 cups melted vanilla ice cream
225 g (1½ cups) self-raising flour

Preheat your oven to 175°C.

Spray and flour a bread tin (approximately 12 × 20–22 cm).

Mix the flour and the ice cream together until just combined but still a little lumpy.

Dollop the mix into the bread tin so it fills the corners and is level at the top.

Pop in the oven for 50 minutes or until the loaf is golden, crusty and cooked through.

Ease the loaf out of the tin and cool. Or eat straight away with butter.

MAKES 1 LOAF

TIP

Another cool use for melted vanilla ice cream, shared by a canny Queensland ABC radio type, is to make a cheat's prawn cocktail sauce. Mix 150 g of melty vanilla ice cream with 50 g mayonnaise, 60 g tomato sauce and a dash of both soy and Worcestershire sauce.

3 ways with FLATBREAD

THE FLATBREAD

1 teaspoon dry yeast
350 ml warm water
1½ tablespoons sugar
475 g plain flour
1 teaspoon salt flakes
1 tablespoon olive oil

Or just make the hack flatbread on page 120!

Mix the dry yeast, warm water and sugar together. The warmth activates the yeast and the sugar feeds it. Never add the salt here or you'll kill the yeast. Leave for 5 minutes.

Mix the flour and the salt in a separate large bowl. Make a well in the centre. Pour in the yeasty water and the olive oil. Using a knife, 'cut' the liquid into the flour. When the liquid is all mixed in pull together the resulting dough into a ball.

Flop the dough onto a floured surface and knead until the dough feels springy and silky. Push your thumb into the dough – if it comes out clean the dough is ready. If not, knead some more!

Oil a bowl twice the size of your dough ball. Throw in the dough. Toss it around, cover with a damp tea towel and leave in a warm place to prove for at least half an hour.

Tip the risen dough back onto a floured surface and 'punch back' the puffiness, or rise, in the dough. Cut into 8 equal-sized balls and roll out on a floured surface to very thin discs.

Toast each disc in a hot dry pan, in a pizza oven, or on the oiled flat-plate of the BBQ. Serve these flatbreads warm or reserve and reheat in the toaster, in the frying pan, in the oven wrapped in a clean, damp tea towel or even – in an emergency – very quickly in the microwave.

MAKES 8 × 20 CM ROUND PIECES OF FLATBREAD

1. THE ACAPULCO FLATBREAD

4 tablespoons olive oil
2 × 400 g cans black turtle beans, rinsed and drained
1 teaspoon sweet paprika
salt flakes and freshly ground black pepper
8 pieces of flatbread
3 limes, peeled and segmented
2–3 green chillies, finely diced
1 red onion, finely sliced
coriander sprigs
1–2 canned chipotle chillis (depending how hot you like it), rinsed, deseeded and chopped
400 g crème fraîche or sour cream

Heat the oil in a hot pan, add the beans and paprika and fry for a couple of minutes. Season with salt and pepper.

Take a flatbread and layer on the beans and the lime pieces.

Scatter over green chilli and red onion slices, a few coriander sprigs, some of the chipotle chilli and a dollop of crème fraîche. Repeat and serve.

MAKES 8

2. SIZZLING PRAWN WRAPS

24 peeled prawn tails, shell at the tip removed
½ cup Japanese Kewpie mayo
3 drops of Maggi seasoning
3 fresh limes
1 avocado, cut into cubes
bunch of coriander leaves, picked
½ head iceberg lettuce, shredded
8 pieces of flatbread
salt flakes

3.

Skewer the prawn tails in sets of 3 on soaked wooden skewers and BBQ.

Mix the Kewpie mayo with the Maggi seasoning.

Cut 2 of the limes into thin wedges and grate the zest of the third over the cubed avocado.

When the prawns are cooked, squeeze over the juice of the zested lime.

Ask guests to assemble their own wraps with the prawns, coriander leaves, shredded lettuce and flatbreads. Season with salt, at will.

MAKES 8

3. THE ENGLISH SOUVA

2 garlic cloves
salt flakes
juice and zest of 1 lemon
500 g Greek yoghurt
1 long (continental or telegraph) cucumber
¼ bunch mint, leaves picked and roughly torn
splash of olive oil
about 800 g lamb shoulder or leg, cut into top of thumb-sized chunks
2 teaspoons coriander seeds, lightly crushed
8 pieces of flatbread
3–4 tablespoons mint jelly
extra lemon wedges, to serve

Pick out the little hot root from the middle of each clove of garlic. Crush the remaining garlic flesh to a paste with some salt.

Combine the garlic paste with half the lemon zest,

keeping the other half of the zest for later. Stir this combo through the yoghurt along with a good squeeze of juice from half the lemon. Set aside to let the flavours mingle.

Using a vegetable peeler, remove the skin from the cucumber, then still using the peeler slice long ribbons of cucumber stopping before you start peeling into the seeds in the middle. Tumble the cucumber ribbons with the mint leaves.

Heat the oil in a frying pan on high heat or on a BBQ. When the pan's sizzling, throw the lamb and coriander seeds on the heat and fry until crispy, turning from time to time. It will take about 4–5 minutes.

Remove the lamb from the heat and place in a warmed bowl. Squeeze over the other half of the lemon and add the zest.

Serve the lamb with the warm flatbread, yoghurt, cucumber ribbons, mint jelly and the lemon wedges on the side, and ask your guests to assemble at the table. Good times!

MAKES 8

PAIN ROULÉS

There are several reasons to go to Paris but none seem quite as persuasive as the promise of the *pain roulés* at my favourite bakery in the world, Du Pain et Des Idées in the 10th *arrondisement* – where I took Dan and Emma at the end of *MasterChef* Season 5.

These tasty savoury rolls are like the posher, tastier ancestors of our cheesymite scrolls – crustier on the outside and far more deliciously elastic on the inside.

My wonder-baker Kate, with a little help from French pastry wunderkind Gontran Cherrier, has perfected this far easier, and proudly Aussie, version of *pain roulés*.

½ teaspoon dry yeast
245 ml tepid water
435 g bread flour
2 teaspoons salt flakes
80 ml olive oil

FILLING
200 g streaky bacon (about
  6 medium rashers), cut into
  lardons
1 small red capsicum, sliced into
  1 cm strips
150 g cheddar cheese, sliced

Put the yeast into 100 ml of the tepid water and leave for 10 minutes. Place the flour and salt into the bowl of an electric mixer with the dough hook attached. While the hook is turning add the remaining amount of water, the water with yeast and the olive oil, and leave to knead for 5 to 10 minutes. When the dough is ready tip it into a clean, lightly oiled bowl, cover with plastic wrap, and leave to rise for 6–8 hours, or overnight, until it has doubled in size.

Preheat your oven to 250°C.

When the dough has risen, tip it onto a floured bench, punch out the air and divide in half. Using one half at a time roll out your dough to a 50 × 15 cm rectangle. Place the filling ingredients of your choice down the centre of the rectangle and fold each flap over to seal. Trim the ends and cut into 6 equal-sized pieces. Place the rolls seam-side down on a baking tray (non-stick or greased with oil) and leave to rise again for 30 minutes.

Bake in the oven for 10–15 minutes until puffed and slightly golden. Serve warm.

MAKES 12

Alternative filling options

1. 200 g camembert cheese, sliced, with 4 sprigs of picked thyme and 4 chopped sage leaves

2. 2 onions, sliced and caramelised with 150 g Cracker Barrel cheese

3. 120 g streaky bacon, cut into lardons, with 80 g pitted prunes

'AS WE HAVE COME LONG
AFTER THE ROMANS AND HAVE
HAD THE BENEFIT OF THEIR
EXPERIENCE, IT IS NO MARVEL
THAT WE SHOULD HAVE GREATLY
SURPASSED THEM ... THOUGH ...
RIBBON MACARONI IS BETTER
PREPARED IN NAPLES AND
SICILY THAN ANYWHERE ELSE
IN THE WORLD.'

Andrew Valentine Kirwan, 1864

PASTA

INDIVIDUAL MAC 'N' CHEESE

Simple question with no trick answers. What is the best part of macaroni cheese? If you said the crusty bit around the edge of the pan you'd be right – and you'll love this recipe, which aims to bring you way more crusty edges by dramatically increasing the amount of mac 'n' cheese in contact with hot metal. Besides having more toasty edges, these mini mac 'n' cheeses are a handy size for a light lunch, or for a mac 'n' cheese snowball fight. Just be careful of the sharp, extra-crunchy edges of their spiky macaroni tops, which can cause a nasty abrasion if you are not careful!

500 g macaroni

70 g butter

35 g (¼ cup) plain flour

500 ml (2 cups) milk

250 g tasty cheese, grated

½ cup freshly grated parmesan

salt flakes and freshly ground black
   pepper

⅛ nutmeg, freshly grated (a couple
   of grates

2 fiore di latte or 10 bocconcini balls

Preheat the oven to 200°C.

Bring a large saucepan of well-salted water to the boil. Cook the macaroni for 1–2 minutes short of the timing on the packet instructions, then drain in a colander. The pasta needs to be a little hard because it will cook more when in the oven.

Generously butter two 6-hole Texas muffin pans, or ramekins, and place them in the fridge to chill.

Heat approximately 40 g of the butter in a large heavy-based frying pan over medium heat. Add the flour and cook for a few minutes, stirring with a wooden spoon. This will 'cook out' the floury taste and let the butter brown a little.

When this roux starts to thicken, add the milk, a little at a time, stirring to incorporate. (Roux is a fancy French word for a flour and butter mixture that thickens things.)

Add most of the tasty cheese (about 200 g) reserving a handful for the topping. Add the parmesan and stir in the pasta. Over medium heat, stir until most of the cheese has melted and you have a lovely gooey sauce.

Season with salt, freshly ground pepper and a touch of nutmeg. Leave to cool.

Fill the chilled muffin pans, or ramekins, with the cooled macaroni. Tear the fiore di latte into pieces and stuff a piece in the centre of each one. Fork up the macaroni on the top so it has rough edges that will get lovely and brown in the oven. Place in the fridge to chill for 30 minutes.

Remove from the fridge, scatter over the remaining cheese and bake in the oven for 15–20 minutes until the tops are golden and the edges crispy.

MAKES 12

PRAWN PASTA *with* CHERRY TOMATOES *and* PANGRATTATO

Did I ever tell you about the time we broke down on the Falls Road in Belfast in an unmarked army vehicle and how our best attempts to look like a gang of long-haired blokes en route to Sunday mass were foiled by the most chinless officer in the British army deciding he'd hop out of the van and strut around it in his tweed jacket and cavalry twill pants 'assessing the situation'. I didn't? Well, it's probably a good thing because it didn't end well and it's a classic example of never judging a book by its cover.

A bit like this pasta really – on the face of it, it looks pretty pedestrian, but once you try the pop of the prawns against the warm tangy burst of those heat-plumped tomatoes and the golden crunch of those breadcrumbs you'll be smitten. A bit like that army officer …

Cook the pasta as per packet instructions. Just remember to have plenty of very well-salted water and stir in a cup of cold water after adding the pasta, to stop it sticking.

Heat 60 ml of the oil in a pan over medium heat. When sizzly, throw in half the garlic and stir for a minute before adding the breadcrumbs and chilli flakes. Season with salt and pepper and continue cooking until the bread has sucked up all the oil and is super golden and crunchy.

Tear in half the parsley leaves and the lemon zest and toss through. This is your pangrattato and it adds a delicious crunch.

While the crumbs are cooking, grab another pan – it needs to be a decent size because you'll be tossing the pasta in here. Now heat 40 ml of oil, add the rest of the chopped garlic and cook for a minute until it's just starting to get some colour. Don't let it burn because you'll get a bitter flavour.

Now tip in the star attraction – your prawns. Sear the prawns for 1½ minutes on each side, until they lose that translucent look and their tails turn bright pink.

Season with salt and a good twist of pepper and turn up the heat before adding the wine and cherry tomatoes. Cook for another 2 minutes; the wine will reduce a little and the tomatoes will soften.

Drain off the pasta reserving 2 tablespoons of pasta water. Tip the cooked pasta and the 2 tablespoons of pasta water in with the prawns and toss through gently and quickly to coat.

Divide the prawn pasta between serving bowls and throw over some of the crunchy, garlicky pangrattato. Finish with a scatter of fresh torn parsley leaves and an extra drizzle of oil.

SERVES 4

500 g pasta, such as spaghetti

about 120 ml (½ cup) extra-virgin olive oil

4 garlic cloves, finely chopped

½ loaf of rustic white bread, roughly torn into quite small pieces

½–1 teaspoon chilli flakes, depending how hot you like things

salt flakes and freshly ground black pepper

½ bunch flat-leaf parsley, leaves picked

zest of ½ lemon

12 green prawns, peeled, deveined, heads removed, tails left on

250 ml (1 cup) white wine

12 cherry tomatoes

Aussie Carbonara

I have a confession to make. In the last book there was what we in the trade would call a 'conceptual dish'. This loosely translates as 'a bit of a wank'. To make matters worse it was a riff on a carbonara – Australia's most loved pasta dish. Adding insult to injury, it also really wasn't as good as the bog-standard carbonara in my first book.

What I should have done is put in this version, which is inspired, like so many of the great moments in history, by pizza. (Do you think man would have gone to the moon if pizza wasn't round? How else do you think the ancient Sumerians got the idea for that first wheel?)

My thinking went like this. What is an Aussie Pizza if it is not just a carbonara without the pasta? So then I thought, stuff it, let's just make an Aussie carbonara! Forget the debate about *guanciale* or pancetta and just get real celebrating our Aussie bacon, Aussie eggs, Aussie tasty cheese and, at the risk of rotating my Grandpa, some Aussie cream.

PS. While this all seemed quite heretical when I first wrote it, I have more recently discovered that carbonara was never the 'charcoal burner's spaghetti' of legend and only appears in Italian cookbooks and records after the American GIs landed at Salerno in 1943. Apparently the invasion left the Allies having to supply food to the hungry Italian people after Mussolini was deposed and their government surrendered. Hence this famous pasta made from American cheese and American bacon was born. It seems that pecorino and *guanciale* were a later Italianisation of carbonara.

400 g spaghetti

splash of local olive oil

200 g Aussie streaky bacon, cut into 1 cm-wide strips

150 ml Aussie cream

150 g Aussie tasty cheese, finely grated, plus extra to serve

6 local egg yolks

Aussie salt flakes

freshly ground black pepper – yeah, OK, that can be from overseas! But you can get Aussie black pepper if you want to …

½ bunch flat-leaf parsley, chopped

Boil a large pot of water that's as salty as the sea. Throw in the spaghetti. Stir so it softens. Pour in a glass of cold water and stir to stop the pasta sticking together. Bring the pasta back to the boil and then simmer until it's almost al dente.

Splash a smidgen of olive oil in a large frying pan, toss in the bacon strips and fry.

Whisk the cream with the grated cheese and 2 of the egg yolks. Season with salt and a twist or two of pepper.

When the spaghetti is cooked but still has a little resistance, lift it from the cooking water and toss it in the bacon pan. Some of the starchy pasta water will come with it. This is good. Over a medium flame toss the pan so the bacon fat and the pasta water emulsify to make a sauce.

Warm four bowls by pouring the remaining hot pasta water into them. Leave for a minute.

Toss the pasta some more. Seat your guests or family. Now back to the bowls, empty them of water and wipe them dry.

Now work quickly to stir the creamy cheese sauce into the hot pasta and stir to coat. Divide the pasta across the 4 warmed bowls and place an egg yolk in the middle of each mound of hot pasta. Get your guests to toss their pasta, further dressing it with bright yellow egg. Finally, get them to throw in parsley and more black pepper with a patriotic green-and-gold Aussie fervour. Add an extra sprinkle of cheese for good luck and dig in!

SERVES 4

·NOTE

Yes, the heat of the pasta will cook the egg yolk but if your guests are squeamish just add the yolks to the cream and cheese and beat.

LEIZA'S GREEK PASTICCIO
made by AN ASIAN

Surely one of the best things about Australia is the cross-pollination that comes from all the culturally blended families. This recipe is a case in point. Taught by a Greek mother-in-law to her half-Chinese daughter-in-law to ensure her darling son remained well fed, it is the best pasticcio – but actually now made better by the Asian than by the Greek *yiayia*. Some might see this as sacrilege but I see it as rather beautiful.

If you can find *kefalotyri* at a local Greek deli use it – this pale, hard sheep's milk cheese is great for grating and has an edge that mellow old parmesan lacks.

50 g olive oil

1 large brown onion, finely chopped

500 g beef or veal mince

500 g pork mince

1 teaspoon ground cinnamon

2 bay leaves

salt flakes and freshly ground black pepper

200 g tomato paste

350 ml water

1 litre (4 cups) milk

115 g butter

125 g flour

1 teaspoon ground nutmeg

180 g *kefalotyri* cheese or parmesan, grated

450 g N°2 macaroni or penne

1 egg, lightly beaten

Heat the olive oil in a large pan and fry the onion over medium heat until soft.

Add the meat and fry until the moisture from the meat has evaporated and the meat is starting to brown, about 10 minutes.

Add the cinnamon and bay leaves and season with salt and some pepper. Stir in the tomato paste and water and leave to simmer slowly until the liquid has almost gone, but not completely. Turn off the heat, remove the bay leaves and leave to cool until needed.

Meanwhile, put a large pot of salted water on to boil.

To prepare the béchamel, pour the milk into a saucepan, heat to boiling point and then set aside.

Melt the butter in another large saucepan, remove from the heat, add the flour and combine well. Return to the heat and stir until the flour begins to swell.

Slowly add some of the milk and continue whisking the butter to combine with the milk. Do this in stages until all of the milk has been whisked into the butter and the sauce begins to thicken.

Add the nutmeg and 80 g of the cheese and season well with salt and pepper. Cook for another 5 minutes or so.

Preheat the oven to 180°C.

When the water for the pasta has come to a rolling boil, add the pasta and cook for 2 minutes less than the cooking time on the packet.

Drain and refresh with cold water to stop the cooking process.

Toss through the beaten egg and the remaining cheese.

Butter a large roasting dish (about 36 × 28 cm) and line up two-thirds of the pasta neatly along the bottom.

Spread all of the meat evenly on top of the pasta and then lay the remaining pasta on top of the meat.

Finally pour the béchamel on top of the pasta leaving no gaps. Bake in the preheated oven for 35–40 minutes. Enjoy hot or even lukewarm, as they do in the Greek islands!

SERVES 8

3 ways with PUMPKIN AND PASTA

There seems to be a primeval understanding between pasta and pumpkin – an almost animal attraction – whether the pumpkin's golden flesh is part of the pasta dough or just dressing its final cooked form. Here are three of my favourite ways to marry pasta with pumpkin.

1. PUMPKIN GNOCCHI

This recipe is one of the three reasons that I knew I had to marry the woman I love. The other two were her deep knowledge of the Chelsea Football Club's injury list and the fact that she is unlike any other woman that I've ever met. That's in a good way, obviously – she doesn't have three toes or an extra set of nipples or anything weird like that … Oh, and while there might be three recipes here this is actually just one of the three ways with pumpkin and pasta.

1 kg pumpkin
250 g (1⅔ cups) flour, plus more for dusting the board
150 g (1½ cups) grated parmesan
salt flakes
pinch of freshly grated nutmeg

Preheat the oven to 180°C.

Cut the pumpkin into large chunks. Place on a baking tray lined with baking paper, cover with foil and bake for 40 minutes until the pumpkin is tender but not golden.

Scrape the pumpkin from the skin, tip it into a non-stick saucepan and mash. The pumpkin will be a bit too wet to make the dough so put your pan over a low heat and stir to reduce the liquid and dry it out. You should have about 2 cups of puréed pumpkin left.

Leave the pumpkin to cool completely, stirring it occasionally to release the steam and thus reducing the moisture content.

Now, you're ready to make the dough. Tip the pumpkin into a large bowl and add the flour, parmesan, salt and nutmeg. Bring your dough quickly together using a fork or palette knife. Don't overwork the dough – you want your gnocchi to be light fluffy pillows of pumpkin.

Lightly dust your working surface with flour and line a tray with baking paper. Tip the dough out and divide it into 6 equal pieces. Lightly roll each piece of dough into a cylinder about 2 cm in diameter and cut into 1.5 cm-long pieces. Transfer the gnocchi to the baking sheet and cover them with a clean, damp towel while you are working. Repeat the process until all the dough has been used.

Bring a large pot of salted water to a hearty boil, then lower the heat to a medium boil. Drop the gnocchi pieces gently into the water. When they float to the top and are cooked, remove them with a slotted spoon.

SERVES 4

1A. PUMPKIN GNOCCHI WITH PARMESAN AND NUTMEG

pumpkin gnocchi (see left)
250 g (2½ cups) grated parmesan
30 g frozen butter, cut into cubes
freshly grated nutmeg
freshly ground black pepper

Make the gnocchi. When the gnocchi are cooked remove with a slotted spoon and serve immediately with the grated parmesan, the butter cubes, a small sprinkling of freshly grated nutmeg and a little ground pepper.

1B. TOASTED PUMPKIN GNOCCHI WITH GORGONZOLA

pumpkin gnocchi (see left)
50 g butter
juice of ½ lemon
150 g gorgonzola or other blue cheese

Make the gnocchi. While the gnocchi are cooking, melt the butter in a large non-stick frying pan. When the gnocchi are cooked and drained add to the hot butter in the pan. Leave the gnocchi to cook without stirring until they start to brown. Flip each piece over to toast the other side. When the gnocchi are done, pour in the lemon juice and give a quick stir.

Dot pieces of blue cheese over the top and allow them to melt slightly before serving.

2. ROASTED PUMPKIN, RICOTTA AND FETA CANNELLONI

This is a double-decker cannelloni, which sounds as decadent as it is supposed to. Especially if you know that the secret to this dish is not to be shy with the nutmeg, sage and feta.

1 kg pumpkin, peeled, deseeded and sliced into wedges (approx 650 g without skin and seeds)

4 tablespoons olive oil

6 garlic cloves, peeled and finely chopped

8 sage leaves

800 g fresh, super-ripe cooking tomatoes, diced, or 2 × 400 g cans crushed tomatoes

3 teaspoons sugar

125 ml (½ cup) red or white wine

salt flakes and freshly ground black pepper

700 ml tomato passata

1 lemon

800 g ricotta

300 g feta – 100 g crumbled, 200 g sliced

¼ fresh nutmeg, finely grated

2 × 250 g packets dry cannelloni shells (20 shells per packet)

Preheat the oven to 200°C.

Toss the pumpkin wedges in 1 tablespoon of olive oil and roast in the oven for 20–25 minutes or until soft.

To make the Napoli sauce, heat the remaining oil in a large flat-bottomed pan, add the garlic and half the sage. Cook for a few minutes until translucent.

Add the tomatoes, sugar, wine, a strip of lemon zest, salt and pepper. Simmer uncovered for 15 minutes. Add the passata, bring to a simmer and cook uncovered for a further 10 minutes.

Remove the lemon zest and blitz the sauce with a stick blender, or leave chunky. Check for seasoning. Set aside.

In a large bowl combine the ricotta with the crumbled feta, nutmeg, a pinch of salt and black pepper. Chop the remaining sage and add.

Add the pumpkin and, using a fork, gently mash the ingredients together to combine (leave some chunky bits).

Spoon the ricotta mixture into a strong plastic bag such as a ziplock or piping bag, snip one corner of the ziplock bag, if using, and pipe the mixture into the cannelloni shells.

Cover the bottom of an ovenproof baking dish with Napoli sauce, arrange one layer of stuffed cannelloni on the sauce, then another layer of stuffed cannelloni on top of that. Spoon over more Napoli sauce to cover the cannelloni. Top with slices of feta, so it looks like white crazy paving.

Bake under a foil top for 40–45 minutes until the cannelloni is cooked and the edges of the feta have turned golden brown. Remove the foil for the last 5 minutes to help with the browning.

Remove from the oven. Serve with green salad leaves on the side. If you want to, squeeze some lemon juice over the top of the finished bake.

SERVES 10

3. PENNE WITH PUMPKIN, PANCETTA, PINE NUTS AND SAGE

The name says it all. Well it would have done if someone had the foresight to add the word 'raisins' in there, too.

600 g pumpkin, peeled, deseeded and cut into chunks (450 g after skin and seeds removed)

2 tablespoons extra-virgin olive oil, plus a little extra, for frying

20 g butter

60 ml (3 tablespoons) cream

1 level teaspoon ground allspice

⅛ teaspoon cayenne pepper

1 teaspoon salt flakes

lots of freshly ground black pepper

500 g pasta, such as penne, rigatoni, fusilli

150 g thick-cut pancetta or bacon, cut into lardons

12 sage leaves

2 tablespoons raisins

2 tablespoons pine nuts, toasted

Preheat the oven to 200°C.

Spread the pumpkin on a baking tray, toss with the olive oil and bake for about 20–25 minutes, or until it's soft.

Gently heat the butter, cream and spices together. Add the cooked pumpkin and blitz using a stick blender or food processor to form a smooth sauce. Season to taste but remember the pancetta is salty, so don't overdo it.

Put your pasta on to cook in plenty of salted boiling water and cook as per the packet instructions (but use some good sense too, because you want it to be al dente, not soggy).

Heat a small frying pan with a splash of olive oil over a medium heat and fry the pancetta until crispy. Then add the sage leaves, raisins and pine nuts to the pan and toss for a few minutes until the raisins and pine nuts are glistening, and the leaves are just starting to crisp.

Check the pasta and, if it's ready, drain. Now spoon the sauce over the serving plate, then pile the pasta on top. Pour over the pancetta, raisins, pine nuts and sage and serve. As you serve it, the pumpkin sauce will coat the penne and mingle with the crispy, salty sage, pine nuts, bacon and raisins. Yum.

SERVES 4

• PLUG

If you struggle with getting the sort of perfect pasta that this sauce demands then make sure you purchase my last cookbook, *Fast, Fresh and Unbelievably Delicious*, as you'll find it includes my Ten Rules of Perfect Pasta Cooking.

Greek Pasta

This recipe comes from a period of fridge-shaking when I was looking for a light summer pasta. This one is bright, tasty and does the usual thing that the Italians tease the Greeks about doing with their food – adding sourness to something rich and savoury. The ingredients are basic but I'd advise in this case to use a more expensive brand of imported Italian canned tomatoes along with Greek feta, as these are what give the dish its pep. Well, along with local lemons – ideally stolen from the local Greek or Italian family's tree.

First up, a little preparation. Pluck 10 leaves off the bunch of mint and shred finely; cut a lemon into 6 wedges; cut 50 g of the feta off the block. This will be your garnish.

In a large frying pan heat the olive oil.

Put a large pot of well-salted water onto a good heat.

Throw the onions into the hot pan and fry, stirring occasionally, until browned. When browned – after about 5 minutes – sprinkle the sugar over the onions and toss. Add the garlic and toss for a couple of minutes.

When the water starts to boil add the pasta and stir in a cup of cold water. Return to the boil and then simmer until almost al dente (or still a little firm to the bite).

Stir the canned tomatoes into the onion mixture, mashing as you go. Cook for a couple of minutes.

Now remove from the heat and squeeze in the juice of the other lemon. Finely slice the rest of the mint (it is OK if some of the finer stalks are sliced along with the leaves, assuming you slice very finely) and stir into the sauce.

Drain and stir in the pasta, along with the other 150 g feta, which you should crumble over the pasta. Taste and season with a little salt, pepper and extra lemon juice if the mint flavour is too strong.

Serve the pasta in bowls garnished with the extra mint leaves, some pristine white feta crumbs and a wedge of lemon.

SERVES 4

1 bunch mint

2 lemons

200 g feta

3 tablespoons olive oil

1 small brown onion, halved and thinly sliced crossways

2 teaspoons brown sugar

5 garlic cloves, peeled, bruised and finely chopped

500 g dried angel hair pasta or spaghetti

2 × 400 g cans best-quality canned tomatoes (it's good if these come from Aussie farmers and an Aussie cannery)

salt flakes and freshly ground black pepper

SMOKY CORN MACHERONY

Smoke, corn, bacon and cheese. This mac 'n' cheese has all the deliciousness of the best bits of a New England chowder, but without the starchy flour and potato soupy blandness. Seriously, why did no one think of this before? I call it macherony because that's the original name of macaroni and the soul of this dish dates back 300 years through my family history.

80 g butter, plus extra for greasing baking dish

500 g good-quality macaroni

300 g smoked bacon, diced as finely as you can

1 chipotle chilli

1 teaspoon brown sugar

2 cups frozen or fresh corn kernels

40 g plain flour

700 ml milk

250 g tasty cheese, grated

100 g (1 cup) parmesan, freshly grated

salt flakes and freshly ground black pepper

Preheat the oven to 200°C. Butter a large baking dish (or several individual dishes).

Bring a large saucepan of well-salted water to the boil. Cook the macaroni for 2 minutes short of the timing on the packet instructions, then drain in a colander. The pasta needs to be a little hard because it will cook more when in the oven.

Heat a frying pan over medium heat and cook the bacon until well coloured. Squash a chipotle chilli into the bacon, add the sugar and cook for a minute. Remove the bacon from the pan and set aside.

Add the corn to the same pan, turn up the heat and cook on high for a minute just to get a bit of colour on the corn. Set aside.

Heat 80 g butter in a large heavy-based frying pan over medium heat. Now make a roux by adding the flour and cooking for a few minutes, stirring with a wooden spoon. This will 'cook out' the floury taste and let the butter brown a little.

When this roux starts to thicken, add the milk, a little at a time, stirring to incorporate.

Add most of the tasty cheese (reserving a bit for the top) and parmesan.

Over medium heat, stir until most of the cheese has melted and you have a lovely gooey sauce. Stir in the corn, then gently stir the drained al dente pasta through the sauce.

Season with salt and pepper to taste.

Tip into your buttered baking dish (or individual dishes). Sprinkle with the remaining cheese and bake in the oven for about 20 minutes, until golden brown and crispy on top. Remove from the oven, scatter over the bacon crumble and serve.

SERVES 6

TIP

Chipotle chillis can be canned or dried. To use, rinse and de-stem the canned ones; soak, de-stem and chop the dried ones.

'FISH OF ALL SORTS IS BEST
WHEN SHORT, THICK, WELL MADE,
BRIGHT IN THE SCALES, STIFF
AND SPRINGY TO THE TOUCH, THE
GILLS OF A FRESH RED AND THE
BELLY NOT FLABBY.'

Andrew Valentine Kirwan, 1864

SEAFOOD

A DOZEN OYSTERS *4 ways*

Here are four ways to serve oysters that are a little less confronting to the oyster newbie than the simple spritz of lemon, grind of pepper or dash of Tabasco approach. For a fifth way, see the *sumiso* on page 174.

1. SPICY CUCUMBER ICE

Peel **1 LONG CONTINENTAL CUCUMBER**, cut it in half lengthways and, using the sharp nose of a teaspoon, scrape out and discard the seeds. Cut the cucumber into chunks and freeze in a small plastic container in the freezer. When frozen, blitz with **1 TEASPOON GIN** and the flesh of **½ LONG GREEN CHILLI** (deveined and deseeded). Taste. If you need more heat add the rest of the chilli. The secret to this ice is that you should get intense cold giving way to chilli heat. The texture should be spoonable rather than slushy, but if the ice is too icy then add a little more gin. This variation of texture depends on how juicy your cucumber is and how much moisture is lost in the dehydration that is part of the freezing. Serve the cucumber ice with a spoon alongside your oysters in a small bowl that's been chilled in the freezer.

2. ELEGANT BLOODY MARY SHOOTERS

Process **1.25 KG SUPER-RIPE TOMATOES** with **1 TEASPOON CASTER SUGAR**, ½ **TEASPOON SALT** and the **JUICE OF ½ LEMON**. Line a sieve with double muslin and place over a clean bowl. Pour the tomato juice and pulp into the muslin, tie up the ends and suspend the tomato bag over the bowl for the night in the fridge. The weight of the pulp will gently push out the tomato water. You should get about 500 ml of tomato water. You'll need about 480 ml; maybe less. (Don't throw the pulp away but cook it with a little stock to make a tomato sauce for pizzas or pasta.) Finely dice **1 STALK CELERY**, reserving any pale leaves. Toss **2 DOZEN SMALL, SHUCKED OYSTERS** (reserving their juices) in a glass or ceramic bowl with **1 TABLESPOON DRY SHERRY**, **1 TEASPOON GRATED HORSERADISH** (either fresh or in a good-quality sauce like Newman's) and **1 TEASPOON WORCESTERSHIRE SAUCE**. Now assemble the shooters. Place a little of the fine celery dice at the bottom of each glass. Drop in an oyster after shaking off any excess liquid. Top up with about 20 ml of tomato water, a little of the reserved oyster juices, and garnish with a little grind of pepper and a celery leaf. If you like, add a drop of **GREEN OR RED TABASCO** for a little extra kick.

3. MIGNONETTE DRESSING AND SAUSAGE MEAT

There is something rather classy about serving oysters with this classic, pale pink liquor, but really it's just a shallot vinegar. To make it, peel and then very finely dice **2 GOLDEN SHALLOTS** and mix with ¼ **CUP RED WINE VINEGAR** (the best you can afford!). Let this sit for half an hour to let the flavours meld before using. While this is happening warm about **1 TABLESPOON OIL, LARD OR BUTTER** in a small pan. Pop the filling out of **2 PORK SAUSAGES (OR 4 SKINNY SAUSAGES, LIKE SPICY MERGUEZ)** into the hot fat. Break up the sausage meat as it browns so it forms little nuggets of salty porkiness. Cook until the nuggets are golden and crunchy. Serve **A DOZEN OYSTERS** with two little bowls, one filled with the porky bits, the other with the mignonette dressing.

4. OYSTERS KILPATRICK

At its simplest this is just oysters sprinkled with Worcestershire sauce, topped with bacon and then grilled, but I like to add a little sweetness and texture to the Worcestershire to accentuate the saltiness of the bacon and the freshness of the oyster. Yes, you could just mix equal parts BBQ sauce with the Worcestershire but this is classier. So, fancy-pants, arrange **12 OYSTERS** on a bed of salt in a shallow ovenproof dish. Cut **175 G LEAN BACON** into matchsticks. Lose any rind. Turn the grill to medium–high. In a small pan heat **3 TABLESPOONS WORCESTERSHIRE SAUCE**, **1 TEASPOON SOY SAUCE** and **1 TABLESPOON BROWN SUGAR**. Bring to a simmer so the sugar and evaporation helps thicken things a little. Now whisk in **20 G COLD BUTTER** cut into cubes. Pour or brush this sauce over the oysters in their shells. Top with matchsticks of bacon. Grill for 6–8 minutes until the bacon is crisp and even a little dark at the top edges. Serve with **LEMON WEDGES**.

1.

2.

3.

4.

TENDEREST KIWI CALAMARI *with* GARLIC AIOLI *and* KIPFLER CHIPS

No, this isn't calamari that's obsessed with rugby union, paua, and hanging out at its 'bach' over summer but, rather, calamari that has been tenderised by the interaction with enzymes from kiwifruit juice.

500–600 g kipfler potatoes, skin on, very finely sliced lengthways

salt flakes

3 kiwifruit, cut in half

4 tablespoons plain flour

4 tablespoons fine semolina

freshly ground black pepper

900 g–1 kg (2–3 medium-sized) calamari, cleaned, legs and wings included

lemon wedges, to serve

GARLIC AIOLI

½ head garlic, cut in half horizontally

olive oil

1 egg

juice and zest of ½ lemon

½ teaspoon sweet paprika, plus another sprinkle

pinch of salt flakes

300 ml grapeseed oil

Preheat the oven to 200°C.

Brush the garlic for the aioli with a bit of oil and get a head start by popping it in the oven on a low-sided baking tray while you prepare the chips.

Toss the finely sliced potatoes with 1 tablespoon of oil and some salt and bake on the same tray as the garlic for about 40 minutes, or until golden and crunchy. You may want to toss them halfway. After 30 minutes take the garlic out and allow it to cool off a bit.

Now make the garlic aioli. You'll need a stick blender to do this. Carefully crack an egg and place it in the base of the stick blender's plastic blending cup or something similar. Add the zest and juice of the lemon. Add the paprika, a pinch of salt, then the grapeseed oil. Then squeeze the roasted garlic flesh out of its skin on top.

Place the stick blender in the blending cup and carefully position the head of the stick blender so it covers and encloses the egg yolk. Blitz. Count to three and then, very slowly, pull the blender up through the oil and – voilà – the oil will emulsify with the egg and the lemon juice.

Squish the kiwis through a sieve to extract the juice.

Mix the flour, semolina, salt and pepper.

Cut the calamari tubes into thin rings, the wings into strips and the legs into pairs. Place the calamari, legs and all, in the kiwi juice for 10–20 minutes. Remove from the juice and give it a quick rinse. Pat dry. Toss the dried calamari in the flour mix. Shake off the excess.

Pour olive oil about 2 cm deep in a high-sided frying pan and heat. To test the temperature of the oil, toss in a little piece of bread. If it sizzles immediately it's ready. Fry the calamari in batches for a couple of minutes, but only until golden. Drain the cooked calamari on paper towel.

Remove the potatoes from the oven, sprinkle over some pepper and salt flakes if needed and serve immediately with the pile of calamari, aioli and lemon wedges on the side.

SERVES 4

TIP

For a super-easy option, grab a jar of garlic aioli from the shop and mix in ½ teaspoon of paprika and the zest and juice of ½ lemon.

Scallops with Sauce Jacqueline

Marco Pierre White has an intensity that is largely undeniable. Spend time with him and the stories, advice and history crash over your ears like relentless waves of wisdom. When he told me that I really ought to include a recipe for sauce Jacqueline in this book, and then very generously offered me his, I was hardly going to turn the great man down, was I? It is classic Marco – simple and delicious – and uses a clever technique to turn carrots into a sort of sweet, liquid gold. This sauce goes perfectly with pretty much any seafood, but I love it most of all with scallops. Especially if you can get scallops with the cleverly colour-coordinated roe still on.

Pick a saucepan large enough to hold the carrots. Don't add them yet!

Add the port to the pan, bring to the boil and then cook for 4–5 minutes over a high heat to burn off the alcohol.

Melt the butter in the same pan with the port and throw in the grated carrots and the cardamom pods. Stir and bring to the boil. Now simmer very gently, uncovered, for 30 minutes.

Using a fine sieve, drain the carrot gratings, collecting all the liquid. Apply some pressure to ensure all the carrot juices come free. This should yield about 450 ml of juice. Discard the remaining carrot, or use it to make fritters.

Return the liquid to the pan and reduce by one-third over a gentle heat.

While the sauce is reducing, heat a frying pan until very hot. While it is heating, rub a little grapeseed oil on both sides of each scallop. Sprinkle some salt flakes on the top of each scallop.

Taste the sauce and adjust it with some salt flakes and a squeeze of lemon juice to reduce the sweetness of the port. Keep warm. Oooh, and warm some plates with a good raised rim, or even some shallow bowls.

Lay the scallops in the pan, salted-side down. Don't move them until the pan-side is well browned.

Flip and finish cooking the scallops. You want them to be cooked and brown in places on the surface and only barely cooked through. Ninety seconds on one side and 30 seconds on the other should do it – depending on the scallops' thickness and the heat of the pan, which you want to be really sizzly!

Pour a slick of sauce on each of 4 warm plates. Carefully and quickly place the scallops in the sauce. Garnish with the coriander. Eat immediately.

SERVES 4

750 g carrots, grated
300 ml white port
300 g butter
5 cardamom pods
grapeseed oil
400 g scallops
salt flakes
½ lemon
coriander leaves (ideally baby sprouts), to serve

LOBSTER *with* CHAMOMILE BUTTER

Oh, how we fought over the inclusion of this recipe in the book. The first time I encountered negativity was at our final meeting with 'them' to discuss what recipes were in and out. Picture, if you can, the sort of suave super-villain henchmen you see in Bond movies; all dressed in black and with the ice-cold eyes of hardened killers. Now dismiss that image and replace it with one of a couple of smiling, friendly women from the publishers – but KEEP that feeling of fear and stomach-tumbling dread that you had earlier when you thought about the henchmen. That's what I felt like.

I knew I was about to be 'worked over' because the meeting was happening over the crispy eggplant chips at Melbourne's Dainty Sichuan. This is a dish as guaranteed to make me lose my focus as a woman twirling her hair around her index finger while biting her lip deep in thought. Oops, I don't know where that popped out from but I think I better pop it back in there straight away.

We tussled over a few recipes and 'they' won a few – for example, you didn't get a chowder recipe, a biryani or a spaetzle – and I won a couple. So I hope you like the Shrimp Wiggle and the Sticky Date Pudding with Tangy Butterscotch. When we came to this recipe, however, the great and pronounced tsunami of – rather theatrical to my mind – groaning, sighing and general rolling of eyes reached new heights. Or should that be depths.

Yes, I know lobster isn't an everyday ingredient. Yes, I know it is expensive. Yes, I know that this will probably be the least cooked recipe in this book. Yes, 'they' probably had a point. But this recipe is here because of two very simple reasons: 1) I can still vividly remember the intense emotional reaction I had when I ate it for the first time at a little French bistro opposite my first school, 2) It's an unusual combination that I thinks work very well.

Now, if a rich aunt ever leaves you a lobster in her will you'll know what to do with it!

1 × 1 kg live lobster

140 g unsalted butter

1 heaped teaspoon dried chamomile flowers (chamomile tea)

salt flakes and freshly ground black pepper, to taste

1 lemon, to serve

Place the live lobster in a plastic bag in the freezer for 1½ hours to go to sleep.

Bring a large pot of water to the boil.

Submerge the lobster in the water and boil for 10 minutes, less if it weighs less. Remove the lobster from the water. Empty the water and hang the lobster over the side of the steaming empty pot for about 30 minutes. It will continue to cook.

While the lobster is steaming itself, gently heat the butter in a saucepan with the chamomile flowers. When hot, remove from the heat and keep warm. When cool enough to taste, check for seasoning.

To remove the head from the lobster, hold the head and tail in opposite hands and twist. Break off the legs, but don't let them go to waste. Eat them. With kitchen scissors snip along the hard shell from head to tail, without cutting into the meat. Take a large sharp knife or cleaver and slice through the meat and softer shell of the underbelly. This will leave you with two halves. Remove any intestinal bits.

Serve the lobster with the warm chamomile butter over the top and a good squeeze of lemon.

SERVES 4

SHRIMP WIGGLE

Before there was tuna mornay there was Shrimp Wiggle – which is basically little tinned prawns (or shrimp as they call them over in the 'Americas') cooked in a white sauce using a chafing dish. Shrimp Wiggle, which first appeared in Fanny Farmer's recipe book in 1898, was a staple for a generation of 'liberated' young American women at the turn of the century, who left the home to work or study and often found themselves in shared accommodation or dorms without a kitchen. Recent inventions of the time, such as the chafing dish (which is like a bain marie but heated by a little burner) and the toaster, were thus the only options for a home-cooked meal.

There is something about this sort of camping-cooking indoors that appeals, as does the significance of the dish to these young women as a symbol of both freedom and as a taste of a pivotal time in the history of sexual politics. I also like the name.

Women were first allowed to vote in Australian state elections in 1895, and in 1902 they won the right to stand for parliament – a world first for which every Aussie should be proud.

My food team – all women – were less misty-eyed about the history of the dish, but did grudgingly admit that it is pretty darned tasty – even if the name is silly.

450 g fresh, peeled shrimp (use any good prawns!)

1 lemon

60 g butter

20 g (2 tablespoons) flour

1 teaspoon Keen's mustard powder (or any English mustard powder)

350 ml milk

salt flakes and white pepper, to taste

½ teaspoon Worcestershire sauce, or as desired

¼ teaspoon paprika

½ cup frozen baby peas

30 ml vermouth or white wine

thick slices of toast, to serve

Mix the shrimp with the juice of half the lemon. Cook the shrimp in the butter in a large frying pan over medium heat until just cooked through, about 4–5 minutes. Remove with a slotted spoon and set aside.

Turn off the heat, combine the flour and mustard and add to the pan, mixing with the butter to form a roux. Turn the heat to low and add the milk while mixing constantly. Slowly bring to the boil while still stirring. When the sauce has thickened, season to taste with salt and white pepper and add the Worcestershire sauce and paprika. Add the frozen peas and cook for another minute or so. Add the shrimp and juices back into the pan along with the vermouth and another squeeze of lemon. Taste and adjust the seasoning if necessary.

Serve on a thick slab of toast.

SERVES 2

CHILLI PRAWNS *in a* STORM OF HERBS

Not much to say here, but just muse on how this dish could almost be the culinary colours for multicultural Australia. If you doubt me, think about how many different migrant groups are recognised in these ingredients.

12 jumbo green prawns, in the shell with heads on

100 g butter

1 teaspoon chilli flakes

½ teaspoon chilli powder

¼ bunch basil, leaves picked

¼ bunch oregano, leaves picked

¼ bunch flat-leaf parsley, leaves picked

1 lemon, plus lemon wedges, to serve

To butterfly the prawns, you will need a sharp knife. I find a serrated one works well to cut through the shell.

Lay a prawn on the bench or board. Press firmly with one hand as you cut through the spine of the prawn, starting at the thickest part of the prawn near the head. Continue to cut the prawn through the head and tail, taking care not to severe completely in half.

Strip the prawn of the poo shoot and any unsightly bits in the head. Don't be afraid of the orange soft stuff – it is full of flavour. Open out the prawn.

Preheat your BBQ on high heat or use a griddle plate inside. A frying pan will do too.

Melt the butter in a saucepan with the chilli flakes and chilli powder.

Dunk each prawn in the chilli butter or baste both sides with a brush.

Place the prawns shell-side down on your hot BBQ and cook for about 2 minutes. Turn over and cook for a further minute or so until the shells are red and the flesh is opaque. Take care not to overcook the prawns or the flesh won't come cleanly out of the shell.

Plate up and throw the herbs over the top. Squeeze lemon juice all over and serve immediately with lemon wedges, finger bowls of water and giant napkins.

SERVES 4–6

COCONUT, CORIANDER, CAULIFLOWER *and* PRAWNS

Coconut and cauliflower are unlikely bedfellows – pale and squeaky as they are – and yet they go together really rather wonderfully, especially when coriander and a few prawns join the party.

vegetable oil, for frying

1 teaspoon Keen's curry powder

1 teaspoon ground coriander

½ teaspoon ground cumin

4 cardamom pods, crushed

2 brown onions, finely diced

3 garlic cloves, finely chopped

3 cm knob of ginger, peeled and finely chopped

1 bunch coriander

2 tablespoons neutral oil (grapeseed, rice bran, etc)

60 g (1 cup) shredded coconut

1 teaspoon salt flakes

2 cups grated cauliflower

500 ml (2 cups) chicken stock

600 g shelled green prawns, tails intact

your favourite grain, flatbread, plain yoghurt and mango chutney, to serve

Heat a splash of the vegetable oil in a frying pan and fry the curry powder and spices until fragrant. Stir in the onions and cook over medium heat until softened. Add the garlic and ginger. Cook for 2 minutes.

While you do this, wash and scrape clean the coriander roots. Cut them off along with the stems. Reserve the leaves for garnish.

Blitz the coriander roots and stems and the spicy contents of the frying pan with the 2 tablespoons of neutral oil to make a fine paste. If you want to be fancy, pass the paste through a coarse sieve to collect any stringy bits of coriander root or random flecks of cardamom pod. Reserve.

Wipe the pan clean and dry-fry the coconut with a teaspoon of salt until toasty and golden. Remove and reserve.

Heat a little more vegetable oil in the pan. Add the grated cauliflower and fry until it starts to colour. Add the stock and simmer until the cauliflower is cooked but still nutty. Drain but keep the cooking liquid that you drain off.

You now have a neat line of little bowls with: 1) spice paste; 2) toasted coconut; 3) cooked cauliflower; 4) reserved cauliflower liquid; 5) coriander leaves. Perfect!

Wipe the pan clean. Throw in the spice paste and fry for a couple of minutes. Now add the prawns and cook until they just start to colour and curl (about 4–6 minutes).

Throw in the cauliflower. Moisten with a little of the cooking liquid but not too much (about ½ a cup should do it). You want the mixture to move in the pan but not be sloppy. This is supposed to be a dry-fry curry.

Cook for 5 minutes on a medium heat. Much of the liquid you've added will have evaporated or been soaked up.

Serve on a warm platter garnished with the picked coriander leaves and the toasted coconut. Serve with your favourite grain, flatbread, yoghurt and some mango chutney.

SERVES 4

STEAMED SNAPPER *with* MARCO'S RATHER ELEGANT CUCUMBER SAUCE

There is something calmingly idyllic about pairing cucumber with fish, whether it's as a fresh crunchy salad, tzatziki dolloped on a BBQ'd fillet, sweet pickled cucumber with Thai fishcakes, or just as butter-poached batons. My current obsession, however, is this sauce taught to me by Marco Pierre White. It's fresh, light and delicate and is perfect with an equally delicate steamed white fish like whiting or snapper.

First, get your sauce underway. Use a teaspoon to scrape out the seeds from your cucumber and reserve them. Then roughly chop the cucumber and blitz it in a processor with the blades spinning fast. If it needs more juice to process effectively add some of the juice of the cucumber seeds, but it should look like a green sludge rather than thickened cream.

Now blitz in a little raw, fresh ginger to taste. You want the ginger to be a secondary flavour after the cucumber. Pass the sauce through a fine sieve and set aside.

Steam the cabbage leaves for 4–5 minutes. Slice the leaves in half, then cover and set aside.

Place the fish on a plate in a large bamboo steamer, or on the top tier of a double saucepan, and steam for 8–10 minutes until just cooked through.

While the fish is steaming, gently warm the cucumber sauce in a pan. Don't boil it!

Finish the sauce by whisking in some cubes of softened butter. I reckon about 25 g of butter for every 100 ml of sauce. You'll get about 250 ml, or 1 cup, from 1 telegraph cucumber. Don't let the sauce boil or else you'll lose the fresh flavour of the cucumber and the ginger.

Pour the green sauce onto warmed plates. Lay 3 pieces of cabbage on each plate and top with the steamed snapper fillets.

SERVES 4

1 long (telegraph or continental) cucumber, ends trimmed, cut in half lengthways

3 cm knob of ginger, peeled

6 cabbage leaves, veins and stems cut out

4 × 160 g snapper fillets, skin off

100 g butter, cubed, at room temperature

Ocean Trout Sumiso

Welcome to a new, delicious and rather exciting place … the home of sweet miso.

Sweet miso is a concept that goes back to Kyoto, where they make a miso called 'saikyo' miso – a white miso made with a higher than usual proportion of rice to soy beans so it is sweeter. It's also usually fermented for a shorter time and uses less salt. As it's sweeter, more buttery and more delicate, it's no surprise that it's also much more expensive than normal white miso.

The inspirational Nobu Matsuhisa's cash-canny solution is to take cheap white miso and sweeten it by adding mirin, sake and sugar to use as a glaze for his famous black cod dish. I've moved the paste on by adding rice wine vinegar and ginger juice as well to give it more punch. Adding vinegar makes what the Japanese call a *sumiso*, which is a traditional thing to do.

Once you've made this moreish paste you can use it in a number of different dishes. It works darn well with pork as well as with rich oily fish. You could also spread it neat onto eggplant before grilling, use it as the base for a Japanese vinaigrette, or even loosen the paste with a little warmed sake (warmed so the alcohol is evaporated off) or chicken stock to create a sauce that works well with everything from crispy chicken to BBQ'd lamb chops or green beans!

This notion of slightly charring the miso can also be taken to another level by employing the sushi technique of 'blazing', where ingredients are quickly licked by a flame – perhaps from a blow torch. This paste works decadently well with oysters using this method. Anchor your opened half oysters steadily on a metal baking tray with a little mound of wet salt under each for the shell to nestle into. Squeeze a little Japanese mayonnaise and a dollop of the sumiso paste on each and then blaze each one with a blowtorch or under a hot grill until the mayo tans and the miso blisters. The result is a creamy flavour bomb. These are great eaten straight away – just be careful eating them as the shells can be hot from the flame!

2 × 180–200 g ocean trout fillets

SUMISO PASTE

50 ml sake

50 ml mirin

150 g white miso paste

75 g sugar

40 ml rice wine vinegar

5 cm knob of ginger

Bring the sake and mirin to a boil together. Reduce the heat right down. When the liquid has cooled slightly, mix in the miso paste.

When the mixture is combined and silky, turn up the heat and gradually stir in the sugar. Do not let the mixture stick or burn – stir continuously.

Finely grate your knob of ginger, squeezing to extract juice (you should be left with 2 teaspoons of juice). Stir into the sake mix with the vinegar. (Note that Nobu's sweet miso paste omits this step, so slavishly leave these ingredients out and follow him if you want.)

When the sugar is totally incorporated and the mix is smooth, remove from the heat and let it cool before using on the fish.

Marinate the fish in the cooled paste for an hour or so.

Heat the grill to medium–high and grill the fish on both sides for 3–4 minutes, taking care not to burn.

Serve with white rice and steamed bok choy or choy sum. Or flake it and stir through some warm soba noodles, or push apart and lay on a Japanese coleslaw of carrot, pickled radish and fine shards of red chilli.

SERVES 2

TIP

Yes, this dish works equally well with salmon.

THE

INGREDIENTS...

The hero ingredients in the pages that follow represent what many people see as the nadir of food – ingredients decried for their industrial roots and their lack of gastronomic value. The question is, can I rehabilitate them? Can I make them into something even the nerdiest foodie would see as delicious? So here they are reclaimed, the ingredients ...

AEROSOL CREAM RECLAIMED

Who needs a recipe?

GLASTONBURY BUTTER-POACHED WHITING FILLETS *with* ASPARAGUS

Inspiration can hit you in the weirdest places. I came up with this dish at the Glastonbury music festival in 2013, when I was cooking dinner on a BBQ outside our teepee. Yes, that is quite probably the most pretentious thing you'll read this year, but it's true. We'd been there a few days and it seemed like a good idea to cook up everything we had for a grand dinner before heading out to see the Rolling Stones do their thing. Strangely, when I got home to Australia and tried the dish again, it turned out to be just as delicious as I remembered, even without the mushrooms. And it's made even better by the fact that it uses 'THE MOST BRILLIANT INSTANT MAYONNAISE EVER', which UK *MasterChef* winner, Mat Follas, showed me.

2 bunches asparagus, woody ends snapped off

16 kipfler or small, new potatoes

150 g butter (100 g for melting, 50 g for cooking)

600–800 g whiting fillets, allowing 150–200 g per person

1 lemon

1 bunch chives, finely chopped

1 bunch tarragon, dill or marjoram, leaves picked and finely chopped

INSTANT MAYO

1 egg

juice of ½ lemon

1 tablespoon Dijon mustard

salt flakes

300 ml grapeseed oil

TIP

If you want to make a simple sauce, boil ½ cup of white vermouth in a small saucepan until it has reduced by half. Pour in the poaching liquid from each of the foil boats. Warm them together. Whisk in cubes of chilled butter for a glossy sauce.

Turn the BBQ on high. Grill one bunch of asparagus until they are gnarly and a little charred in places, then keep warm and set aside.

Place the potatoes in a large saucepan of cold water to cook over a good heat.

In a small saucepan, melt 100 g of the butter. Heat until it just starts to colour and smell nutty, then remove and set aside.

Now blanch the other bunch of asparagus in a pot of boiling water, cooking for a couple of minutes until it turns bright green. Refresh it in iced water, remove and pat dry. Cut off the tips of this blanched asparagus and reserve.

Slice up the blanched stalks. Using a stick blender, blitz the stalk pieces. We're going to fold this through my …

Instant Mayo! You'll need your stick blender to do this, too. Carefully crack the egg and place it in the base of the stick blender's plastic blending cup. Add the lemon juice, mustard and a pinch of salt, then pour over the grapeseed oil.

Place the stick blender in the blending cup and carefully position the head of the stick blender so it covers and encloses the egg yolk. Blitz. Count to three and, very slowly, pull the blender up through the oil and – voilà! – the oil will emulsify with the egg and the lemon juice. So, there's instant mayonnaise with no need for the stress and slow dribbling – of olive oil that is. Gently fold through the blitzed asparagus stalks.

Now fashion four aluminium-foil 'boats', each big enough to hold a whiting fillet. Use a strong sheet of aluminium foil or, ideally, double it over and ensure that all four edges are turned up. This 'origami' has been a traditional part of our Glastonbury adventures for over three decades now. Butter the boats.

Butter the whiting fillets, season and grate a little lemon zest over each one. Pop each buttered fillet in a 'boat' and place on the BBQ to cook slowly and gently (this will take about 5 minutes). You could use a 200°C oven for this instead.

Drain the cooked potatoes and return to the pan. Toss through a blizzard of chives.

When the fish is almost cooked, lift the boats off the grill and carefully carry them inside to plate up.

Serve the just-cooked fillets on the grilled asparagus with the lightest dusting of chopped tarragon or dill. The steamed tips should be strewn over the plate and the chive-boiled spuds tossed in. Drizzle over some of the fish-poaching liquid and add generous dollops of the asparagussy Instant Mayo.

SERVES 4

SALMON *with* SAUTÉED KALE *and* TOO MANY CAPERS

Bitter loves salt the way that misery loves company and the way TV 'talent' loves someone whispering in their ear telling them how great they are – especially if they aren't. Like me. Both of these elements – bitter and salt – play a great role in this dish by bridling in the richness of the salmon.

2 × 200 g salmon fillets, skin on and bones removed

salt flakes

olive oil, for frying

2½ tablespoons capers, drained

1 garlic clove, sliced

1 bunch kale, well washed, tough stalks cut out

zest and juice of ½ lemon, plus wedges, to serve

freshly ground black pepper

Pat the skin of the salmon dry with kitchen paper, then rub it with salt and leave it for 30 minutes. The salt will draw the moisture from the salmon and help make a delicious, crispy skin.

Scrape the excess salt from the skin (you can use the blunt side of a knife), and pat it dry.

Add a splash of oil to a heavy-based frying pan and bring it to a medium heat. Cook the fillets for about 4 minutes, skin-side down, until crisp, then gently flip and cook for a further 2–3 minutes, depending how you like your salmon cooked. Don't forget that the heat will keep cooking the fish after you take it off the stove, so don't overcook it. It should be soft and flake easily.

While the salmon is cooking, heat about 2 cm of oil in another pan over medium to high heat. When the oil is hot, flash-fry the capers for 30 seconds, then remove from the oil and set aside.

Now, in the same pan, sauté the garlic for 30 seconds before adding the kale, moving it around to coat with the oil. Add the zest, a squeeze of lemon, pepper and half the capers and toss in the pan just long enough to wilt the kale (don't let it go soggy).

Place a bed of kale on each serving plate, lay the salmon fillets on top and throw over the remaining crispy capers. Serve with a wedge of lemon on the side.

SERVES 2

Roasted Salmon with NYC Celeriac

Undervalued … it happens to vegetables just like it happens to people at work, or in relationships. Celeriac's only role seems to be as a purée under beef or game, or as crunchy batons in a remoulade. Its versatility and sheer deliciousness – somewhere between parsnip and celery – is seldom seen elsewhere. Yet it makes a delicious creamy soup and is really outstanding used instead of potatoes in a mash.

Everything in this dish has one role – to make the celeriac look good! It is based on a simple bowl of celeriac purée slathered with melted butter and vinegary hot sauce that I ate in Brooklyn on one of those magical, memorable nights when a table for six ended up as a table for 38, as more and more of the *MasterChef* crew stumbled in out of the night. The place was run by Aussies, so they seemed to understand that sort of thing. I don't remember getting home but I do remember the celeriac.

For the salmon, firstly pat the skin dry with paper towel. Rub the skin with salt flakes and set it aside for at least 30 minutes while you attend to the other elements of this dish. The salt helps draw the moisture from the skin.

When it's time to cook, scrape the salt off with the blunt side of a knife.

For the fennel, preheat the oven to 180°C.

Toss the fennel halves or quarters generously with olive oil. Lay on a baking tray with the thyme and garlic.

Bake for 30–40 minutes until cooked and coloured, turning once at the halfway mark. Add the garlic cloves at this point. When it's all cooked, remove from the oven and drizzle over the red wine vinegar.

Cook the celeriac while the fennel is in the oven. Put it in a pan with the milk and bring to the boil. Skim the scum, if there is any. When soft (after about 20 minutes), drain and reserve the milk. Blitz with a stick blender, using enough of the reserved milk to make it smooth and creamy. Add the cream and season to taste.

Always start the fish in a cold, wide-based, heavy frying pan with a touch of oil and bring it to a medium heat.

Cook skin-side down for 4–5 minutes until the skin is golden and crispy.

Gently flip the fish over and continue cooking for a further 2–3 minutes, depending how you like your fish cooked. Remember the fish will keep cooking through with residual heat once off the flame.

To serve, smear a generous mound of celeriac purée over a large share platter. Dot with butter, which will melt, and shake a few drops of Tabasco over the celeriac. Lay the fennel and garlic over the top and crown with the salmon fillets.

SERVES 4

4 salmon fillets, skin on and bones removed

salt flakes and freshly ground black pepper

4 baby fennel, halved or quartered, depending on size

olive oil

8 thyme sprigs

6 cloves garlic, unpeeled

50 ml red wine vinegar

1 kg celeriac, peeled and grated

1 litre (4 cups) milk

125 m (½ cup) cream

knob of butter

Tabasco sauce

'AS TO POULTRY, IT MAY GENERALLY BE REMARKED THAT BARN-DOOR FOWLS ARE PREFERABLE TO THOSE FED IN COOPS. A POULTRY YARD ... SHOULD BE WELL SHELTERED, WITH A WARM ASPECT AND SUFFICIENTLY INCLINED TO BE ALWAYS DRY ... THERE SHOULD BE ALSO A SUPPLY OF RUNNING WATER, OF WHICH POULTRY ARE FOND. A GREEN PATCH OF EARTH SHOULD BE NEXT TO THE POULTRY-YARD TO ALLOW THE FOWLS FREE EXERCISE.'

Andrew Valentine Kirwan, 1864

CHICKEN and a DUCK

AUNTIE KIRSTEN'S STICKY CHICKEN DRUMMIES

Strange but true that some people look at me and fail to see the suave, svelte sophisticate that I see staring back at me from the mirror every morning. I suspect that my fondness for simple, finger-sucking dishes like this might be partly responsible for the abject failure of my marketing division to brand me as the 'Aussie George Clooney'. At least we didn't call the dish 'Hot Auntie Kirsten's Sticky Bingo Wings' as I originally wanted to! Or even worse, 'Auntie Kirsten's Drumettes' which sounds too much like a marching band from *Toddlers and Tiaras*.

2.5 kg chicken drumettes or wings
500 ml (2 cups) soy sauce
¼ cup dark brown sugar
3 large garlic cloves, crushed
3 tablespoons grated ginger

Rinse the chicken drumettes and pat them dry with paper towel.

Place all of the marinating ingredients in very large bowl and stir to dissolve the sugar.

Add the chicken, toss the pieces around so that they are nicely coated and then cover with plastic wrap.

Leave them to marinate for at least 3 hours, or overnight, in the refrigerator.

Preheat your oven to 180°C.

Remove the drumettes from the marinade and put them side-by-side in two large baking dishes.

Bake them for 1 hour until they are dark and sticky.

Remove the baking dishes from the oven and stir the chicken pieces to make sure they are coated with the juices.

Cover with aluminium foil and cook for another 10 to 15 minutes.

SERVES 10–12

3 ways with CHICKEN MINCE

In these health-conscious days, I love chicken mince, you love chicken mince, we all love chicken mince – but only if it is judiciously seasoned and carefully cooked. The key question is, what to do with it? As well as my handy list below, here are three of my favourite ways to cook an Australian ingredient whose popularity is rising almost as fast as quinoa and chicken thighs.

30 other things to do with chicken mince

1. Chicken bolognese
2. Larb gai
3. Chicken meatball sub, wrap or sanger
4. Chicken and lemongrass bun cha
5. Chicken kofta
6. Cabbage rolls
7. Chicken arancini
8. Stuffed capsicums filled with spiced rice and chicken mince
9. Chicken and thyme rissoles
10. Chicken burgers with tarragon mayonnaise
11. Chicken mince and mushroom lasagne
12. Chicken gyoza
13. Chicken and shiitake ravioli
14. Chicken chilli con carne
15. Chicken herder's pie (like shepherd's pie, but cluckier)
16. Chicken and spinach cannelloni
17. Chicken momos – which are very similar to dumplings, but speak with a Nepalese accent
18. Chicken wonton soup
19. Chicken Scotch eggs (those are the ones that ran away at Culloden. Sorry, there was only so far I could go before a dad joke blurted out)
20. Chicken, jalapeño and iceberg tostadas
21. Chicken tostadalitas (which is the name I've just made up for teeny tostadas)
22. Chicken pide
23. Chicken samosa
24. Chicken roulade
25. Butter-fried chicken balls in parmesan soup
26. Chicken mousse
27. Savoury chicken mince with peas and feta (see page 27 and improvise!)
28. Minced chicken and prawn dumplings in sticky rice flour wrappers
29. Chicken and pistachio pâté
30. Chicken and pork terrine with Dijon mustard sauce.

1. THAI CHICKEN SAUSAGE ROLLS

FILLING
500 g chicken thigh mince
500 g chicken fillet mince
200 g sweet potato, peeled, cooked and roughly mashed
1½ teaspoons grated ginger
2 garlic cloves, peeled and crushed
3 kaffir lime leaves, finely shredded
1 red onion, finely diced
1 egg, lightly beaten
¼ cup sweet chilli sauce, plus extra, to serve
1½ cups fresh breadcrumbs
½ bunch coriander, leaves and stalks
2 teaspoons salt flakes
freshly ground black pepper
crushed peanuts, but you can leave them out if these are going to school

PASTRY
5 sheets puff pastry
1 egg, lightly beaten
2–3 tablespoons white or black sesame seeds

Preheat the oven to 200°C. Line two trays with baking paper.

Combine the filling ingredients in a large mixing bowl.

Cut the pastry sheets in half. Roll some mince and lay it along the long edge of the pastry. Brush or use a finger to rub a little water along the other long edge. Starting with the meaty side, roll to enclose the pastry – it should overlap a bit.

Cut into whatever size rolls you like and arrange them on trays, seam-side down (but don't overcrowd the trays).

Brush the tops with egg and, if you like them, sprinkle with sesame seeds. Repeat with the remaining sausage meat and pastry. Bake for about 20 minutes until golden and cooked.

Serve with sweet chilli sauce.

MAKES 16–20

2. MINCED CHICKEN SALAD

1 tablespoon peanut or vegetable oil

1 stalk lemongrass, white part only, finely chopped

3 teaspoons minced ginger

4 garlic cloves, finely chopped

5 coriander roots, scraped clean and finely chopped

1 teaspoon coriander seeds, crushed

500 g chicken thigh mince

1½ tablespoons hoisin sauce

1 teaspoon salt flakes

½ red onion, finely diced

150 g canned water chestnuts

150 g rice noodles

½ bunch coriander, leaves picked

DRESSING

2 tablespoons peanuts, crushed

2 tablespoons sugar

½–1 teaspoon chilli flakes

3 tablespoons lime juice

1 tablespoon fish sauce

TO SERVE

1 tablespoon peanuts

1 red chilli, finely sliced

3 spring onions, finely sliced

½ bunch Thai basil

To make the dressing, combine all the ingredients and set aside.

Heat the peanut or vegetable oil in a frying pan or wok over medium–high heat. Add the lemongrass, ginger, garlic and coriander roots and seeds and keep moving in the pan for a couple of minutes until fragrant. Turn the heat up high, if it isn't already, and add the chicken mince, breaking it up as you go. Keep turning it until it's cooked through. Add the hoisin and salt and stir through. Add the red onions and toss through before adding the water chestnuts last. Remove from the heat.

Cook the noodles as per packet instructions. Drain and toss through a little of the dressing, but leave some for plating.

The chicken should now have cooled off a bit, so you can add the coriander leaves without them wilting immediately.

Lay some noodles in a plate or bowl and add a little more dressing, but don't drown. Heap the chicken on top and finish with the peanuts, chilli, spring onions and sprigs of Thai basil.

SERVES 3–4

3. CHICKEN LOAF

2 tablespoons olive oil

1 brown onion, finely chopped

2 garlic cloves, crushed

2 celery stalks

6 thyme sprigs

20 sage leaves, finely shredded

70 g (a scant ½ cup) pine nuts, chopped and toasted

1 kg chicken thigh mince

1½ cups fresh breadcrumbs

1 egg, lightly beaten

2½ tablespoons Dijon mustard

2½ teaspoons salt flakes

freshly ground black pepper

ONION JAM

1 kg (8–10) onions, peeled, halved and thinly sliced

olive oil

1 kg sugar

75 g mustard seeds

400 ml red wine vinegar

300 ml sweet chilli sauce

Preheat the oven to 190°C. Line a loaf pan approximately 8 cm deep × 10 cm × 25 cm with aluminium foil and then with baking paper. Make sure the sides and ends overhang enough to wrap and enclose the whole loaf.

Heat the oil in a frying pan over medium heat. Add your chopped onion, garlic, celery, thyme and sage and cook until softened, about 8–10 minutes. Add the toasted pine nuts. Set aside to cool. Remove the thyme stalks.

Combine the chicken mince, breadcrumbs, egg, mustard and onion mixture and season with salt and a few good twists of freshly ground pepper. Mix well. Spoon the mixture into the loaf pan, pressing it down firmly but forking up the top a little for some craggy peaks. Bake for 40 minutes.

Remove the pan from the oven and transfer the loaf in its foil and paper onto a shallow baking tray. Open up the wrapping to expose the loaf and spoon a generous amount of onion jam over the top and sides as a glaze. Place under the grill for a few minutes, or back into a hot oven, to get some colour and burny bits on the jam.

Remove from the heat and let sit for 10 minutes before cutting and serving.

SERVES 10

ONION JAM

Cook the onions in a pan with a small amount of olive oil until softened, which will take about 20–30 minutes.

Add the sugar and mix, stirring over the heat until dissolved.

Add the mustard seeds, vinegar and the sweet chilli sauce.

Boil for about 30 minutes, or until reduced and thickened.

To test if the jam will set, drop some jam onto a saucer and place in the freezer for 2 minutes. If the jam forms a skin when pushed gently with your finger, it is ready.

When the jam is cooked, pour it into sterilised jars, wipe the mouth of the jars with vinegar and seal.

MAKES ABOUT 6 × 250 ML JARS

TIP

You can keep your onion jam on the pantry shelf, but after opening it store it in the fridge.

THE BEST FRIED SCHNITZEL THAT ISN'T

If you ever journey to Malta to see the 4000-year-old, four-aspe Tarxien temple of Borg In-Nadur near Birzebbuga you will find a small stone plaque embedded in the original megalithic 4.5 m stone wall to the west side of the site. The words on it, weathered and faint now from centuries of sun, rain and sea spray, and from the constant tracing of tourist fingers, are simple. 'There is one rule and one rule alone. No Matt Preston cookbook can be complete without a recipe from Jen the country cook.'

Rules is rules, so here it is – about the cleverest thing I've seen done with chicken thighs since George Calombaris learnt to ride a bicycle. You will not believe these aren't fried in oil!

Preheat the oven to 180°C. Line 2 low-sided baking trays with baking paper.

Flatten the chicken thigh fillets between baking paper using a mallet or rolling pin, just so they are even in thickness. Cut into tiles about 3 cm square.

Toss the chicken in the melted butter then into the panko crumbs to coat.

Lay the chicken nuggets on the baking trays, leaving enough room between each nugget to allow crisping. Sprinkle with salt flakes.

Pop them into the preheated oven for 15–20 minutes or until cooked and golden, turning once halfway through cooking.

Serve with my . . .

INSTANT MAYO

You'll need a stick blender to do this. Carefully crack the egg and place it in the base of the stick blender's plastic blending cup. Pour over the grapeseed oil, add the mustard and a good squeeze of lemon juice and salt.

Place the stick blender in the blending cup and carefully position the head of the stick blender so it covers and encloses the egg yolk. Blitz. Count to three and then, very slowly, pull the blender up through the oil and – voilà! – the oil will emulsify with the water in the egg white and the lemon juice, thanks to the yolk.

SERVES 6

12 (about 1.5 kg) chicken thigh fillets
80 g butter, melted
120 g (2 cups) panko breadcrumbs
salt flakes

INSTANT MAYO
1 egg
300 ml grapeseed oil
1 tablespoon Dijon mustard
juice of ½ lemon
salt

MATT'S CORONATION CHICKEN
with INSTANT MAYONNAISE

This is the result of a 'recipe-off' between my Coronation Chicken recipe and that of my friend Marnie. She's one half of the cabal of smart, sassy women who help with my recipes, and provide excellent, if sometimes unwelcome, comments on how I could become a better person as well as a better cook. She believed her recipe was better because it came from the kitchen of a posh bush homestead. I believed mine (probably given to my family as a gesture of thanks from a grateful Princess Elizabeth after her Coronation) was surely better – if only because it comes from the UK, where this creamy chicken dish was created. The trouble was that when we read each other's recipes we realised they were pretty much the same. This means that you are now staring at the only Coronation Chicken recipe you'll ever need.

2 litres (8 cups) chicken stock

4 chicken breasts (about 1 kg), skin off

2 tablespoons apricot jam

1 lemon

3 green cardamom pods, crushed

12 dried apricots, chopped into 1 cm dice

1 egg

300 ml grapeseed oil

3 teaspoons tandoori paste or curry powder

salt flakes

100 g flaked almonds

200 ml cream

coriander leaves, to serve

iceberg lettuce, celery and cucumber, to serve

small boiled potatoes, butter and dill, to serve

TIPS

1. Any leftover Coronation Chicken can be used in sandwiches. Just use soft white bread to highlight the silkiness of this chicken salad.

2. If you are feeling posh, pistachios make a nice change from almonds.

Pour the stock into a pot and bring to the boil. Throw in the chicken breasts, then bring the stock back to the boil. Cover and turn off the heat, but leave on the stove.

Let the chicken breasts steep in the stock for 45 minutes, then check to see if they have firmed up, which shows they are cooked. Remove from the broth (keep the broth for a simple soup another day).

Cover the poached breasts and put them in the fridge to chill until needed. When the chicken is cool, chop it into thumb-sized chunks.

While the chook is poaching make the dressing. Melt the apricot jam over a low heat with a squeeze of lemon. Stir in the cardamom and apricot pieces. Bring to a simmer then remove from the heat and leave to cool.

Now make the Instant Mayo. You'll need a stick blender to do this. Carefully crack the egg and place it in the stick blender's plastic blending cup. Pour over the grapeseed oil, half the tandoori paste or curry powder, a good squeeze of lemon and a pinch of salt.

Place the stick blender in the blending cup and carefully position the head of the stick blender so it covers and encloses the egg yolk. Blitz. Count to three and then, very slowly, pull the blender up through the oil and – voila! – the oil will emulsify with the egg and the lemon juice.

Toast the almonds in a dry frying pan. Watch them as they have a tendency to burn and you want them to be golden and crunchy but not black in any way.

Whisk the cream until it is soft and billowy. Do not over-whisk.

Fold the mayo into the cream with half the cooled apricot mixture. Taste the mayo and flavour it with some more salt, curry paste/powder or lemon juice, as you think fit. For my palate I usually add all the curry flavourings and a little bit more of the apricots to counteract the richness of the dressing.

Spoon the dressing over the chook and turn lightly to coat. Don't overdo it. You can always serve extra dressing on the side. Scatter on the coriander leaves and toasted almonds and serve with a salad of lettuce, celery and cucumber and small boiled potatoes.

SERVES 8

Apricot Chicken

You'll find new takes on a few retro classics dotted through this book – savoury mince, Coronation Chicken, meatloaves, jaffles, sticky toffee pudding – but all with a neat new spin.

None, however, are quite as 'scrape-the-sticky-burny-bits-off-the-bottom-of-the-baking-tray' delicious as this reinvention. Herbs, olives and caperberries move this dish as far from the seventies classic of tinned apricots and chook as that recipe was from the original tagines that inspired it. And look how short the method is … that means it is dead simple to make!

8 chicken thigh chops, on the bone with skin

80 ml olive oil

12 garlic cloves, smashed in their skins

1 heaped tablespoon dried Greek oregano

10 thyme sprigs

24 (about 150 g) dried apricots

24 caperberries

24 green olives (I use Sicilian)

1 strip orange rind

2 bay leaves

1 teaspoon salt flakes

freshly ground black pepper

120 ml sherry vinegar

250 ml (1 cup) verjus or white wine

2 tablespoons brown sugar

flat-leaf parsley leaves, to garnish

In a bowl or large ziplock bag combine the chicken with the oil, garlic, oregano, 8 thyme sprigs, apricots, caperberries, olives, orange rind, bay leaves, salt and pepper and the sherry vinegar.

Place in the fridge for at least 2 hours, or overnight if you can, to allow the flavours to infuse.

Preheat the oven to 180°C.

Lay the chicken and all the marinade ingredients in a large baking dish. Add the verjus or wine to the dish and sprinkle over the sugar. Bake in the oven for an hour.

Remove the chicken from the oven and leave it to rest for 5 to 10 minutes before sprinkling over the parsley and some fresh thyme leaves stripped from the remaining 2 stems.

SERVES 6

TIP

This is delicious served with green beans. Oh, and rice or crushed waxy potatoes.

BURNISHED ROAST CHICKEN *with* BURNT LEMON GRAVY

We are in a culinary era of bitterness. This most elegant of the five tastes is currently all the rage, whether it is ice clinking in a glass of Campari, short shots of coffee, or kale … everywhere. Another great source of bitterness is the pith of lemons. This recipe plays on that by partnering the rich toasty citrus notes of a lemon roasted in chicken fat with the saltiness and umami-richness of juices from the oven-browned chook. When you blitz these two together and season well, you're left with a thick, complex gravy in which that slight pithy bitterness balances against all the schmaltzy richness of the chicken juices.

You can salt the chicken hours before, or even the night before, for extra-crispy skin.

To do this, dry the skin of the bird and cavity. Stuff 2 lemon halves into the cavity, along with the garlic and rosemary sprigs. Rub the entire bird – breasts, bottom, legs and wings – with olive oil and salt. Grind over a little pepper.

If you're doing this the night before, or well ahead of time, put the chicken in a dish or on a plate and keep it in the fridge. You'll need to bring the chicken back to room temperature before roasting.

Otherwise, place it in a roasting pan. Nestle the other 2 lemon halves face-down in the pan (you want these to burnish in the heat).

Preheat the oven to 200°C.

Bake for 1 hour, basting with juices periodically.

When the juices run clear at the thigh or your meat thermometer reaches 68°C, remove and rest for at least 15 minutes before carving.

To make the burnt lemon gravy, pour the pan juices and the toastiest lemon half into a processor, or use a stick blender and blitz (including the skin of the lemon). Season to taste, or add the juice of the other cooked lemon if you think it needs more zing.

SERVES 4

1 × 1.6 kg free-range chicken

2 thin-skinned lemons, halved

3 garlic cloves, smashed in their skins

2 rosemary sprigs

lots of good-quality salt flakes and freshly ground black pepper

2–3 tablespoons extra-virgin olive oil

SHREDDED CHICKEN *on* CORN DISGRACE

Each time I write a cookbook I'm teased about my ingredient obsessions by Marnie and Kate, the wise women who keep me in line and who improve my recipes when my back is turned. In the last book I obviously had a thing for oranges, zucchini, yoghurt, feta, figs, bread and caramels. In the first book mangoes, chocolate, eggs, onions and beef littered the pages.

I'm not sure what will be the most-used ingredients in this tome but one thing is for sure, bacon or prosciutto, chicken, corn, parmesan, butter, herbs, lemon, cucumber, feta and iceberg lettuce will all be prominent because they always are in my cooking. Perhaps that is why I love this recipe so much; because it uses all my favourites in one dish! Oh, and because the sloppy corn pudding is just pure pleasure food. It may not look too good but let's face it, as you get older you get to learn that the best pleasures leave everyone a little dishevelled; a little disgraced but loving it!

4 tablespoons butter

1½ cups diced onion (about 2 small onions)

15 sage leaves, 5 of them very finely shredded

220 g (about 2 cups) small button mushrooms, wiped clean

2 cups frozen corn kernels, or 5 corn cobs

2 tablespoons flour

160 ml (⅔ cup) cream

160 ml (⅔ cup) milk

90 g prosciutto or bacon, cut into strips

¼ cup grated parmesan

salt flakes and freshly ground black pepper

1 supermarket roast chook (I prefer free range)

zest and juice of 1 lemon

1 iceberg lettuce, shredded

1 cucumber, peeled, halved, deseeded and cut into crescents. Keep the seeds!

100 g feta

Preheat the oven to 160°C.

Melt 1 tablespoon of butter in a large pot over a gentle heat. Throw in the diced onion with the 5 finely shredded sage leaves and cook until it starts to soften.

Melt 1 tablespoon of butter in another pot and cook the mushrooms. While the mushrooms are cooking, briefly pulse the frozen corn kernels in a food processor. If using fresh corn, coarsely grate the corn from the cobs.

Remove the mushrooms from the heat when they are cooked but have yet to reach that really slippery stage (a couple of minutes).

Stir the flour into the onions. Then add the corn. Turn up the heat and cook for 3 minutes.

Next pour in the cream and cook gently for another 3 minutes.

Add the milk, prosciutto, parmesan and the reserved mushrooms. Stir and cook for 2 more minutes. Season to taste.

Pour the mixture into a well-buttered baking dish and place it in a high-sided baking tray filled with warm water halfway up the side. Place the baking tray with the corn pudding basin in the oven and bake for about 40 minutes until it is cooked but still has just a slight jiggle left in it.

While the corn pudding is baking, shred the meat from the chook. Just before the pudding is ready melt the rest of the butter. When it is foamy throw in the remaining sage leaves so they go crisp and flavour the butter, which will start to go nutty – but don't let it burn!

Serve a spoonful of your Corn Disgrace (disgraceful because it is so delicious!) topped with the shredded chook, crispy sage leaves and drizzled with the sage butter and a little lemon zest.

Serve with a simple salad of shredded iceberg and cucumber crescents dressed with the juice of the lemon blitzed with half the cucumber seeds and the feta.

SERVES 6

MARNIE'S TAUT CHICKEN THIGH BAKE

I have yet to cook this dish for anyone who hasn't loved it. The same set of ingredients work well with fillets of salmon too. I'm not so sure Marnie is keen on the name – but then, it is her recipe and it would be rude not to credit her!

¾ cup sweet chilli sauce

2 garlic cloves, crushed

1 teaspoon finely grated ginger

½ bunch coriander

24 Thai basil leaves (optional)

3 kaffir lime leaves, super-finely cut

1 teaspoon salt flakes

½ teaspoon sesame oil (optional)

8 chicken thigh fillets, without skin

Scrape and clean the coriander roots. Chop them, along with the stems, reserving the leaves for your garnish.

Combine all the ingredients (except the coriander leaves) in a bowl or large ziplock bag. Gently massage the flavours into the chicken. Leave this to sit for at least 2 hours or overnight in the fridge.

Preheat the oven to 200°C.

Lay the chicken along with the sauce in a large baking dish and cook for 25–35 minutes. Check at the 25-minute mark; the chicken should be all sticky with dark caramelised bits. If it's still a little pale, turn up the heat for a further 10 minutes to get more colour.

Serve immediately with a scatter of fresh herbs, such as coriander and Thai basil.

This chicken is fabulous the next day on its own or stuffed into a baguette or wrap with fresh herbs.

SERVES 4

FESENJOON (PRONOUNCED: FESSENJUNE)

I fell in love with this dish at a long-gone Persian restaurant rather epically called Nights of Shiraz, but the laborious nature of the recipe made me seriously debate whether to find shortcuts or just not put it in this book at all. The thing is that the result is just so unusual, so naggingly sweet 'n' sour and moreish, that I felt it had to stay.

Blanch the walnuts for 5 minutes in 1 litre (4 cups) of boiling water. Drain and refresh in cold water, then repeat. Tip the walnuts onto a clean tea towel and dry very thoroughly.

Pound the dry walnuts to a fine meal in a mortar, or pulse in batches in a food processor. Take care not to over-process them into butter.

Throw the ground walnuts into a wide pan and dry-fry them until toasty and fragrant, about 6 minutes. Stir every so often so they don't burn – especially at then end when they are more likely to catch. Sprinkle on 1 teaspoon of turmeric and stir.

The secret to this dish is to go slowly. Pour 750 ml (3 cups) of the stock into the walnuts. When it starts to steam, lower the heat to the merest bubble. Cook for 90 minutes, checking every 15 minutes or so. The walnuts need to stay moist and yield up their oils, so add more stock if needed. Take care they don't catch on the bottom of the pan.

After 90 minutes start your chook thighs. Tuck in their sides to form tight little bundles. Add a big splash of oil to a large, lidded oven pot set on a medium heat. Throw in the onions to make a raft and pack the thighs on top, rounded sides up. Turn everything over after 5 minutes and sprinkle with the rest of the turmeric. Check after 5 minutes and lift out any thighs that have coloured all over. When all are browned, remove from the pan along with the browned onions.

Deglaze the chook pan with 250 ml (1 cup) chicken stock.

Tip the soupy walnuts into the canister of a stick blender, adding a splash of stock if they are very thick. Blitz to a purée then pour into the chook pan. Add another 250 ml of stock – or more – until the walnutty sauce is the consistency of light cream.

Stir in about ½ cup of pomegranate molasses then taste and season well with salt. If it's too sweet, add a squeeze of lemon. Or, if you prefer, add more of the pomegranate molasses.

Add the bay leaves, saffron threads and their soaking liquid, then add the onions and pack in the chook thighs. They should be covered by walnutty sauce, so top up with extra stock if need be.

Simmer gently for 30 minutes, or until the chicken is tender and the sauce has thickened. Stir occasionally to stop things sticking to the bottom of the pot.

Taste and adjust the lemon, salt or molasses as needed.

Garnish with pomegranate seeds, coriander sprigs and lemon wedges and serve with buttered rice.

SERVES 8–10

500 g walnut pieces

3 teaspoons ground turmeric

2 litres (8 cups) chicken stock (some may be left over)

3 brown onions, finely diced

1 teaspoon saffron threads, infusing in 1 tablespoon boiling water

18 chicken thighs (about 2.5 kg), skin off

olive oil

scant ¾ cup pomegranate molasses (some will be left over)

salt flakes

5 fresh bay leaves, or 2 dried

fresh pomegranate seeds, to serve

buttered rice, to serve

lemon wedges, to serve

half a bunch of coriander, sprigs picked, to serve

TIP

This dish is typically served with butter-crusted chelo rice. You'll find a recipe in my first cookbook, *Matt Preston's 100 Best Recipes*. It is also good with nutty brown rice. Those of you who are regular visitors to my cookbooks will realise I find it hard to resist subversive marketing messages like that last one. Sorry. Oh, and add some sour little barberries to garnish the rice too.

PAN-FRIED CHICKEN BREAST *with* CASHEW MISO 'BUTTER'

To paraphrase *House of Cards'* Machiavellian senator, Frank Underwood – and let's try and say this with his molasses-slow but good bourbon–smooth, Southern drawl – chicken loves creaminess more than sharks love blood. This is just my attempt at a healthier play on this combo by using the creaminess of cashews instead of dairy. It's also a quick-fix dish that can be accessorised for any season, which is always good to have in your repertoire.

2 × 350 g boneless chicken breasts, skin off

155 g (1 cup) unsalted cashews

2 level tablespoons miso paste, ideally white miso

about 4 tablespoons hot water

juice of ½ lemon

Cut the tenderloins from the chook breasts (see Tip 3 below for how to use these in another dish). Beat the breasts flat between two sheets of baking paper using a rolling pin, meat mallet or a wine bottle. You don't want them too thin, about 1–2 cm is fine, but even is important.

Blitz the cashews with half the miso and 2 tablespoons of hot water. Taste. Add more miso until its flavour is there as a warm glow. I reckon you'll need about 2 more tablespoons.

Now, drop by drop, add the lemon juice if you want the mellow-salty-savouriness of the cashew butter to have some citric acidity. Work in more hot water if you want a looser sauce to pour over your chicken. I like it more dollopable than runny, but each to his own.

Now place a non-stick frying pan over medium to high heat, pop in the breasts and fry until they're golden on both sides. You won't need any oil. When the chicken is just cooked (about 4 minutes) remove and keep warm for a minute or two to rest. Serve with cashew miso butter.

SERVES 4

TIPS

1. In summer, serve the chicken with a cool salad of finely sliced iceberg, chunks of radish, sliced celery and quartered lychees. The cashew butter can be stretched into a dressing by the addition of a couple of extra tablespoons of hot water, a tablespoon of lemon juice and a splash of soy.

2. When the weather's cold, partner the chicken with some comfort food. Roast some sweet potato, carrot and pumpkin pieces and toss them through 2 cups of cooked brown rice with some fried corn kernels and a handful of craisins for added zing. Stir through plenty of fresh chopped coriander, drizzle with runny honey and season with a pinch of salt flakes.

3. Chicken tenderloins are delicious buttered, crumbed and baked like the recipe on page 191, or grilled and added to the black quinoa salad on page 94. Or maybe just use the pistachio tarator recipe on page 94 and serve over shredded iceberg lettuce.

Antique French Chicken

Cream, mustard, thyme. This holy trinity is central to so many of the classic French-inspired chicken and rabbit dishes my grandmother cooked in her old wood-burning Aga. This version has all the deliciousness of the original but with the flavours amped up through the umami boost of shiitake mushrooms. Umami wasn't something that was discussed in my grandmother's day – perhaps because it was identified as a fifth taste in 1908 by a Japanese scientist, Kikunae Ikeda. It was another, Akira Kuninaka, who discovered in 1957 that shiitake mushrooms were loaded with the ribonucleotides that help give that umami savouriness. You see, my grandfather was a veteran of WWII in Burma and so the Japanese were never mentioned. On a lighter note, throwing in potatoes and peas with walnuts and parmesan add another couple of chapters to the umami story of this dish.

butter and oil, for frying

700 g skinless chicken breasts, cut in 3 cm, equal-sized chunks

4 celery stalks, cut into 1 cm dice

1 red onion, finely diced

500 g mushrooms, sliced (any will do but ideally use darker mushrooms and at least 100 g of shiitake if you can find them)

2 garlic cloves, thinly sliced

¼ cup Dijon mustard

250 ml (1 cup) sweet sherry

1 bunch thyme

500 ml (2 cups) chicken stock, simmering

500 g frozen peas

200 g walnut pieces

100 g parmesan, finely grated

salt flakes and freshly ground black pepper

1 tablespoon grapeseed oil

120 ml (½ cup) cream

12 small boiled potatoes, to serve

1 bunch flat-leaf parsley, leaves picked and chopped

In a large pan over a medium heat melt a little butter in olive oil, then fry your chicken breast chunks in two batches until golden edged. Add half the celery dice and all of the onion to the second batch. Remove each batch when the chook is still a little squidgy and undercooked in the middle. Tip out the veg, too, and keep everything warm.

Throw your mushrooms into the now empty chook pan and sauté them until they start to soften. Add the garlic and the Dijon mustard. Cook for 2 minutes. Whack up the heat and when the pan is very hot (after 2 minutes) pour in the sweet sherry and half the thyme, the leaves still attached to the branch. Everything will bubble furiously. Let the sherry reduce by half and add half the stock. Let this reduce by half again. Remove the thyme.

Drop the frozen peas into the remaining simmering chicken stock for about a minute, until they are just done. Drain the peas, reserving the stock. Crunch 50 g of the walnuts and toss in with the reserved peas in their pan.

Using a stick blender blitz the rest of the walnuts with the parmesan; drizzle in the reserved chicken stock to lubricate this process. Season well – it should almost taste salty but not quite. Check the consistency – creamy is the word that should leap to mind. Now turn the stick blender back on and slowly drizzle in the grapeseed oil. The walnut dressing should fluff up a little.

Throw the chicken back in with the sweet, stocky mushrooms and add the rest of the uncooked celery. This will give the finished dish some fresh crunch. Pour in the cream and stir. Let the cream bubble, the sauce thicken and everything get nice and toasty. Taste and season if required; it usually is.

Dress the chook with the leaves picked from the rest of the bunch of thyme. Serve with boiled potatoes (buttered and tossed with chopped parsley) and the peas and walnuts draped with walnut 'oli' (that's an 'aioli' without the 'ai'!).

SERVES 4

TIPS

1. Those peas and walnuts with the rich walnut dressing are wonderful tossed through pasta with parmesan and lemon.

2. Or, fry the chicken pieces in butter with ½ bunch chopped tarragon. When almost cooked, remove the chicken and keep warm. Throw in a handful of seedless grapes and, with the pan over the heat, give them a toss for a minute. Now deglaze the pan with ¼ cup white wine vinegar. Leave the grapes in. When the gravy is reduced and you've scraped off all the tasty burnt bits, pour in 200 ml of cream and stir. Let it bubble away for a couple of minutes. Return the chook to the pan, plus another handful of small seedless grapes and the remaining tarragon. Stir to coat and warm. Serve on mash with a crisp salad.

BUTTER CHICKEN

Some dishes are like butterfly kisses, some are like a big fat smoocheroo. This one is more like sinking into a long, slow hug with someone built for comfort rather than speed.

1 kg chicken thighs, cut into 2–3 cm cubes

2 tablespoons tomato paste

80 ml plain yoghurt

3 large garlic cloves, minced

¼ teaspoon chilli powder

1 kg very ripe tomatoes, roughly chopped

1 large red onion, roughly chopped

2 tablespoons coconut or olive oil

5 green cardamom pods

½ teaspoon ground mace

1 teaspoon ground coriander

2 tablespoons chopped ginger

80 g butter

1 tablespoon sugar

1 tablespoon dried fenugreek leaves (if you can find them. If not, leave them out)

1 teaspoon garam masala

salt flakes

100 ml cream

In a large bowl mix the chicken with the tomato paste, yoghurt, half the garlic and chilli powder and set aside.

Place the chopped tomatoes and onion in a large frying pan over a medium heat and bring to a simmer, then simmer, uncovered, for 10 minutes.

Meanwhile take another frying pan and heat the coconut or olive oil over a medium to high heat. When the oil is hot, add the cardamom pods, mace, coriander, the remaining garlic and the ginger. Fry for a few minutes and then add to the tomato mixture and stir through. Remove from the heat and cool for a few minutes, before puréeing in a blender.

Strain the tomato mixture through a colander, pressing with the back of a spoon to push them through, then pour back into the large frying pan, add the sugar and return to the heat. Discard what is left in the colander.

In the smaller frying pan melt the butter over a medium heat and, when frothy, add the chicken and cook for 5 minutes. Remove from the heat then pour the chicken with the butter into the tomatoes. Simmer gently, uncovered, for about 10 minutes, to allow the chicken to cook through.

Add the fenugreek leaves and garam masala and stir through. Add salt to taste and leave to simmer for another 10–20 minutes to allow the sauce to thicken. Taste and adjust the seasoning if necessary. Add the cream just before serving.

SERVES 4

CHICKEN SAUSAGES *with* ROASTED BREAD PUDDING

Old chums will know that I have a bit of a thing about stale bread. It is such a symbol of starvation rations, of that depravation diet fed to prisoners with water, that I love turning it into something delectable. It's sort of like origami, folding dry bread into a form unrecognisable from the original, something that is, frankly, quite beautiful. I'm not sure that these toasty, chooky puddings are all that pretty but they *are* really, really tasty. So much so it's almost not worth twisting and replacing the seal on that bag of sliced white!

200 g breadcrumbs (about 2 firmly packed cups), made from blitzing stale bread

40 g melted butter, plus an extra 30 g, for greasing muffin pan

400–500 ml good chicken stock

1 bunch flat-leaf parsley, leaves picked and chopped

8 (about 600 g) chicken sausages

20 Brussels sprouts

4 bacon rashers

4 spring onions, sliced into discs

30 g extra butter

50 g slivered almonds, toasted

To make the mini bread puddings, first toast the breadcrumbs in a dry pan until crisp and a little golden (you'll need to keep them moving in the pan by tossing often). Then stir in the melted butter and cook the crumbs for a couple of minutes.

Next, little by little, slowly add the chicken stock and a handful of the chopped parsley. The crumbs will swell and soak up the stock until they reach a polenta-like consistency. This process will take up to 10 minutes – keep stirring as you go. Add a little more chicken stock if you think the crumbs will take it, but don't leave the mixture too wet or the puddings will not firm up in the oven.

Now pour the mixture into a buttered 12-hole mini muffin pan and pop it in the fridge for about 30 minutes to cool and firm up.

Preheat the oven to 200°C.

Cook the sausages in a pan over medium heat (or on the BBQ) until they have browned and cooked all the way through.

Pop the Brussels sprouts in a double saucepan to steam until cooked but still nice and firm. This will take 6–8 minutes depending on the size of the sprouts.

While the snags and sprouts are cooking, bake the mini bread puddings until warm in the middle and golden and crusty on the outside. This will take about 20–25 minutes.

After about 15 minutes, fry the bacon until crispy and brown. When it's cooked to your liking, drain the Brussels sprouts, cut them into quarters and throw them in the pan with the bacon, the spring onions and the extra butter. Toss and tan the sprouts up a little.

Serve up two snags, two mini bread puddings and a slice of bacon on each plate. Top each with a tumble of the sprouts and garnish with the rest of the parsley and the toasted almonds.

SERVES 4

Thai Red Duck and Pumpkin Curry

If velvet was edible this is what it would taste like. What with the silkiness of the sweet lychees, the satin-smooth pumpkin flesh and the lycra of the duck skin this is more like a haberdashery than a Thai dish. Although you can't eat a haberdashery can you?

Little known fact: although haberdasheries are rather indigestible, you could quite easily eat a haberdasher if you had the appetite. Daniel Defoe, who wrote *Robinson Crusoe*, and US President Harry S. Truman were both haberdashers, but there is no record that either were eaten. The only haberdasher who, legend has it, was eaten – by Hawaiians no less – was Capt. James Cook. Cook had served as an apprentice haberdasher before he took to the sea. The truth of the matter, however, is that while the Hawaiians baked him in an oven after they'd killed him, this was to prepare the bones as holy relics rather than to eat him. There is no record of whether the roasting flesh smelt like red duck and pumpkin curry but one suspects that if it did – and someone was tempted to take a nibble – they would have kept it a secret anyway.

Pour half of the coconut milk into a medium-sized saucepan and heat for a few minutes until simmering.

Add the curry paste and cook for 4–6 minutes.

Tip in the palm sugar and the fish sauce, then the rest of the coconut milk and allow to simmer for a couple of minutes until the sugar dissolves.

Now add the pumpkin, the strips of duck breast and the kaffir lime leaves to the sauce. Simmer uncovered for another 15 minutes or so, until the pumpkin is just tender.

Add the lychees, along with some water if the sauce is too thick, and bring back to a simmer. Lastly add the lime juice and most of the Thai basil, give it a stir then turn off the heat.

Garnish with freshly sliced red chilli, the rest of the Thai basil leaves and a drizzle of coconut milk.

SERVES 2–4

REVERSE TIP

What did you do with the duck skin and duck fat when you made this dish? Tell me at @mattscravat

400 ml coconut milk, plus a little extra, to serve

2 tablespoons red curry paste

60 g (2 tablespoons) palm sugar

2 tablespoons fish sauce

200 g pumpkin, peeled, chopped into 3 cm chunks

2 × 200 g duck breast fillets, fat removed, meat sliced into thin strips

4 kaffir lime leaves, finely sliced or torn

100 g canned lychees

juice of 1 lime

1 small bunch Thai basil, leaves picked

1 long red chilli, finely sliced, to serve

'MAKE YOUR BILL OF FARE ACCORDING TO THE SEASON AND THE NUMBER OF YOUR COMPANY. WHEN YOU HAVE TWO ROASTS THEY SHOULD BEAR NO RESEMBLANCE TO EACH OTHER. THE ART OF ROASTING IS CONSIDERED AN ESPECIAL ART … IT IS VERY TRUE, THAT THERE IS NO PROCESS IN COOKERY SO SIMPLE, AND YET VERY FEW CAN ACCOMPLISH IT PROPERLY.'

Andrew Valentine Kirwan, 1864

MEAT

4 ways WITH BURGERS

I wouldn't be doing my job if I didn't question everything and search for simpler, better ways to do things. Burgers have been a research project of mine for over four decades now and here are four examples of how challenging orthodoxy can make a burger that tastes better and eats better.

1. CHICKEN BURGER

I reckon a chicken breast is way too cumbersome to go in a roll. The solution is to cube it up and set these cubes into patties mortared together with softened butter which then set in the fridge. This results in a super-juicy and very decadent burger that won't pull all the bits out of your bun when you bite into it.

2 chicken breasts, cut into 1 cm chunks

40 g butter, at room temperature

salt flakes

2 white rolls that are soft in the middle

a few lettuce leaves – cos, butter or iceberg

4 rashers bacon, fried

freshly ground black pepper

mustard

lemon

Mix the chicken with a little of the soft butter. Shape the chicken into patties using an egg ring or a ramekin lined with plastic wrap. Refrigerate to chill.

Once the patties have set (so the butter holds them together), carefully remove the wrap and sprinkle with salt. Heat a non-stick frying pan then add the patties and fry until golden on both sides and cooked through.

Serve your patties in a soft-hearted white roll with little more than lettuce, bacon, black pepper, mustard and a squeeze of lemon. Mayo and sauce are optional extras for the greedy amongst us.

SERVES 2

2. BRISKET BEEF BURGER

This is the perfect burger. Simple – because your butcher's meat grinder does all the work – and small, so it cooks quickly. Allow for two burgers per person if your guests aren't greedy.

500 g brisket with 150 g smoked pork belly or kaiserfleisch, coarsely minced (ask your butcher to do this for you. A quarter-inch grind is fine)

salt flakes

olive oil, for frying

8 slices plastic cheese (that's the processed cheddar most kids love)

¼ cup mayonnaise

8 small white dinner rolls, lightly toasted

¼ iceberg lettuce, finely shredded

2–3 tablespoons Dijon mustard

8 small pickled cucumbers

Shape lumps of your minced meat into patties, matching the size of the patty to the roll, then put into the fridge to chill for at least 30 minutes.

Then salt the sides and fry the patties in a hot pan with a splash of olive oil. When you flip, top these beauties with a square of very politically incorrect plastic cheese.

To serve, spread some mayo on the bottom half of each lightly toasted roll, followed by shredded iceberg, a cooked patty and a dollop of Dijon mustard. Finish with long slices of pickled cucumber on top.

SERVES 4

4 ways WITH BURGERS

3. FISH FINGER BURGER

You could just make this burger with fish fingers but I'm not supposed to tell you that, as this recipe is far more 'artisan' which is apparently 'very good for sales'.

60–80 g (1 cup) panko or fresh breadcrumbs

zest and juice of ½ lemon

½ teaspoon salt flakes

freshly ground black pepper

300–350 g flathead fillets, cut in half lengthways
   if they are long

2 eggs, lightly beaten

3 tablespoons aioli

80–100 ml olive oil, for shallow-frying

4 slices of white bread, lightly toasted (rolls if you prefer)

butter

2 soft lettuce leaves, such as butter, gem or cos

2–3 spring onions, cut into small coins

2 tablespoons dill fronds

Combine the panko crumbs, lemon zest and seasoning in a shallow bowl or plate.

Dip the fish fillets in the egg, then coat in panko crumbs. Lay on a plate and refrigerate while you prepare the other ingredients.

Squeeze some lemon into the aioli and set aside.

Heat the oil in a flat pan over medium heat. Cook the fish until golden and cooked through, about 2–3 minutes on each side.

While the fish is cooking, toast the bread and butter it while still hot.

To assemble your burgers, lay a lettuce leaf on the bottom slice of toast. Place the fish fillets on top. Spoon a whopping dollop of aioli on top, scatter over spring onions and dill, squeeze over a bit more lemon and top with another piece of toasted buttered bread.

SERVES 2

TIP

If you are using thin-sliced white bread, pop two slices together into one of the toaster slots. Then you get a fish finger burger sandwich that is crunchy on the outside and pillowy-soft on the inside. And then this journey of the tooth is repeated with the fish burger itself.

4. SALMON BURGER

Yes, slicing the salmon and setting it seems like a lot of hassle but once you discover how easy this is to do, you'll be hooked.

2 × 200 g salmon fillets, boned
  and skin removed
oil, to fry
2 burger buns or rolls, lightly toasted
2 tablespoons cream cheese
3 chopped gherkins
1 tablespoon capers, drained
1½ tablespoons mayonnaise
2–4 gem hearts lettuce leaves, or any other

Cut each salmon fillet into thin, wide slices horizontally across the grain. Pile at least three of these slices on top of each other, wrap tightly in plastic wrap and then place in the fridge to chill for at least an hour to set.

Once chilled and set, lightly oil the patties and cook in a non-stick pan until golden edged and just cooked through. The texture should be robust but still coming apart easily when bitten into.

Line the toasted buns' bases with a mixture of cream cheese, chopped gherkins, capers and mayo, topped with the cooked salmon patties and then a couple of little lettuce leaves. Perfect.

Hooked!!! See what I did there?

SERVES 2

FALSE MEMORIES OF THE ABRUZZO
Polenta with Sausage Ragu

There is something alluring about the food of Abruzzo. So often it seems to be at odds with what you'll find further to the north and south of Italy. Like the idea of pouring a volcano of runny polenta onto a large wooden board about the size of a small door and serving it in the middle of the table, the crater filled with a rich gooey ragu. In the Abruzz', that sauce may feature snails, liver sausages or a white sauce of rough local snags, egg and hilltop pecorino. This here is a far more approachable version that's simple to make and delicious to eat. You can individually plate this dish but it's far better to have the family share a board and all race to eat in towards the centre.

2 tablespoons grapeseed or other neutral oil

1 kg pork and fennel sausages, skins removed and meat squeezed out in chunks

1 carrot, finely diced

1 onion, finely diced

30 g butter

2 celery stalks, finely diced

4 garlic cloves, crushed, peeled and chopped

½ teaspoon chilli powder

½ teaspoon fennel seeds

2 baby fennel bulbs, tough skin removed, cut into 3 mm slices (save any fronds)

2 × 400 g cans crushed tomatoes

oregano leaves, to serve

extra parmesan, to serve (optional)

POLENTA

500 g polenta (instant is fine)

1.5 litres (6 cups) boiling water

500 ml (2 cups) beef or chicken stock

100 g parmesan or pecorino, grated

75 g butter

Heat your heaviest casserole dish with a little oil in the base. When hot, brown the sausage meat.

Drain off any excess oil. Now toss the diced carrot in with the sausage meat and cook for 2 minutes.

Add the onion, along with the butter. Stir and cook for 2 minutes.

Finally stir in the celery and cook for 2 minutes.

Now stir in the garlic along with the chilli and the fennel seeds.

Throw the finely sliced fennel on top of the sausage meat. Carefully pour in the canned tomatoes, breaking them up if required. Bring to the boil and then reduce to the barest simmer. Cook for 15 minutes, or until the sauce thickens slightly and the sausage meat is cooked through.

While the ragu is thickening on the stovetop, cook the polenta according to the packet instructions. As a rough measurement, I like to have 1.5 litres (6 cups) of water boiling with 500 ml (2 cups) of stock before I whisk in my polenta. It is most important to follow the polenta's packet instructions, but maintain this 3 parts water to 1 part stock ratio.

When the polenta is cooked, stir in the cheese and butter, and you might want to add a little extra hot water to ensure the polenta is not too stiff.

I like to serve the sauce dolloped in the middle of a crater of polenta and garnished with oregano leaves, but you can also serve it in individual bowls.

SERVES 4–6

THE MEATLOAF, REBUILT

There is nowt as confusing as the names of sauces. Sunny Thousand Island dressing actually originated up on the chilly St Lawrence River, the classic French dressing mayonnaise is actually named after the capital of the Balearic island of Minorca, while Cumberland sauce originated in Germany rather than the north of England. Thank heavens, then, for the prosaically named meatloaf, which has no such airs and graces. The porkiness of this meatloaf means that the sweet tang of the Hanover sauce – my variation on a Cumberland – goes rather well, as opposed to the BBQ sauce I use on my bog-standard meatloaf.

500 g beef mince

500 g pork sausage meat

½ red onion, finely chopped

3 garlic cloves, finely chopped

125 g (1 cup) rolled oats

1 egg

250 ml (1 cup) milk

salt flakes

100 ml port

1 orange, zest cut into long strips and thinly sliced, orange juiced

1 × 200 g jar redcurrant jelly

1 teaspoon English mustard

freshly ground black pepper

red wine vinegar

mashed potatoes, with butter and milk, to serve

hot English mustard, to serve

TIP

This Hanover sauce is also great with duck, ham, venison or chunky pork sausages.

Preheat the oven to 180°C. Line a baking tray with foil and with baking paper.

Place the beef mince and the pork sausage mince into the bowl of an electric mixer fitted with a paddle attachment. Start mixing on low to medium speed.

Add the onion, garlic, oats and egg, mixing until combined. Then gradually add the milk and a pinch of salt, mixing until very well combined. Yes, you can do this with clean hands if you'd rather – either way, just don't overwork the meat and make it sticky, or you'll end up with a dense loaf.

Hand-shape the meat mixture (wetting your hands first helps with this) into a long loaf of equal thickness on the tray.

Now, into the oven it goes to bake for 30 minutes.

Meanwhile, make the Hanover sauce. Pour the port into a small saucepan and bring it to the boil. Reduce the heat and simmer for about 5–10 minutes to reduce the port by a third.

When the port is reduced, whisk in half the orange juice, the redcurrant jelly and mustard until the redcurrant jelly melts into the sauce. Taste. Now season the sauce with salt, a good grind of black pepper and a splash of red wine vinegar. You'll need a couple of teaspoons to balance the sweetness of the jelly and the port. Simmer the sauce for 6 minutes to thicken.

Take the sauce off the heat. Remove half the sauce to a separate container to glaze the meatloaf. Add the orange zest to the other half of the sauce in the saucepan to serve with the cooked meatloaf.

After the first 30 minutes of meatloaf cooking has elapsed, remove the meatloaf from the oven and brush the Hanover sauce from the separate container over the top and sides. Repeat until the meatloaf is well glazed.

Return the meatloaf to the oven for a further 30 minutes or until cooked through. If you're checking it with a meat thermometer, the internal temperature should reach 65°C.

When the meatloaf is cooked, remove the loaf from the oven and set it aside to rest for 5 minutes before carving.

Reheat the sauce with the remaining orange juice to freshen it. When it's hot, pour into a warmed jug.

To serve, carve the meatloaf and place on a board. Serve with the Hanover sauce, potato mash and lashings of hot English mustard.

SERVES 8

SALTY, SWEET, SOUR – PULLED PORK, RED CABBAGE *and* DIJON APPLE SAUCE

Classic flavours never go out of style and they don't get more classic than apple and pork. Well, assuming that you've got a pagan, or a Christian, Northern European heritage. Pagans will be especially impressed by the use of apples as they have great significance in Celtic, Druidic and tribal traditions. In fact, cut an apple in half around its circumference and you find a pentangle – a pagan, pre-Christian symbol attributed with its own powerful magic. Its five points symbolise the five elements: earth, air, water, fire and spirit. Which is a bit like how the five tastes – sweet, sour, salty, bitter and umami – come together in this dish.

Mix the salt and paprika together and rub half of it all over the pork skin and fat but not directly onto the meat. Set aside in the fridge for at least a couple of hours, but ideally overnight. This will help dry out the skin to achieve crispy crackling. Rub the rest of the paprika salt on just before you put it in the oven.

Return the pork to room temperature before cooking.

Preheat the oven to 220°C.

Place the pork in a baking tray and roast on the top rack to prevent the bottom from burning. Roast for about 30 minutes, then baste with any juices, cover with foil lined with baking paper to prevent sticking and lower the oven temperature to 160°C. The pork can be on a lower rack once the oven temperature is lowered. Continue cooking on the lower heat for a further 3 hours, basting from time to time.

Toss the sweet potato in the oil and roast for 45 minutes before you want to serve.

Remove the covering from the roasting dish and roast for a further 30–45 minutes to allow the crackling to crisp up again. If it needs a little more crunch, pop it under the oven grill and keep an eye on it.

To make the red cabbage, melt the butter and throw in the cabbage with a splash of water. Add half the honey and vinegar and slowly cook down the cabbage until soft and buttery, about 15–20 minutes. Stir occasionally to prevent it from sticking. Throw in the caraway seeds, currants and the rest of the honey and vinegar. Stir over the heat to combine.

To make the Dijon apple sauce, melt the butter and stir in the mustard. Toss the apples through before adding the lemon juice, verjus (or apple juice) and ½ cup of water. Slowly cook down to a chunky apple sauce, or blitz if you prefer it smooth. Add a touch more water if necessary to loosen.

To serve, remove the crackling from the pork and set it aside. Shred the pork flesh. Serve the pork on a bed of the buttery sweet and sour cabbage with some apple sauce on the side. Top the lot with pieces of crackling, some chopped parsley, a pinch of salt flakes and the zest of the lemon sprinkled over. Oh, and a couple of pieces of sweet potato per person, on the side.

SERVES 6–8

2 teaspoons salt flakes

1 teaspoon sweet paprika

1 × 1.25 kg pork shoulder, boned, rolled and scored

4 sweet potatoes, peeled and cut into thumb-sized pieces

1 tablespoon olive oil

½ bunch flat-leaf parsley, leaves picked and chopped, to garnish

RED CABBAGE

50 g butter

1 smallish red cabbage, cored and very finely sliced

2 tablespoons honey

5 tablespoons cider vinegar

1 teaspoon caraway seeds

1 cup currants

DIJON APPLE SAUCE

50 g butter

1 tablespoon Dijon mustard

5 Granny Smith apples, peeled, cored and cut into chunks

zest and juice of 1 lemon

½ cup verjus or apple juice

Pork and Cider Casserole

Growing up, cider was my poison: the 'goon' or *kalimotxo* of its day. I should have realised cider wasn't a good idea when the barman ignored my fake ID and poured me a 'snake bite'. I've never been good at noticing omens, plus I was young and foolish, and the 1-litre bottles had a Norman knight on the label, which made me feel butch. I'd like to say that this dish was one of my early attempts to tame those cider demons, but I think it was more likely a way of using up flat cider so I didn't have to drink it.

200 g (about 2) red onions, finely diced

3 rashers middle bacon, cut into thick matchsticks

olive oil, for frying

3 garlic cloves, crushed and finely chopped

200 g celery (about 3 stalks), cut into 1 cm pieces

1 kg diced pork (shoulder is good)

150 g (1 cup) plain flour

500 ml (2 cups) cider

500 ml (2 cups) chicken stock

1 tablespoon Dijon mustard

1 tablespoon runny honey

600 g (about 3) carrots, cut into 4 cm chunks

salt flakes and freshly ground black pepper

2 Granny Smith apples

juice of 1 lemon

TO SERVE

potatoes, to mash

broccoli, to steam

zest of ¼ lemon

chopped flat-leaf parsley leaves

Preheat the oven to 170°C.

In a trusty frying pan fry the onions and the bacon in a little oil until soft. Add the garlic and about three-quarters of the celery – no need to be too exact here. Soften over a medium heat for a couple of minutes. Scrape the bits into a large (2 litre or bigger) casserole.

Now dust the pork pieces with flour, turn up the heat and fry in the same frying pan, until the pieces are brown on all sides. Do this in two or three batches to keep the pan hot. Throw the browned pork into the casserole.

Use half the cider to deglaze (or scrub off) the nice browny bits from the bottom and sides of the frying pan. Pour this cider and the scrubbings over the pork in the big casserole along with the rest of the cider and chicken stock. Also stir in the mustard, honey, the carrots and some salt and pepper.

Cover and cook in the oven for 2 hours, or until the pork is tender.

THE FINAL COUNTDOWN

45 minutes before serving, put on the potatoes for the mash and proceed to make it as you prefer.

15 minutes before serving, taste and season the casserole. Put on the broccoli to steam (but don't leave it so long that it goes grey and overcooks).

10 minutes before serving, peel and chop the apples into bite-sized chunks. Toss in half the juice of the lemon.

5 minutes before serving, throw the apple pieces and the remaining celery into the casserole. Stir. The apple pieces will warm up but not cook; retaining their freshness against the richness of the casserole.

Take the casserole out of the oven. Taste and season. Garnish the pork and gravy with chopped parsley, a little lemon zest and a squeeze of lemon.

Serve in the pot on the table with the steamed broccoli and buttery mashed potatoes.

SERVES 4–6

TIP

To fancy-up this dish, cook the onions with 2 teaspoons of crushed coriander seeds or fennel seeds. Finish the dish with ½ a cup of sour cream, stirred through just before serving.

TWICE-COOKED STICKY RIBS

There is something 'dirty-good' about eating ribs; part primeval, part Alabama truck driver. These ribs might have an American pedigree but they also have a distinct Chinese accent, which always makes me think of the fictional West's most famous pig farmer: Mr Wu of Deadwood, South Dakota.

2 kg American-style pork spare ribs
on the bone

MARINADE
2 cinnamon sticks

2 star anise

120 ml (6 tablespoons) light soy
sauce

4 teaspoons ground ginger

6 tablespoons brown sugar

4 garlic cloves, crushed

1 teaspoon Sichuan peppercorns
(optional)

160 ml red wine

SAUCE
120 ml (6 tablespoons) light soy
sauce

80 ml (4 tablespoons) Chinese
rice wine

8 tablespoons brown sugar

2 teaspoons malt or cider vinegar

Combine all the marinade ingredients. Cover the ribs with marinade, place in the fridge and marinate for at least 8 hours, preferably overnight.

Take the ribs out of the fridge and leave for about 30 minutes to return to room temperature before cooking.

Preheat your oven to 200°C.

Remove the pork from the marinade (reserve the marinade) and place on a roasting rack. Place the rack over a baking dish half-full of hot water. Cover the whole tray completely with foil and steam the ribs for 30–45 minutes. This can also be done on a stovetop steamer.

Add the reserved marinade to a pot along with the sauce ingredients, bring it to the boil for 5 minutes and then simmer to reduce, stirring regularly.

Now, remove the pork from the oven and take off the foil. Baste the ribs on both sides with the sauce and put them back in the oven for another 30 minutes or so, until they are dark and sticky.

Serve the ribs on a big plate or tray and pour over any extra sauce.

SERVES 4

SLOW-ROASTED LAMB – *Then and Now*

The heady smell of oregano always takes me back to a summer I once spent in the Cyclades. I had paid a peppercorn rent for a small hut in an olive grove. It had a lock and an old metal bed and not much more. We washed from the large cistern at one end, our nights lit only by the moon, and when we cooked, we cooked over a small fireplace on old olivewood that spat and hissed.

The grove sat a little way back from the beach, up in the hills above the little village. There were only three ways into the village. By boat, by foot, or, if you were posh, you could take a donkey along the stony goat track that wound 8 km from the only road on the island and along the course of a dry riverbed lined with large bushes of wild oregano past my hut.

Back then, Vathi was a simple place of two tavernas, a blue-domed, white-washed church and a handful of houses perched on a rocky bay that was a perfect protected anchorage. It was quiet until mid-morning, when the tiny, ancient ferry from the ugly port belched its way into the bay carrying ice and chattering Scandinavian backpackers.

Early in the evening the smell of lamb cooking over coals, doused with wild oregano, would snake across the beach carried on wispy fingers of smoke – each local taverna competing for the custom of the backpackers who had stayed to bathe in those last rays, or for the yachties rolling into the bay enjoying the sunset. It was the most persuasive of all adverts.

Each night we'd share a plate, my blonde Norwegian and I, in one tavern or the other. The achingly slow-cooked and tan-crusted meat always fell apart in strands like a fraying rope, each piece laced with fresh lemon and another big fresh handful of oregano. The herb was everywhere: on the salad of soft local goat's cheese with fat tomatoes and black olives, and thrown like a green blizzard over the chunks of cooled cucumber that came with the inevitable ouzo. It was always a long dinner, the meat punctuated with endless backgammon and broken Greek; by laugher and music, always music. Careening, whirling tunes of love, loss and goat prices played on a cracked-cased old bouzouki by a man with a face as brown and scrunched as a walnut.

Sometimes we danced, close or wild, and then later, in the dark, we'd walk home up the dry river bed, lips and fingers sticky with lamb fat, brushing against those wild oregano bushes, so we'd arrive home with our clothes and bodies richly perfumed by the herb.

500 g Greek yoghurt

1 cup chopped oregano, plus another couple of branches for dressing

2 lemons

50 g ground coriander

2 garlic cloves

1.5 kg boned, butterflied lamb shoulder (ask your butcher to peel off the tough outer bark to reveal the milky fat beneath)

100 ml olive oil

80 ml white wine vinegar

salt flakes

8 ripe tomatoes, cut into chunks

1 large red onion, finely diced

1 cup pitted black olives

100 g feta, crumbled

2 cucumbers, skin on, kept in the coldest part of the fridge

250 ml (1 cup) ouzo, plus more to drink

Blitz the yoghurt with the oregano, the zest and juice of one of the lemons, the ground coriander and the garlic. Slather the marinade on the lamb shoulder then cover and leave it to marinate in the fridge overnight or up to 24 hours.

Preheat your oven so it's really hot. 200°C should do it.

Remove the lamb from the marinade, but leave on any oregano paste that is clinging to it. Place the lamb on a metal rack over a roasting pan, drizzle on half the olive oil and pop it in the oven. Blast with heat for 30 minutes.

Add 180 ml water and the vinegar to the pan. Now turn the oven down to 150°C and leave the lamb alone for 3–4 hours. If it needs a little crisping up on the outside you can grill the top for 5–10 minutes.

When the meat is cooked, and by cooked I mean crusty on the outside and falling apart in the middle, pull it out and leave it to rest for at least 15 minutes covered in a sheet of foil, with some old copies of newspaper on top, to retain the heat.

To serve, place the lamb on a large wooden board and shred the meat from the shoulder so it falls in shards across the board. Season with salt flakes. Now sprinkle the lamb with the tomato chunks (complete with seeds), red onion, black olives and more oregano leaves. Squeeze over the juice of the second lemon, scatter over the feta, and drizzle on the rest of the oil.

Place on the table along with the cucumber (freshly cut into batons straight from the fridge) dunked into four small glasses of ouzo. Share. Dance. Live.

SERVES 8

OVEN-BAKED LAMB ON TOMATOES, RISONI AND ANCHOVIES

This is a beautifully simple way of taking the family Sunday roast on a holiday to the other side of the world. I first had this dish on a grey winter's day at my friend Jen's place. The canned tomatoes brought sunshine from the other side of the world and the little grains of pasta soaked up all those lip-smacking lamb juices so it became something really rather special. I keep thinking this dish would be delicious customised with black olives, anchovies and salted ricotta instead of haloumi. Or how's about using feta rather than haloumi and serving the whole shebang in the baking dish covered in a confetti of gremolata made from combining a bunch of freshly chopped mint, parsley and lemon zest, with lemon juice for added freshness?

800 g boneless lamb shoulder, trimmed and cubed

2 large brown onions, chopped

4 bay leaves

½ teaspoon ground cumin

½ teaspoon paprika

1 × 400 g can chopped tomatoes

1½ cups risoni or *kritharaki* pasta

750 ml (3 cups) boiling water

½ teaspoon salt

150 g haloumi, grated

Preheat the oven to 180°C.

Place the lamb in a small baking dish along with the chopped onion, bay leaves and spices. Pour over the chopped tomatoes and cover the dish tightly with foil or a lid. Bake in the oven for 1½ hours.

Take the cover off the dish and turn the meat and cook, uncovered, for another half an hour or so, to brown.

Add the pasta, boiling water and salt to the dish.

Cover again and bake for another 40 minutes. If the pasta is looking dry add some more water during the cooking process.

Serve hot topped with the grated haloumi.

SERVES 4

TIP

Kritharaki, orzo and risoni are all types of rice-shaped pasta.

BLACKENED LAMB BACKSTRAPS
with TURKISH MUHAMMARA

Coffee, garlic and lamb have long been a favourite combination of mine – well before an understanding of flavour compounds revolutionised modern cookery and people started mixing caviar with white chocolate. I just did it because my best mate's grandmother did!

With this recipe, I've amped up the quantities dramatically. The dark and slightly bitter crust – reminiscent of the burnt char that's so Mugaritz 2004 – hides beautifully pink lamb and that slight touch of coffee bitterness is balanced by the sweetness of the roasted red peppers in the *muhammara*.

While I fell in love with this walnut and red capsicum paste in Istanbul, it exists on menus from all across the sphere of influence of the old Byzantine/Ottoman empire. I suspect it might even be related to the *romesco* sauce invented in the southern Spanish town of Tarragona, which was also under Muslim control for 200 years around the turn of the first millennium. While *muhammara* is largely served as a dip, this Spanish sauce marries hazelnuts, almonds and roasted capsicum to dollop on chicken, seafood, or even lamb. Once again proving that smart new ideas have often been done before!

1 tablespoon coriander seeds

½ teaspoon black peppercorns

1 teaspoon salt flakes

1½ tablespoons instant coffee granules

4 garlic cloves, unpeeled

60 ml olive oil

2 × 300–400 g lamb backstraps

fresh herbs such as mint, flat-leaf parsley, or coriander, chopped, to serve (optional)

TURKISH MUHAMMARA

½–¾ cup mild extra-virgin olive oil

2 red capsicums

100 g (1 cup) walnut pieces

80 g (1 cup) fresh breadcrumbs

juice of ½ lemon

1 teaspoon ground cumin

salt flakes and freshly ground black pepper

TIP

If you want to give your *muhammara* a little extra pep add a tablespoon of pomegranate molasses. For extra sweetness add a tablespoon of honey.

Grind the coriander seeds, peppercorns, salt and coffee granules using a mortar and pestle or bang them in a bag. Add the garlic and smash before adding the oil and mixing it all together.

Tip the marinade into a plastic bag or place in a container and rub it all over the lamb. Leave to marinate in the fridge for a couple of hours.

Now make the muhammara. See below.

Heat your BBQ, pan or grill plate on medium to high heat. Sear the straps for 2–3 minutes on each side. Leave them to rest, covered, for at least 5, and preferably 10 minutes, before cutting into slices.

Slice each fillet and arrange the lamb on a plate or board. Spoon over the muhammara or serve it on the side.

Finish with a scatter of fresh chopped herbs of your choice.

TURKISH MUHAMMARA

Preheat the oven to 200°C.

Rub a little oil on each capsicum, wrap individually in foil and cook in the oven for 1 hour. Once soft, remove the capsicums from the oven, allow to cool sealed in the foil until you can touch them. Peel and deseed and return the flesh to the base of the oven on a baking tray to dry out. Check every 15 minutes or so. Remove when they're no longer slippery, but are still sticky.

Blend the capsicum with the walnuts and breadcrumbs. Keep the blender going and add ¼ cup of the olive oil. Add the lemon juice, cumin, salt and freshly ground black pepper to taste. Add more of any of the ingredients if you think it needs it.

Add up to another ¼ cup of olive oil to finish. The texture should be somewhere between a paste and a dip.

SERVES 4

4 International ways with MEATBALLS

1. CHICKEN POLPETTE

There's something very Italian about meatballs, even if it took the Italian-American kitchen to elevate them to cult status.

Preheat the oven to 180°C Soak **1 CUP FRESH BREADCRUMBS** in ⅓ **CUP MILK**. Gently fry **100 G FINELY CHOPPED PANCETTA**, a **LARGE MINCED CLOVE OF GARLIC** and a very **FINELY CHOPPED ONION** until translucent. Cool. In a large bowl mix together **500 G CHICKEN MINCE, 1 LIGHTLY BEATEN EGG, 1 TABLESPOON TOMATO PASTE**, the **ZEST OF ½ LEMON, ½ BUNCH OF CHOPPED FLAT-LEAF PARSLEY** (reserving the other ½ for garnish), **1 TEASPOON SALT**, the oniony pancetta and the breadcrumbs (squeeze out the milk first). Chill. Then measure it into 20 equal dollops about 35 g each – you do the maths! Shape into golf-ball-sized balls with damp hands. Place on a metal tray lined with baking paper. Smear the top of the meatballs with a glaze of spicy tomato paste made from blending **½ A DEVEINED, DESEEDED LONG RED CHILLI** and **1 TABLESPOON TOMATO PASTE** with a **SCANT TABLESPOON OF OIL, A SPLASH (½ TEASPOON) VINEGAR, 1 TEASPOON SUGAR** and a good **PINCH OF SALT**. Add more chilli if you like it hot. Bake for 30 minutes or until cooked through.

Serve tossed through a sizzling hot pan of spaghetti with **A WHOOSH OF GOOD OIL**, a **SPLASH OF CHICKEN STOCK**, the **REST OF THE PARSLEY** and **A BLIZZARD OF FINELY GRATED CHEESE**.

MAKES 20

2. KEFTA

Change the spices and the cooking technique and suddenly you've got Middle Eastern kefta. Just knead together **1 KG MINCED LAMB** with **1 LARGE GRATED ONION** and **A HANDFUL OF FINELY CHOPPED FLAT-LEAF PARSLEY AND CORIANDER**. Season and add **1 TEASPOON TOASTED GROUND CUMIN** and **A LITTLE PAPRIKA**. Work the meat until it feels a little sticky and then press around metal or wooden skewers. Grill over coals or on the BBQ and serve with warm mountain bread, a tabbouli salad and a squeeze of lemon.

MAKES 16

3. KEFTEDES

Even strong Greek men get misty-eyed at the very mention of their mother's keftedes and the Greek meatball recipe I use is based on one from my 'Aussie mum', Mary Calombaris. Start by soaking **3 SLICES OF WHITE BREAD** in **ENOUGH MILK TO COVER THEM** for 5 minutes and then squeezing out the excess milk. Now mix the bread with **500 G MINCED LAMB**, a **FINELY DICED ONION** and **2 GARLIC CLOVES, A COUPLE OF MIXED TABLESPOONS OF OREGANO** and **MINT** and about the same amount of **FLAT-LEAF PARSLEY**. Mix this up with a **LOOSELY BEATEN EGG**, some **SALT TO SEASON** and **2 TEASPOONS VINEGAR** and spoon into a large ziplock bag. Massage the mix for a couple of minutes to combine and then chill it in the fridge to firm up. When cool roll out two dozen footie-shaped meatballs, toss them gently in plain flour to coat their outsides and shallow-fry them in **A LITTLE OLIVE OIL** for about 6 minutes or until cooked through and golden. Do this in batches so you don't overcrowd the pan. Feel free to add **A LITTLE NUTMEG** to the mix like naughty little George does when his mum's not looking.

Serve with **RIBBONS OF FRESH CUCUMBER** and a drizzle of dressing made from whipping together **1 CUP GREEK YOGHURT** with **50 G CREAMY FETA** and a **SQUEEZE OF LEMON**.

MAKES 16

4. SCANDI MEATBALLS

Swedish meatballs are some of the most famous. Finnish meatballs are, however, no less venerated and when I make them I'm inspired by one of my favourite food writers, Tessa Kiros, who flavours hers with allspice. I use **1 TEASPOON ALLSPICE** for every **500 G MIXED PORK** and **BEEF MINCE** used. Bind the mix with **1 EGG** and **1 THICK SLICE OF WHITE BREAD** soaked in, and them squeezed free of, **MILK**. After rolling into walnut-sized balls, brown their sides by frying in a mix of **BUTTER** and **OIL** until golden. Finish cooking them very gently for 10 minutes in sour cream sauce. For the sauce, over the heat whisk **60 G FLOUR** into **40 G MELTED BUTTER**. When combined and just colouring up whisk in **200 ML SOUR CREAM** and **200 ML WATER**. The sauce will bubble and thicken it. Add **MORE WATER** (up to about 200 ml) to loosen the sauce until it coats the back of a spoon. Serve with cranberry sauce 'cos the traditional lingonberry jam is hard to find outside of IKEA.

MAKES 20–24

1.

3.

2.

4.

HONEST BEEF PIE

This is no-fuss – the sort of dinner that not only fills a horde but also makes the whole house smell amazing. Assuming you love the smell of the three beautiful Bs – baking, beef and beer!

1 kg chuck steak, or gravy beef, diced

4 tablespoons flour

salt flakes and freshly ground black pepper

4 tablespoons oil

1 large onion, diced

200 g thick-cut, streaky bacon, sliced into batons or lardons

300 ml dark ale

500 ml (2 cups) beef stock

2 carrots, chopped

4 thyme sprigs

2 bay leaves

1 tablespoon dark brown sugar

1 tablespoon balsamic vinegar

2 tablespoons tomato sauce

PASTRY

200 g unsalted butter, chilled

250 g plain flour

salt flakes

125 ml sour cream

1 egg, beaten with a little water, to glaze

Heat the oven to 160°C.

Toss the meat with the flour and some salt and pepper.

Heat half the oil in a large frying pan and fry the meat in two batches until brown, then transfer the meat into a large, ovenproof casserole dish.

Add more oil to the pan, if needed, and fry the onion until just softened, about 2–3 minutes. Add the bacon and cook until just coloured. Add the onion and bacon to the meat.

Deglaze the pan with some of the ale and add to the casserole along with the remaining ingredients. Bring the casserole to a simmer on the stovetop and then cover and place in the oven for 2½ hours. Remove from the oven, remove the lid and continue cooking on the stovetop until the liquid has reduced and thickened and the meat is very tender. This filling can be made ahead of time and kept in the refrigerator until needed.

To make the pastry, dice the butter and place in a food processor along with the flour and a pinch of salt, and pulse until the mixture resembles fine breadcrumbs. Add the sour cream and continue to pulse until the dough combines. Turn out onto a clean surface and quickly form into a ball. Wrap in plastic wrap and place in the refrigerator until needed.

When you are ready to bake your pie, preheat the oven to 180°C.

Place the meat in a small oven dish, about 24 × 18 cm. Roll the chilled pastry out until 3 mm thick, lay it over the top of the pie and trim the edge. You can trim the pastry to a little larger than the dish and fold it back onto itself or cut out some shapes to decorate the top, as you like.

Brush the top of the pie with an egg glaze and bake in the oven for about 30 minutes. The top of the pie should be golden brown and the filling piping hot.

SERVES 6

PROPS

Maggie Beer championed this sour cream pastry that works so well given the acidity of the sour cream.

AUTHENTIC BEEF RENDANG

Beef rendang is one of the most abused South-East Asian curries. It should be fragrant and dry rather than sloppy. A bit like this one, which comes primarily from my friend Heng's sister, Soo Chi, but with some tips and tweaks from Heng's close friend Julia Chua and my mate, the very wise Tony Tan.

Sear the beef pieces in hot oil to brown. Do this in batches. Remove the beef and set aside.

To start the sauce, toast the coconut over low heat, without oil, until it is slightly brown. Remove from the pan and set aside to cool.

For the spice paste, blitz all the ingredients (except the fish sauce) in a food processor until you have a fine paste. Add the fish sauce last, dripping it in until its flavour is almost offensive. Fry the spice paste in a splash of oil in the same pan you used to start the sauce until it smells fragrant and a little toasted.

Add in the beef and stir-fry until well blended. Now stir in the toasted coconut and the kaffir lime leaves. Cook for a couple of minutes.

Lastly add the coconut cream, brown sugar and the water. Bring to the boil then reduce the heat to low and cook uncovered for about 3 hours until the meat is soft and the sauce is thick. You may need to add a touch more water from time to time if the meat starts catching.

When it is cooked, add salt to taste. The beef should be a little sticky and dried out. I always think a good rendang is a little 'squeaky' in the mouth.

Serve with boiled rice and the sweet pickled cucumbers below.

SERVES 4

SWEET PICKLED CUCUMBERS

To make the pickles, mix the sugar and salt in a small non-reactive bowl (i.e. not metal) and then throw in the cucumber chunks and stir to cover them with the sweet–salt mix. I find it easiest to cover the bowl securely with plastic wrap and then tumble the cucumber around to coat it.

Leave for 15 minutes and drain. Splash in the vinegar and leave for half an hour.

TIPS

1. You can also use this rendang recipe to make a lamb rendang with diced lamb shoulder or a chicken rendang using chicken thighs. Just add the browned meat to the spice paste before the coconut and kaffir lime, omitting the water unless the meat starts to dry and catch. The chicken will take less time to cook down than the lamb.

2. Kaffir lime leaves keep really well in the freezer.

THE MEAT

1 kg oyster blade or other braising beef, like chuck or cheek, cut into 4 cm cubes

grapeseed oil or peanut oil, for frying

SPICE PASTE

2 brown onions, chopped

4 garlic cloves, peeled

6 red fresh chillies, tops trimmed

5 candlenuts (buah keras) or 8 macadamias

2 sticks of lemongrass, white parts only, smashed/bruised with the back of a knife and finely chopped

1 cm fresh galangal, peeled and finely chopped

2 teaspoons ground turmeric

a little grapeseed or peanut oil

1 tablespoon fish sauce

SAUCE

3 tablespoons fine desiccated coconut

6–8 kaffir lime leaves, thinly sliced

1 × 400 ml can coconut cream

1 tablespoon brown sugar

250 ml (1 cup) water

salt flakes

SWEET PICKLED CUCUMBERS

1 tablespoon caster sugar

1 teaspoon salt flakes

1 long (continental or telegraph) cucumber, deseeded, quartered lengthways, and cut into bite-sized chunks

2 tablespoons vinegar (coconut or rice wine vinegars are best)

BEEF A LA MODE

This is my modernised version of an original handwritten recipe from my great-great-great-great-great-grandmother's home recipe book penned in 1765. Mine has a little bit more to it, but is still delicious.

1.2 kg beef cheeks, trimmed of sinew and silver skin

salt flakes and freshly ground black pepper

6 long bacon rashers

3 tablespoons sherry vinegar or red wine vinegar

splash of olive oil

2 garlic cloves, peeled and smashed

12 golden shallots, peeled and left whole

3 celery stalks, finely diced

a few grates of nutmeg

400 ml red wine

500 ml (2 cups) beef stock

3 fresh bay leaves

6 thyme sprigs

18 small chat potatoes (I like to peel them, but this is optional)

12 (about 2 bunches) baby carrots, leave a bit of the green tops on

zest of ½ lemon

20 g butter

½ cup coarsely chopped flat-leaf parsley

Preheat the oven to 160°C.

Season the beef cheeks well with salt and pepper.

Cut the bacon rashers in half. Cut the meaty pieces into lardons and set aside. Throw the fatty bits into a heavy-based, ovenproof casserole dish over low to medium heat and cook long enough to release the fat into the pot. Brown the beef cheeks in the bacon fat for a couple of minutes on all sides. Remove from the dish and set aside.

Deglaze the pot with 2 tablespoons of the sherry vinegar. When syrupy, add a splash of olive oil and brown the garlic and shallots before adding the celery and nutmeg. Cook for a further 2 minutes.

Return the beef cheeks to the pot. Stir in the wine, stock, bay leaves and thyme. Bring to the boil, then cover the casserole and put in the oven to slow-cook for 2½–4 hours, or until the meat is falling apart.

About 30 minutes before you're ready to eat, steam or boil the potatoes and then, 15 minutes later, steam the carrots.

When the casserole is nearly ready, heat a pan over medium heat and sauté the bacon lardons. When the bacon is well cooked, add the lemon zest and a splash of sherry vinegar to the pan. Take off the heat.

The meat should now be tender and succulent and the sauce reduced a fair bit. If the sauce is not reduced enough, remove the meat and onions from the dish and set the pot over medium to high heat on the stovetop for a couple of minutes.

Stir the butter through the sauce before serving.

When ready to serve, add the parsley leaves to the bacon and toss.

Serve the casserole as a shared dish with the bacon and parsley piled on top and the potatoes on the side, or serve individually with a bit of everything on warm plates.

SERVES 6

THE SECRET RECIPE FOR PERFECT 24-HOUR CHILLI CON CARNE

There is much debate about the perfect chilli. The English serve it on white rice or even baked potatoes while New Yorkers may plump for sloshing it on their hot dogs to make a chilli dog. The 'chili queens' – the Hispanic street vendors of San Antonio, who really took ownership of chilli in the 18th century when they sold it to the Spanish divisions parading in the city's Military Plaza until 1887 – served theirs with tortillas. They also used chunks of meat rather than the more familiar mince, and game meat such as venison as often as they used beef. Furthermore, the presence of beef suet was another essential element of their spicy stews.

For me there is only one essential in this recipe – well, other than the sour cream, coriander and grated cheese to garnish – and that is time. The best chilli I have ever eaten was in an East End pub, where the myth was that the giant lunchtime chilli pot was replenished every day as had been done for a decade, ensuring that the complexity of the chilli continued. I never got sick but I still wouldn't recommend this!

Fry the onions in a little oil in a large pot for about 5 minutes, or until soft.

While the onions are cooking crush the coriander and cumin seeds together with the coriander stems using a mortar and pestle.

Add the garlic and the crushed seeds to the onion. Stir over the heat for a minute or two until things start to get fragrant. Now add the mince. Stir through with the heat under the pot to brown the meat a little.

Scrape the mince back from one side of the pot and moving that side directly over the flame, tilt the pan towards that side and pour in the vinegar. Let it bubble away with the juices that flow from the meat for a minute. Now stir it in with the chilli flakes and the oregano (or epazote if you are using it).

Add the cinnamon stick, the tomatoes, a pinkie-sized strip of orange zest, the beef stock and half the beans. Stir and break up the tomatoes if needed. Bring to the boil and then reduce to the merest bubble on a low heat for a couple of hours, stirring every so often when you pass the stove.

Let the pan cool and place overnight in the fridge to let the flavour develop.

An hour before you want to eat, pop the potatoes into a preheated 180°C oven to bake.

Put the chilli back on the stove and bring to the boil. Add the remaining beans and the diced red chillies. Boil for a couple of minutes and then reduce to a simmer until you want to eat. Lay the 4 long green chillies on top of the chilli and leave them there to soften.

Remove the potatoes when soft and serve, split in half, filled with chilli and topped with a dollop of sour cream.

Garnish with grated orange zest and coriander leaves. Serve with a bowl of grated cheese and a bowl of the finely sliced green chilli on the side.

SERVES 6–8

TIP Dump the baked potatoes for tortillas if you want to be 'authentic'. The 'chili queens' sold a big plate of chilli, refried beans and a tortilla on the side for a dime!

2 onions, diced

olive oil, for frying

2 teaspoons coriander seeds

1 teaspoon cumin seeds

1 bunch coriander, stems cleaned and chopped, leaves reserved

2 garlic cloves, crushed

1 kg beef mince

1 tablespoon red wine vinegar

1 teaspoon chilli flakes

1 teaspoon dried Mexican oregano (what, you don't have it and can't get it? Well shame on you – just leave it out, and use the more classic epazote leaves instead. Or the usual fresh or dried oregano)

1 cinnamon stick

1 × 400 g can crushed tomatoes

1 orange

500 ml (2 cups) beef stock

2 × 400 g cans kidney beans, drained and rinsed (banned from US chili competitions since 1999)

6 large potatoes

4 long red chillies, finely diced

4 mild long green chillies, finely sliced

300 ml sour cream

200 g grated cheddar (or Monterey Jack if you are making this in the US), to serve

2 jalapeño or other green chillies, finely sliced, to serve

Cottage Pie

It's pretty obvious why a shepherd's pie is called that. It's made with lamb. Why, then, is beef mince cottage pie called a cottage pie and not a drover's pie or a cattleman's pie? After all, they are pretty much the same thing, just differing in meats. Is it because shepherds were an itinerant lot and slept in the field with their flock whereas the drovers had cottages? Is this more of the insidious class difference rife in middle England? A sign that there was obviously a hierarchy in the fields back in the day? Mull on this, as well as the conundrum of why only the cottage pie has carrots in it, as you are tucking in to this country favourite. Just don't ever get drawn into the debate about why no country trade has claimed mince un-topped with potato. Why is that just 'savoury mince'?

80 ml (4 tablespoons) olive oil

1.25 kg beef mince

2 anchovy fillets

2 brown onions, finely chopped

3 carrots, diced

2 celery stalks, diced

2 garlic cloves, finely chopped

3 tablespoons plain flour

1 tablespoon tomato paste

250 ml (1 cup) sherry

800 ml beef stock

2 tablespoons Worcestershire sauce

2 tablespoons soy sauce

6 thyme sprigs

2 bay leaves

salt flakes and freshly ground black pepper

MASHED POTATO

1.5 kg potatoes, peeled and cut into 2 cm chunks

200 ml milk

20 g butter

a couple of grates of nutmeg

salt flakes

200 g strong cheddar, grated

Heat 1 tablespoon of oil in a large saucepan and fry the mince in batches until it's brown, making sure to break up any lumps as it cooks. Mash in the anchovies and then remove the meat and set aside.

Add the remaining oil to the pan, add all the chopped veggies and cook on a low to medium heat, stirring every now and then, until they start to caramelise. This will take about 20 minutes. Add the garlic, flour and tomato paste, increase the heat and cook for a few minutes.

Return the beef to the pan. Pour over the sherry and boil to reduce it slightly before adding the stock, Worcestershire sauce, soy sauce and herbs. Bring to a simmer and cook, uncovered, for 45 minutes.

While the meat is cooking, put the potatoes on.

The filling is ready when the gravy is thick and coating the meat. If the liquid isn't reducing after about 30 minutes, turn up the heat to help it along. Season with salt and pepper to taste. Discard the bay leaves and any woody bits from the thyme.

While the meat is cooking, drain and mash the potatoes, then stir in the milk, butter, a grate or two of nutmeg, some salt and about half the cheese. The potato will sit better on the meat if it has cooled off before layering it on the meat.

Spoon the meat into one big ovenproof dish, or smaller individual ramekins. Spoon the mash on top or pipe over for a fancy finish.

Preheat the oven to 200°C.

Sprinkle over the remaining cheese and pop the dish in the oven for 20–25 minutes until the cheese is melted and golden.

SERVES 6–8

TIP

For better mash, when the potatoes are cooked, drain and return them to the hot dry saucepan (burner off, lid on) and let them steam dry before adding the other ingredients.

JUDE'S SHORT-RIB BRAISE

A couple of years ago I wrote a rather po-faced and sentimental piece about how recipes were living things, designed to evolve. Then about 18 months after my first cookbook was published I was sent an ace photo by someone who had made the mother-in-law's lamb, pineapple and walnut dish and opined that it was even better with beef short ribs. She may have a point – even if it is hard for me to admit in print. Either way, this rich gravy is still addictively good in an extremely moreish sweet-and-sour way.

2 kg beef short ribs

2 tablespoons flour

2 tablespoons oil

3 garlic cloves, peeled and smashed

2 teaspoons curry powder

1 × 140 g can tomato paste

500 ml (2 cups) pineapple juice

80 ml (4 tablespoons) soy sauce

2 tablespoons vinegar

2 tablespoons brown sugar

1 cm knob ginger, grated

75 g (¾ cup) walnut pieces

salt flakes and freshly ground black pepper, to taste

Preheat the oven to 170°C.

Toss the ribs in the flour. Heat the oil in a large ovenproof pot over high heat and fry the ribs on all sides until brown. Remove and set aside.

In the same pot, fry the garlic, then add the curry powder and cook for a minute before adding the tomato paste.

Add the pineapple juice, soy sauce, vinegar, brown sugar and ginger, and bring to the boil, gently scraping up any browny bits at the base of the pot with a wooden spoon.

Put the beef ribs back into the pot and spoon over liquid to cover the meat. Cover and cook in the oven for about 2½ hours.

When cooked, stir through the walnuts and season to taste.

Serve with rice, ideally brown, or risoni, and your favourite greens.

SERVES 6–8

AN OSSO BUCO *with* MORE FRONT THAN MEYER *and a* KALE GREMOLATA

The Meyer lemon is a strange-tasting hybrid that is more like gently tart orange or mandarin than bright, sour lemon. Because the Meyer doesn't work like a true lemon it tends to be relegated to the role of stand-in fruit for a citrus cordial, lemon delicious or the fourth fruit in four-fruit marmalade (when cumquat is otherwise engaged).

But then I went to a lunch cooked by one of my favourite chefs, Riccardo Momesso, and Meyer lemon was served to be squeezed across paper-thin, golden-crumbed veal schnitzel or fillets of whiting on a rich tomato sauce loaded with borlotti beans.

This made me think of using it in my osso buco and the results were great. It lifted this hearty, peasant stew into something a little more fragrant, a little more elegant. If you can't get Meyer lemons, a mix of lemon and orange or mandarin zest will do instead.

Preheat the oven to 180°C.

In a large heavy pot with a lid make a *soffritto* (or *battuto*, if you love calling the old ways by the old names) over a medium heat on the stovetop. To do this, melt half the butter in half the olive oil. When it's hot, fry the carrots, celery and onions. At the end, stir in the garlic and the finely chopped parsley stalks for a minute. Remove and reserve with a slotted spoon, leaving the butter and oil behind.

Toss the veal shank slices in flour seasoned with salt. Heat the remaining butter and oil in the pot. Then fry the shank slices in batches until they are browned. As they brown, remove them from the pan and set aside.

Deglaze the empty pan with the red wine. When it has lost the winey smell and you've scrubbed the tasty bits into the reduced wine, throw in the tomatoes, bay leaf and stock. Stir and bring to the boil. Grind in a good couple of twists of black pepper. Add the pieces of zest from the Meyer lemon. Add the vegetable soffritto. Place the browned shanks on the top. Cover and pop in the oven.

Braise in the oven for 90 minutes. Taste, season and stir. Check the meat. It should be slipping off the bone. If not, give it another 15 minutes.

Now start your kale gremolata (see below).

When the meat is done, remove from the oven and stir in the parsley leaves.

Serve with the kale gremolata and either mash or a simple butter and parmesan risotto flavoured with a few strands of saffron.

KALE GREMOLATA

Throw the kale stalks into a small pan with some hot oil and butter. Fry. When the stalks have softened (about 5 minutes) throw in the kale leaves. Turn down the heat. Pop on a lid. Give the pan a good shake every few minutes until the kale looks glossy and very green. This will take about 5 minutes. Throw in the sliced garlic and toss. Cook for 2 minutes. Remove to a warm serving dish and keep warm in the oven until serving.

Just before serving with the osso buco, grate over the remaining zest of the Meyer lemon and add a good squeeze of the juice. Squeeze the other half of the Meyer lemon over the osso buco pot.

SERVES 6

100 g butter

2 tablespoons olive oil

2 carrots, cut into 2 cm chunks

3 celery stalks, cut into 1 cm dice

2 large brown onions, cut into 1 cm dice

3 garlic cloves, crushed

1 bunch flat-leaf parsley, leaves chopped and stalks reserved

800 g veal shank (with good marrow in the bones), cut crosswise into steaks

flour

salt flakes

125 ml (½ cup) cup red wine

2 × 400 g cans crushed tomatoes

1 bay leaf

500 ml (2 cups) beef stock

freshly ground black pepper

2 × 2.5 cm pieces of zest from a Meyer lemon (you'll need the lemon for the gremolata too)

KALE GREMOLATA

1 bunch kale, well washed, stalks cut into 1 cm pieces and leaves cut crossways into 2 cm-wide strips

olive oil

butter

2 garlic cloves, finely sliced

zest and juice of 1 Meyer lemon

'THE DESSERT, IF BY THAT WORD BE UNDERSTOOD THE AGREEABLE MINGLING TOGETHER OF CAKES, OF FRUITS, AND SWEETMEATS, IS AN ITALIAN INVENTION. IT WAS CRADLED IN THE SWEET SOUTH, AND IS THE OFFSPRING OF BEAUTIFUL GARDENS, AND FLOURISHING CITIES AND TOWNS, CLUSTERING WITH GRAPES AND PEACHES. A DESSERT SHOULD, ABOVE ALL THINGS, BE SIMPLE'

Andrew Valentine Kirwan, 1864

DESSERTS

ICE CREAM PEANUT BUTTER SANDWICH

HACK

We all have our guilty secrets in the kitchen; things that we shouldn't do but, for a number of reasons, we do do. Doobie, doobie, do! Mine revolve around cheesy packet snacks and peanut butter. My love affair with junky chips, however, is but a snog behind the bike sheds when compared to the Romeo and Juliet–sized love (and lust) affair I have had with peanut butter over the years.

As a child I'd run home from the local bakery with a squidgy white loaf hot from the ovens burning my hands and chest, such was my anticipation of slathering thick slices with slabs of cold butter from the fridge, a nice thick layer of crunchy peanut butter and a smear of jam. Strangely, in spite of all this running, I wasn't a skinny child … Later, the heady mix of chocolate and peanut butter in US candies like Reese's Peanut Butter Cups came hand in hand with my discovery of older women – in this case, the visiting American students at my sister's school who came bearing candy.

Once I started cooking, I used peanut butter to make everything from satay sauces to slices, but it always tastes best straight from the jar. That's why I've always been thankful for my long, fast fingers that could delve into the deepest corners of the jar to chase out the last vestiges of nutty goodness and still retract before the accusing eyes of my mother/wife/children could catch me red-handed – or more accurately, peanut butter–handed.

More recently I have discovered that most of the attraction of peanut butter comes down to my slavish appreciation of the junk food trinity of sugar, salt and fat. The advent of low-salt, low-sugar peanut butter dramatically reduced its appeal. At last I felt I was free of its sticky grip – until these biscuits and this dessert.

As a homage to my first great love affair I've paired these simple biscuits with PB's old friend jam, for an ice cream sandwich that will have your friends and family regressing back to days of skinned knees, double art and an aching crush on that dreamy teacher.

SIMPLE PEANUT BUTTER COOKIES

1 cup crunchy peanut butter

1 cup sugar, plus extra for sprinkling

1 egg

salt flakes

ICE CREAM PEANUT BUTTER SANDWICH

1 jar of raspberry, apricot or strawberry jam

1 tub of decent-quality vanilla ice cream

8 peanut butter cookies (above)

TIP

Break the biscuits up and serve as part of a layered trifle with vanilla ice cream, fresh berries and a raspberry coulis.

Preheat the oven to 190°C.

To make the peanut butter cookies, mix all the ingredients together.

Using a dessertspoon and fingers dipped into a little bowl of water, shape nuggets of the mixture into decent walnut-sized balls. Lay these balls on a greased or baking paper–lined baking tray.

Press down with a wet fork. Sprinkle with salt and a little extra sugar.

Bake in the oven for 10–12 minutes, or until golden brown on the edges.

Let the biscuits cool on the baking tray until firm enough to ease off and put onto a cooling rack.

ICE CREAM PEANUT BUTTER SANDWICH

Spread 4 cookies thickly with your favourite jam.

Load with a pat of vanilla ice cream.

Place the second biscuit on top. Press together. Serve.

Repeat, if you and your guests are feeling greedy.

MAKES 8 BISCUITS (4 SANDWICHES)

INDIVIDUAL BLACK FOREST MERINGUES

I've had a long-running obsession with hybridising the Black Forest gateau with other classic desserts. My first attempt, the rather embarrassing 'Black Forest meringue-en-bouche', remains online complete with a particularly unappealing picture (please don't google it). It is as if, like Dr Frankenstein, I mocked God and so God has mocked me by ensuring that my creation will live on in the ether long after I've gone. These Individual Black Forest Meringues are a far more alluring proposition – even if the name isn't nearly as good!

180 g dark chocolate

5 egg whites

250 g caster sugar

250 g cherries in kirsch, pitted,
**   3 tablespoons kirsch reserved**

500 ml (2 cups) cream

20 g flaked almonds, toasted

Preheat your oven to 120°C. Line two baking trays with baking paper.

Roughly chop 80 g of the chocolate, melt it over a double boiler and leave to cool.

Beat the egg whites to soft peaks then slowly add the sugar bit by bit until the sugar has dissolved and the mixture is stiff and glossy. Test the mix by rubbing a little between your fingers. If you can feel any grains of sugar, keep beating.

Now, pour the cooled but still runny chocolate over the meringue and, using a palette knife or spatula, swirl the chocolate around a couple of times, being careful not to blend it with the meringue. You want it to streak through.

Spoon three large rounds of the meringue onto each of the prepared baking trays. Then, using the back of the spoon, scoop out the centre of each one to create a well. Pop the tray into the oven and bake for about 1 hour. Remove from the oven and allow to cool completely.

When you are ready to serve, melt another 50 g of the chocolate over a double boiler and mix with the 3 tablespoons of kirsch to make a sauce. Leave it to cool a little.

Grate the remaining chocolate. Whip the cream and divide it between the meringues. Drain the cherries and place on top of the cream. Garnish with some chocolate sauce, a smattering of the toasted almonds and the grated chocolate and serve.

SERVES 6

3 ways with ICED LOLLIES FOR GROWN-UPS

First we had the muffin, then the cupcake and then the cake pop. Right now there is nothing more on-trend than making your own iced lollies – whether as a healthy, additive-free treat for the kids, or something decadent (but equally unadulterated) for yourself. Here are three of my favourites.

1. RASPBERRY, LIME AND GINGER BEER

2 tablespoons icing or caster sugar

juice of 2 limes

200 g raspberries, frozen or fresh

about 320 ml ginger beer, left to go flat (otherwise it'll expand out of the mould when freezing)

Dissolve 1 tablespoon of the sugar in the lime juice.

Dissolve the remaining tablespoon of sugar in the raspberries and mash or blitz to combine.

Fill the tip of each iced lolly mould with a touch of lime juice, then place in the freezer. When the juice is frozen, add the blitzed raspberries. Freeze this before topping up with the ginger beer and returning to the freezer.

MAKES 4

TIP For an adult touch, add vodka to the raspberries.

2. HONEY, ALMOND MILK, WHITE CHOC AND PISTACHIO

1 tablespoon honey
400 ml sweetened almond milk
200 g white chocolate, melted
3 tablespoons pistachio kernels, finely chopped

In a saucepan, gently heat the honey until it is runny. Add the almond milk and stir over the heat just to ensure the honey infuses into the milk. Remove from the heat and allow to cool. Pour into iced lolly moulds and freeze.

When ready to eat, melt the white chocolate in the microwave or over a double boiler. Allow to cool down a bit. Unmould the iced lollies. Dip the top third in white chocolate or drizzle it over the top. Working quickly, press nuts into the melted chocolate before it sets. Eat straight away or re-freeze for later.

MAKES 4

3. PINEAPPLE AND COCONUT

200 ml coconut milk
70 ml milk
1 × 440 g can crushed sweetened pineapple, drained, juice reserved (you'll have some pineapple left over, so use it in a smoothie or quadruple this recipe for more delicious iced lollies!)

Pour the coconut milk, milk, 100 g of the crushed pineapple and 100 ml of the pineapple juice into a tall vessel. Using a stick blender or mini processor, blitz to combine.

Pour the pineapple–coconut milk to the three-quarter mark of your moulds. Freeze these before topping the level up with the reserved pineapple juice, to create a striped effect.

MAKES 4

AN ALL GROWN-UP LEMONGRASS JELLY

I have a thing for jelly. It is simultaneously funny and sexy. Usually, however, it's too sweet and the flavours are too artificial. This is not that sort of jelly. This is an elegant jelly; the sort that you could take to a posh restaurant and it would know its way around the European page of the wine list, or talk knowledgably with your posh friends about the latest Balkans crisis and the complex duology of Malevich's later work. Pretty as a picture, it would have them transfixed with both its shimmering beauty and its exotic sophistication. Heck, sounds an awful lot like dating me, well apart from … hmmm … well, apart from all of it!

3 large stalks lemongrass, white parts only, chopped and bruised

30 g palm sugar

2 kaffir lime leaves

250 ml (1 cup) cold water

1 × 750 ml bottle ginger beer

8 gold-strength gelatine leaves

TO SERVE

4 scoops coconut ice cream (for a simple recipe see page 266)

1 mango, thinly sliced

PRALINE

½ cup caster sugar

1 tablespoon water

2 kaffir lime leaves, finely shredded

Place the lemongrass, palm sugar, kaffir lime leaves and cold water in a clean saucepan. Agitate the contents to help release the flavours into the water.

Bring to the boil, then reduce to a simmer. Continue simmering for about 5 minutes – the liquid will reduce a bit.

Now add the bottle of ginger beer. Bring the mixture back to the boil, then turn down and simmer for another 10–15 minutes. Strain the liquid through a fine sieve.

Soak the gelatine leaves in cold water for a couple of minutes until soft, then wring the water out with your hands. Add the gelatine leaves to the hot liquid and stir to dissolve. You will be left with about 800 ml liquid.

Line a plastic container (or containers) with two layers of plastic wrap. Pour in the liquid to fill the container 2.5–3 cm deep and allow to set in the fridge. This will take about 4–5 hours.

Now, make your praline. In a clean saucepan, dissolve the sugar in the water over low heat. Turn up the heat a little and continue to cook until you have a light golden toffee.

Pour onto a baking tray lined with baking paper and quickly scatter over the shredded kaffir lime. Leave to set before breaking into shards or chopping into a toffee crumble.

Remove the jelly from the container once set and cut it into cubes. Arrange over four plates and serve each with a scoop of coconut ice cream, some fresh mango and a scattering of praline shards.

SERVES 4

TIP

Try adding cubes of this lemongrass jelly to the top of a pavlova with chunks of pineapple or slices of mango, or serve with the coconut panna cotta on page 307.

FUDGY CHOCOLATE TART
with WHITE CHOCOLATE NOODLES

Every cookbook needs a chocolate tart. This one is rather nice because it has a fudgy base and pretty white chocolate squiggles that add some crack against the rich velvetiness of each mouthful. That's an idea I nicked from Laura and Georgia from season six of *MasterChef*. They were a little obsessed with piping melted white chocolate into iced water to make crunchy white chocolate noodles. It's a lot of fun; try it yourself. You can make twigs, branches or even fine lacy latticework to add to desserts. Even sillier is to mix in 100s and 1000s or even popping candy to thicker applications!

TART CASE
200 g plain flour

2 tablespoons cocoa powder

80 g icing sugar

100 g butter, plus extra for greasing

100 g (1 cup) ground almonds

2 egg yolks

1½ tablespoons iced water

FILLING
300 g milk chocolate

200 g cream

30 g butter, diced

WHITE CHOCOLATE NOODLES
150 g white chocolate

2 litres (8 cups) iced water

TIP

For a more sculptural form to top your tart, just pipe white chocolate noodles into the iced water and place a jumble of them straight onto the tart before serving.

To make the tart case, place the flour, cocoa powder, icing sugar and butter in a food processor and pulse until the mixture resembles coarse breadcrumbs. Add the ground almonds and combine. Add the egg yolks and then add the water a little at a time until the dough begins to combine. Tip the dough onto a clean surface and bring quickly together to form a disc. Wrap in plastic wrap and refrigerate for 2 hours.

Preheat your oven to 170°C. Grease a 21 cm tart ring or fluted tart case with butter. Roll out your dough to about 5 mm thick and quickly line the tart ring and transfer to your baking tray. Place in the refrigerator for 15 minutes and then bake in the oven for 15 minutes. Remove and leave to cool completely.

When your tart case is cool, chop the chocolate into small pieces and place in a clean bowl. Bring the cream to the boil and then pour it over the chocolate. Leave for a few minutes to melt then, using a wooden spoon, stir in small circles from the centre until the chocolate begins to amalgamate with the cream. Continue stirring until all the chocolate and cream have combined. Add the butter and combine. Pour into the tart case and place in the refrigerator to set for at least 2 hours.

To make the white chocolate noodles, put the white chocolate into a bowl over a small saucepan of boiling water and leave to melt, making sure the bowl does not touch the water. Remove the chocolate from the heat when it is about 90 per cent done and set aside to allow the rest of the chocolate to melt. Give it a stir and pour into an empty squeeze bottle or a piping bag with a fine nozzle. Pour the iced water into a bowl about the same circumference as your tart, and begin to squeeze the chocolate evenly into the water to form a lacy pattern the same shape and size as your tart (the chocolate will harden as it hits the icy water and then float to the surface). Make sure the chocolate is not too thin in parts. When you have created a disc shape, carefully lift it out, place it onto a non-stick baking tray or a large plate and put it in the freezer to harden. When it is quite firm, gently pat the disc dry and place it upside down on your tart.

Remove the tart from the refrigerator about 40 minutes before serving.

SERVES 8

Mulled Wine Pears

There are few things that say winter to me as eloquently or evocatively as mulled wine, glühwein or glogg. At the same time, red wine-poached pears are the perfect winter dessert. So why not marry the two and drape the hot pear with a fat slice of rich brie that will gently melt over it? This is a far classier alternative to a dollop of cream and plays on the top restaurant idea of what they like to call a 'composed cheese course'. This is basically a cheese-based dish that combines sweet and savoury elements.

Place the wine, sugar, spices and honey in a saucepan just large enough to hold the pears. Bring to the boil and stir to dissolve the sugar.

Add the pears, top up the pan with water if you need to cover the pears and bring to a simmer.

Cut a circle of baking paper the size of the pan, cut a small circle in the middle and place it over the pears. (This is to slow down the reduction of liquid.) Simmer the pears over a low heat for an hour.

Remove the pears and the baking paper from the wine and set aside. Turn up the heat and continue to reduce the wine to a thick syrup.

Serve the pears with a slice of brie and some of the syrup.

SERVES 4

750 ml (3 cups) red wine, such as merlot or shiraz

100 g raw sugar

4 star anise

1 teaspoon ground cinnamon

2 cloves

2 tablespoons honey

4 beurre bosc pears, peeled, stalks left on

slices of brie, to serve

SOUR CHERRY *and* COCONUT RIPE SUNDAE

HACK

I sometimes think that the only reason my mother visits Australia is to top up on two things – Cherry Ripes and the coconut ice cream at Longrain. Slightly miffed by this, I thought it might be fun to combine the two in an ice cream sundae that might make *me* the centre of attention on her next trip. Fingers crossed! To be honest, this recipe was also a chance to play with my favourite 'instant ice cream' technique in a new way and to marry it to a great and stupidly simple chocolate sauce that sets hard when poured over cold ice cream like magic. Just don't tell my mum!

CHERRY ICE AND CHERRY SYRUP

1 × 680 g jar of pitted morello cherries, drained, syrup reserved

70 g sugar

2 egg whites

splash of cabernet or port for an adult touch (optional)

COCONUT ICE CREAM

400 ml coconut milk (not cream)

200 ml sweetened condensed milk

2 egg whites

ICY MAGIQUE

220 g good-quality, dark chocolate buttons

120 g coconut oil

ASSEMBLING THE SUNDAE

8 scoops of cherry ice cream

8 scoops of coconut ice cream

1 bottle of icy magique

cherry syrup

24 fresh cherries, halved and pitted (optional)

coconut flakes (optional)

TIP

If you are in a hurry, you can skip the perfectly frozen scoops and serve your ice cream straight from the freezer. The coconut ice cream will start melting quickly though.

CHERRY ICE AND CHERRY SYRUP

Place the cherries in a large ziplock bag, seal and press them so they flatten out and crack a little. (Otherwise they'll just rattle around like marbles in the food processor when you come to blend them later.)

Freeze the cherries for at least 8 hours. Also place a metal baking tray in the freezer – this isn't essential but it will make for a classier result.

At least an hour before you want to eat the ice cream, make it! Place the frozen cherries in the food processor with the sugar. Blitz until they become an icy crumb. Now add the egg whites with the blades still turning. The blades will whip the eggs, the cherries will flavour it and the cold will freeze everything into a smooth lactose-free gelato. Place 8 or so scoops of the cherry ice cream on the chilled baking tray and return to the freezer to firm up.

To make the cherry syrup, pour the reserved cherry juice into a pan and gently cook it until syrupy, about 10 minutes. Cool. Note that the syrup will thicken when it cools so don't reduce it too much. Think syrup, rather than treacle.

COCONUT ICE CREAM

Pour the two 'milks' into a large ziplock bag or clean plastic take-away container. Stir together. Freeze for at least 8 hours.

At least an hour before you want to eat the ice cream, make it! Roughly break up the frozen milk and place in the food processor. Blitz until it becomes an icy crumb. Now add the egg whites with the blades still turning. The blades will whip the eggs, the coconut will flavour it and the cold will freeze everything into a smooth, sweet ice cream. Place 8 or so scoops of the coconut ice cream on the chilled baking tray and return to the freezer to firm up.

ICY MAGIQUE

Melt the chocolate and oil together in a small pan over low heat until combined. Pour into a bottle or canister, ready for sundae assembly. If the sauce hardens up in the bottle it can always be re-liquefied by placing the container in warm water.

To assemble the sundae, pile 2 scoops of each flavour ice cream onto 4 chilled plates and throw some fresh cherry halves on top. Drizzle over a little of the cherry syrup.

Drizzle on the icy magique at the table and sprinkle with coconut flakes if using.

SERVES 4

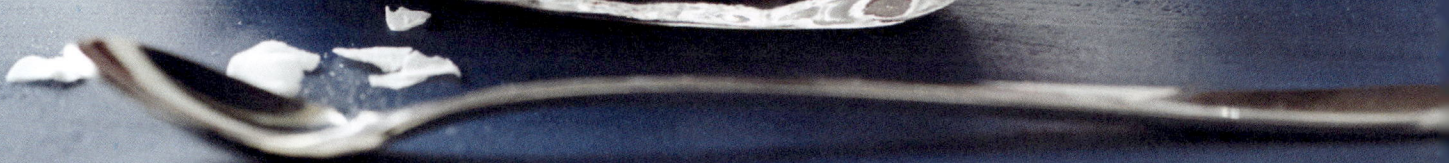

Stone Fruit Snowdrift

Here's another brilliant new idea of mine ... that I've discovered was actually was invented 500 years ago! In the *Propere Newe Booke of Cokerye*, printed in 1545, there is a recipe for a sweetened white cream folded together with whipped egg whites and a little rosewater called 'A Dyschefull of Snow'. The only way to explain this odd coincidence is that I was a feast-loving Elizabethan noble in a previous life. That would also explain my love of doublet and hose. And why this dish reminds me of you, as chaste as unsunned snow.

½ cinnamon stick

½ star anise

4 allspice berries

1 clove

2 tablespoons caster sugar

8 apricots, quartered

4 peaches, quartered

6 plums, quartered (or any combination of stone fruit that takes your fancy)

zest of 1 lemon

2 tablespoons honey

300 ml cream

200 ml plain yoghurt

2 egg whites

a few rosemary leaves, to serve

Preheat your oven to 200°C.

Use a mortar and pestle to grind the spices and mix with the sugar.

Lay the cut fruit, skin-side down, on a baking tray. Sprinkle over the sugar-and-spice mix and lemon zest, drizzle over the honey and bake in the oven for 10 minutes until firm but now nicely oozy and caramelised.

While the fruit is in the oven, whip the cream and yoghurt together until soft and billowing, being careful not to over-whip.

In another bowl, whip the egg whites to soft peaks. Add the whipped whites to the cream mixture, gently lifting from the bottom of the bowl and cutting them in to keep the mixture light and fluffy.

To serve, arrange a selection of the stone fruits in low serving bowls and generously spoon over the caramelised juices. Using a large spoon, drape the cream over the fruit. You want the colour to peek out from under the cream as if it's been snowed on. Finally, add a delicate smattering of small rosemary leaves to mimic pine needles.

SERVES 6–8

TIP

You can use tiny fronds of dill, instead of the rosemary, to suggest pine needles. Or even pine needles! But do not eat them; just enjoy the fragrance.

APRICOT CHEESECAKE *with* *a* SPICED BASE

There are certain flavour combinations that resonate more intensely with me than others. Cardamom and apricot is one of these. Make it part of a cheesecake with a biscuit base that's 50 per cent gingernut biscuits and we have something rather special on our hands. Subtle but special. I want to say 'elegant' here but I suspect that I've already used that word far too much in this book. The thing is, my brief to myself for the food in this tome was to be somewhere between a country kitchen, a cool beach shack and a slightly dishevelled and disreputable gentleman's club: all faded elegance and barely whispered scandals. The woman I love tells me to stop being a pretentious idiot and that this is 'only a cookbook' and not some work of great literature. I suspect we can all agree that she has a point.

Preheat the oven to 160°C. Line the base and sides of a 23 cm springform cake pan with baking paper.

Finely grind the biscuits in a food processor along with the sugar and the ground cardamom. Stir the melted butter into the crumbs until combined. Press the crumbs evenly and firmly into the prepared tin and bake in the oven for 12 minutes. Allow to cool.

Soak the gelatine leaves in cold water and then dissolve in the boiled water and leave to cool. If using powdered gelatine, dissolve in the hot water and allow to cool.

Beat the cream cheese with the lemon zest until soft and smooth, add the gelatine and mix through. Now add the condensed milk and continue beating until combined. In a separate bowl, beat the egg whites to soft peaks and fold gently through the cream cheese mixture. Pour the cheese mixture over the base and refrigerate until set.

Place the apricot jam, the 2 tablespoons of brown sugar and the Grand Marnier in a small saucepan and stir to mix. Bring to the boil and simmer for a few minutes until the sauce has thickened. Turn off the heat and add the orange blossom water and the apricots and stir to coat the fruit.

When the fruit is cool, remove the cheesecake from the cake pan and place onto a serving plate. Pile the apricots on top in a mound. Drizzle with some syrup and sprinkle with the chopped macadamias. Enjoy!

SERVES 8–10

BASE

150 g sweet biscuits (½ gingernut, ½ Marie biscuits)

40 g brown sugar

¼ teaspoon ground cardamom

60 g unsalted butter, melted

FILLING

3 gold-strength gelatine leaves (or 9 g powdered gelatine)

30 ml boiling water

500 g cream cheese, at room temperature

zest of 1 lemon

320 g sweetened condensed milk

2 egg whites

TOPPING

2 tablespoons apricot jam

2 tablespoons brown sugar

50 ml Grand Marnier or Cointreau

1 teaspoon orange blossom water

4 fresh apricots, sliced into quarters

40 g macadamias, chopped

PRETENTIOUS WINE TIP

Serve with a chilled glass of Mr Rigg's Sticky End Viognier or an older bottle of De Bortoli Noble One Botrytis Semillon.

COCONUT JELLIES

Sometimes recipes are an expression of cultural pride. Sometimes they are an artistic interpretation that teaches you something new about an ingredient or a flavour. Sometimes they aren't either of those things. This recipe is colourful and silly, and valued for those reasons alone.

This recipe uses brown coconuts, which are those hairy ones with the husk removed that line old-world coconut shies at fairs in forties musicals. It also uses clear coconut water, which is really rather trendy, so maybe play that card if making these jellies for a kids' party where worthy, New Age parents might be present.

3 brown coconuts

1 litre clear coconut water

9 gold-strength gelatine leaves

about 80 g sugar

food colouring

To split your coconuts, place one of the coconuts in the palm of your hand and, using the blunt side of a heavy mallet, hit the coconut around its circumference until you make a crack. Continue around the whole coconut until you meet the other side. At this point you can prise the two halves apart. Discard the contents.

When you have all your coconuts ready, fill each half with water and pour into a bowl to measure the total volume of clear coconut water you will need. Round up to the nearest 100 ml and add another 200 ml for good measure. Rinse each half with warm water and wipe the insides with paper towel to dry them.

Measure out the coconut water and bring it to a simmer in a saucepan. Add the sugar to taste if your coconut water is unsweetened. Allow the sugar to dissolve and then turn off the heat.

You will need 1 gelatine leaf for every 100 ml of liquid, so if you have 1 litre of coconut water you will need 10 gelatine leaves. Soak the gelatine leaves in cold water for a few minutes until soft then squeeze them out and add to the hot coconut water and stir to dissolve completely.

Leave the liquid to cool before adding your food colouring. Measure enough of the liquid to fill one or two of your coconut halves, pour into a white bowl and colour it to your liking. Sit each coconut half in a small jar or similar container and fill with the coloured liquid, then place in the refrigerator. Repeat with the rest of the coconuts, using different colours if you like. Leave them to set for about 3 hours.

MAKES 6

TIP

Other alternatives to coconut water are fruit juice (fresh or bought), cordial (gourmet or home-made) or lemonade. The rule of 1 gelatine leaf to every 100 ml of liquid should work for a firm-set jelly, or, if using powdered gelatine, use ½ a heaped teaspoon for every 100 ml of liquid.

LUCY'S GRANNY'S LEMON MOUSE

My grandmother, who wasn't a very good cook, lived in a house surrounded by woods and fields. It was perhaps no surprise, then, when we discovered a dormouse nesting in her pantry. To kids who maybe weren't too goot wid spelin' this gave a slightly ominous edge to her signature dessert, a tangy, fluffy cold-set lemon mousse. It was delicious and only very occasionally contained any mouse. Sadly, she took the recipe with her when she went.

I thought I'd never taste it again until Lucy Wallrock, one of our *MasterChef* contestants in 2013, knocked up almost exactly the same dish. Tasting it was like one of those moments in a movie where the image goes all wavy and blurred at the edges and suddenly we're thrust back 40+ years. I'm there in my cowboy suit, six guns stowed politely on the sideboard, as I pour a little 'top of the milk' on a decent scoop of this lemon-scented set foam. I can see the large, ridged, high-sided round white ceramic dish she'd always use. I can feel the bubbles in the mousse popping on the roof of my mouth and taste that special deliciousness that comes from combining creaminess with lemon. All that has changed is the continent and the century. Oh, and me a little bit – although I do still like dressing like a cowboy, obviously.

This is Lucy's own granny's recipe for lemon mousse. It doesn't contain any mouse either. Paradise Lost! Paradise Regained!

2 eggs, separated

150 g caster sugar

zest and juice of 1 lemon (you'll need 40 ml or 2 tablespoons)

40 ml (2 tablespoons) cold water

2 gold-strength gelatine leaves

200 ml cream

Place the egg yolks, sugar and lemon zest in an electric mixing bowl and whisk until light and fluffy.

Gently heat the lemon juice in a pan over a low heat, then add it to the egg and sugar mixture and continue whisking until the mixture reaches ribbon stage. This will take about 15 minutes.

Pour the cold water into a bowl and add the gelatine leaves (you may need to break these up). Place the bowl over a saucepan filled with a little water and gently heat until the gelatine has dissolved.

Meanwhile, whip the cream to soft peaks and fold into the lemon mixture. Then fold in the softened gelatine, along with its soaking water.

Whisk the egg whites to stiff peaks and fold these into the mixture as well.

Divide the mixture equally between 4 ramekins, or other small dishes, and place in the fridge until set. This should take about an hour.

Serve with a soft curl of whipped cream and a sprinkling of lemon zest.

SERVES 4

TIP

If you want the mousse to sit up above the top of the ramekins, before pouring in the mousse, wrap some greased baking paper a few centimetres taller than the ramekin around the outside of the ramekins and secure tightly ('an elastic band works for me,' says Lucy). Pour the soufflé mixture in to about 0.5–1 cm above the rim of the ramekin. Remove the paper before serving.

WHITE CHOCOLATE *and* HAZELNUT BLONDIE *with* WHIPPED CREAM, VANILLA SYRUP *and* GRAPES

I know lots of blokes called 'Brownie' but there can only ever be one woman who answers to the name 'Blondie'. In homage to one of my earliest crushes, this is basically a 'brownie' made without chocolate or cocoa. This recipe uses skimmed milk powder to get even more of the milk solids that taste deliciously brown buttery, without adding extra butter. This, I fear, is the only measure of restraint shown in this recipe, which is a mash-up of an Eton mess and a brownie. I suppose that it is really a 'whitie' or a 'caramelly' but I never had a crush on anyone called 'Whitey'.

PS. Yes, I know, white chocolate isn't chocolate, but it is still jolly good.

Preheat the oven to 190°C.

Line a 28 cm × 18 cm slice pan with baking paper. Use a piece that's large enough to go up the two longest sides. Make it stick to the metal tray by greasing the tray with spray oil first.

In a frying pan over medium heat, melt the butter and stir in the skimmed milk powder. Heat and let the butter and the added milk solids go tanned and smell nicely toasty and nutty, to make a *buerre noisette*. Watch it carefully though – it will very quickly burn once it starts to colour. Pour the browned butter into a bowl and let it cool down.

Now in a large bowl, mix the cooled brown butter with the brown sugar. Stir in the eggs and the vanilla extract.

Mix the flour, baking powder and salt together in a bowl. Fold these dry ingredients into the goopy butter and sugar paste. Finally fold in the chopped white chocolate and the hazelnuts.

Pour this blondie batter into the lined baking tray and bake for 40–45 minutes. Your blondie is ready when it starts cracking a little on the top and a skewer pushed into the centre comes out with a little of the batter still sticking to it. The batter should be moist rather than wet, however.

When cooked, leave the blondie in the slice pan to cool slightly before cutting into roughly 4 cm squares.

While it is cooling make a simple vanilla syrup. Dissolve the caster sugar in the water over a low heat. Once it's dissolved, turn up the heat, add the vanilla and let it bubble until golden and syrupy – but don't take it too far or you will end up with toffee. Take it off the heat; it will thicken as it cools. You want it to be like runny honey, so add more water over gentle heat if it gets too thick.

To serve, take a glass for each person, and lay 3 pieces of blondie into each glass. Spoon in some whipped cream to cover the blondies like a snowy blanket, drizzle over vanilla syrup, then finish with a few of the grape halves.

After making this recipe for four you'll be left with 12–16 pieces of blondie to go in the kids' lunch boxes – or yours. Score!

SERVES 4 (WITH LEFTOVER BLONDIES FOR SCHOOL LUNCHES)

BLONDIE

- 250 g unsalted butter, plus extra for greasing
- 2 tablespoons skimmed milk powder
- 275 g dark brown sugar
- 2 eggs, lightly beaten
- 1 tablespoon vanilla extract
- 250 g plain flour, sifted
- 1½ teaspoons baking powder
- ½ teaspoon salt flakes
- 250 g white chocolate, cut or broken into thumbnail-sized chunks
- 200 g hazelnuts, toasted, skin rubbed off

VANILLA SYRUP

- ½ cup caster sugar
- ½ cup water
- 1 vanilla pod, cut into super-fine shards on the angle

TO SERVE

- 200 ml softly whipped cream
- 200 g seedless red or green grapes (or blueberries), halved just before serving

·NOTE

The white chocolate needs to be cut quite large because white chocolate melts more readily than dark or milk chocolates.

IDIOT CAKE *with* INSTANT APRICOT ICE CREAM

HACK

In recent years there has arisen an internet culture of trying to scam dishes together using as few things as possible. Most of these recipes are 'pants' – the product of stoner cooks answering the sort of stoner questions that should never be answered like, 'Can we made an ice cream out of condensed milk and a can of lemonade?' The answer is 'yes', but it will never, ever replace a Lemon Lime Splice, so why do it?

Then I came across this recipe and, in a looser moment, thought I'd give it a try. It worked but it smelt pretty eggy, which is not something you want in a chocolate cake. This rather sizeable flaw was overcome by my mate George's suggestion of adding a little vanilla to the mix to mask the smell. Genius!

Like the ice cream that it is served with here, it probably shouldn't work, but it does. Which probably makes this a clever cake, actually. Oh, and it's also flourless, which is another plus!

4 large eggs

240 g good-quality chocolate hazelnut spread

1 teaspoon vanilla extract

INSTANT APRICOT ICE CREAM

1 × 825 g can apricots, mostly drained

1 × 395 can sweetened condensed milk

2 egg whites

a splash of any cream (about 1 tablespoon)

TO SERVE

50 g hazelnuts, peeled, toasted and roughly crushed

50 g dried apricots, chopped

30 g raisins or sultanas, chopped

Preheat the oven to 175°C. Grease and line the base and sides of an 18 cm springform cake pan.

In a large, clean bowl, whisk the eggs on the highest speed you have. We want them to billow up to about triple the size and this will take about 6 minutes. (This is far easier with an electric 'stand' mixer than hand beaters.)

Soften the chocolate hazelnut spread with the vanilla extract by stirring in a large metal bowl over a pan of boiling water. (Yes, you can use a microwave for this job too!). We are going to fold the softened spread into the eggs, so we want it soft so that the spread doesn't knock too much air out of the eggs.

When the eggs are pale and billowy, fold a third of them into the softened spread. Repeat the process until the eggs are all combined and the mixture is of a uniform colour and not streaky at all.

Pour the chocolatey egg batter into the cake pan. Bake for about 20 minutes – or until a skewer inserted into the cake comes out nearly clean. Don't overcook it!

The cake will look lovely and domed when it emerges from the oven, but it will collapse a little after cooling. It's supposed to do that.

Serve a scoop of Instant Apricot Ice Cream (see below) on each slice of Idiot Cake and scatter both with a mix of the hazelnuts and dried fruit. Eat immediately.

INSTANT APRICOT ICE CREAM

Pour the apricots and condensed milk into a large ziplock bag or plastic container. Squidge them together, seal and freeze for at least 8 hours, but ideally overnight.

Remove the frozen condensed milk and apricots from the freezer. Tip the contents into your food processor, breaking or chopping up any large pieces. Blitz on high speed until all the big lumps have been broken down. Now add the egg whites while the blades of the food processor are still going fast.

After a couple of minutes you'll notice the mixture start to turn pale. Magically the egg whites will start to turn the sweet apricot ice crumbs into a pale orange soft-serve ice cream. A little splash of cream can help speed up the process but it shouldn't take more than a couple of minutes.

SERVES 6–8

ESCOFFIER'S PEARS BELLE HÉLÈNE – REINVENTED *by* KATE

Paris in the late 1860s was an exciting place. Artists like Monet, Renoir and Sisley were making their first faltering steps towards what was to become Impressionism. Crossing-dressing French noblewoman George Sand was caring for an ailing Chopin in Montmartre and Victor Hugo had just published *Les Miserables*, while Baron Haussman had redesigned Paris into a city of grand boulevards – the unstated aim being to do away with the crooked medieval alleys that were too easily barricaded by the Paris mob in 1832's June Rebellion (that Hugo wrote about).

There was a looseness in the air and nowhere more so than in the streets around the toll gates that stood where the Arc de Triomphe is now. Back then, this was a disreputable area of footpads, 'cocottes' (the street walkers, not the casserole dishes!) and wild drinking holes, but like a Gallic forerunner of Harlem, St Kilda and Kings Cross, it also started to attract the theatrical set and society playboys searching out the artists' models and flirtatious 'grisettes' that frequented the area. This is the part of Paris where Dumas had set his tragic story of a courtesan rescued (aka Camille, or *La Traviata*, or *La Dame Aux Camelias*) and into which walked a diminutive young cook from Nice. It was 1865 and Auguste Escoffier had been recruited to work in a restaurant that would soon be gentrified into Le Petit Moulin Rouge.

Before his arrival the place had been famous as the hangout for the new Romantic movement, who came to eat the kitchen's famous Neapolitan stews, but it was to be here, as a garde-manger chef just entering his twenties, that Escoffier would create the first of his homage desserts that would reach its pinnacle in the Pêche Melba named for our own operatic legend. First, however, was Escoffier's *Poire Belle Hélène* – a dish of cold poached pears with chocolate sauce destined to become one of France's most famous desserts.

The dish was inspired by Offenbach's operetta *La Belle Hélène*, a saucy comedy about the seduction of the world's most beautiful woman by a prince of Troy named, appropriately, Paris. It had opened at the end of December 1864; an instant hit, it was still running when Escoffier arrived in Paris.

It was a suitable choice for, like many of Offenbach's works, this comedy is in a style called *opera bouffe* and 'bouffe' literally translates as 'food'. Furthermore, central to the operetta is Paris's decision to give a golden apple to Aphrodite in return for Hélène's love, although Escoffier chose to use a pear at the centre of his dish.

There is also an odd similarity between Escoffier and Kate, who reinvented this dish by butter-poaching the pears into a caramelly softness; both had a fondness for wearing heels in the kitchen.

50 g unsalted butter

4 firm Buerre Bosc pears, peeled, cored and quartered

100 g sugar

1 tablespoon water

100 g dark chocolate, chopped into small pieces

150 ml cream, plus extra, to serve

Melt the butter in a large frying pan until foaming, throw in the pears and leave to brown for a few minutes, then turn and brown the other sides. Add the sugar to the pan with the water, mix with the butter and leave for 1–2 minutes to caramelise. Remove the pears with a slotted spoon and set aside to cool. Reserve the caramel sauce in the pan.

Make the chocolate sauce by putting the chocolate pieces and the cream into a glass bowl over a saucepan of boiling water. Don't let the bowl touch the boiling water. When the chocolate has melted, stir gently from the centre in small circles until you have dark chocolate sauce.

Whip the cream lightly until you have soft peaks. Resist the urge to over-whip – you want a soft, billowing cream to spoon over your pears.

To serve, arrange the pears on a platter, reheat the caramel left in the pan and drizzle it over the cooled pears, then pour some of the chocolate sauce over the top. Serve extra chocolate sauce on the side, and a bowl of cloud-like cream.

SERVES 4

RASPBERRY AND WHITE CHOC NOT BREAD 'N' BUTTER PUDDING

History is a constant inspiration to me. I have, over the years, enjoyed a number of rather fine bread 'n' butter puddings made with stale croissants rather than bread. None, however, have referenced in their flavourings the apocryphal story of how the croissant was first baked by the Viennese in celebration of the end of the Turkish siege of their city in 1683. As the croissant's shape was inspired by the white crescent on the red banners of the besieging Ottomans, so this dessert takes that inspiration a step further by using raspberries and white chocolate to reference those banners some more. Or maybe I made that up just now to justify the shocking piggery of combining buttery croissants with sticky condensed milk, white chocolate and sweet raspberries. Surely you know me by now!

Preheat the oven to 180°C. Grease an oven-to-table baking dish (about 20–25 cm-wide) with a little butter.

In a large bowl, whisk the sugar, eggs, cream, milk and vanilla pod and extract together to make a custard mixture.

Arrange the croissant pieces in the baking dish, adding a few raspberries and chocolate pieces as you go. Pour over the custard until the croissants are partly submerged. Finish with a scatter of raspberries and chocolate on the top, followed by a drizzle of condensed milk (about 1 tablespoon).

Pop the dish in the oven and bake for about 30 minutes.

Remove your pudding from the oven and drizzle over the remaining condensed milk, or take it to the table. Ice cream and/or cream are delicious with this pudding too. Why not all three?

SERVES 6

TIP

Almond croissants can be used in place of plain croissants, but perhaps cut out the condensed milk.

butter, to grease dish

2 tablespoons soft brown sugar

4 large eggs

300 ml cream

200 ml milk

1 vanilla pod, chopped into fine shards

2 teaspoons vanilla extract

8 croissants, 2–3 days old, cut into 3 on the angle

200 g raspberries, fresh or frozen

180 g white chocolate, cut into chunks or buttons

3–4 tablespoons sweetened condensed milk

'AUSTRALIA DAY' PAVLOVA

As fiercely contested as any Bledisloe Cup is the debate over who invented the pav: Australia or New Zealand. This squabbling seems a little petty, given how our two countries have been through so much together. So let's bury the hatchet, agree to share the pav and celebrate with a glitter-cannon topping of green and gold fruit, suitable for any Anzac Day, or even an Australia Day weekend. You wouldn't want to put kiwifruit on there, so mint can be the green.

6 large eggs, separated

¾ teaspoon cream of tartar

320 g caster sugar

300 ml cream

1 mango, sliced

pulp of 2–3 passionfruit

1 small bunch mint, leaves picked

Preheat the oven to 110°C. Line a baking tray with baking paper and mark an 18 cm diameter circle on the paper.

Whisk the egg whites with the cream of tartar in the bowl of your electric mixer until they form soft peaks. Begin to add the sugar very slowly, bit by bit, beating all the time until the meringue is thick and glossy and all of the sugar has completely dissolved. Test the mix by rubbing a little between your fingers. If you can feel any grains of sugar, keep beating.

Use a large spoon to form a circle of meringue on your baking tray, then use the back of the spoon to make some pretty swirls. Bake in the oven for about 1 hour and 50 minutes. Turn off the oven and leave the door ajar and allow the pavlova to cool before removing it.

When the pavlova has cooled completely, whip the cream to soft billowy peaks and cover the centre of the pavlova. Decorate with the mango and passionfruit pulp, and finally dot around some mint for colour.

SERVES 8

TIP

Strengthen your pavlova's sides by smoothing round the sides with a palette knife neatly before baking.

MIDDLE EASTERN MANDARINS *with* GINGER *and* YOGHURT ICE CREAM

I have a weakness for mandarins but it is a weakness that's only in season from April to September. So set an alarm in your calendar now to remind you to try this recipe in April. You'll love it so much that you'll want to make regular dates with it for the next five months because the flavours of mandarin, ginger and yoghurt go so very well together. Serve the mandarins warm or cold depending on the weather.

2 tablespoons honey

250 ml (1 cup) water

1 cinnamon stick

2 star anise

5 cardamom pods

2 cloves

8 mandarins

zest and juice of 2 mandarins

few drops of orange blossom water (optional)

PISTACHIO PRALINE

50 g sugar

50 g (½ cup) pistachios, shelled

GINGER AND YOGHURT ICE CREAM
(Inspired by the Clarkes of Moro. I love these guys, and their books.)

3 large egg whites

200 g caster sugar

750 g Greek yoghurt

50 g candied ginger, chopped

½ cup ginger marmalade

First, make your pistachio praline. Melt the sugar in a small pan. Let it bubble and turn into a brown caramel. Toss the pistachios into the pan and stir to cover in caramel. Spread them out onto a baking tray lined with baking paper to dry.

Now make your ginger and yoghurt ice cream. Gently mix the egg whites and caster sugar together over a gentle heat. Heat to about 80°C.

Pour into a bowl and whisk for 15 minutes until you have a cold, stiff and fluffy meringue. Keep whisking and pour in the yoghurt. Whisk until combined.

Pour the mixture into a running ice cream machine. As it starts to freeze, drop in the candied ginger and teaspoon-sized dollops of the ginger marmalade. This will marble the yoghurt ice cream. Continue to churn until the ice cream is frozen. Keep in the freezer until required.

Now combine the honey, water, cinnamon, star anise, cardamom pods and cloves in a saucepan and bring to a bubble over a low heat. Simmer gently for 8–10 minutes to let the flavours infuse, and until the mixture thickens to a lovely syrup.

Take the segments from 5 of the mandarins. Using your nails or a sharp knife, peel off as much of the pith as you can. Reserve the segments.

Zest the other 3 mandarins, then juice the fruit.

Add the mandarin segments to the syrup, stirring to heat through, and poach for 3–4 minutes.

Remove the segments, add the zest and juice of the remaining 3 mandarins and reduce over a gentle heat for 4–5 minutes. Finish with a couple of drops of orange blossom water, if using.

Serve the poached mandarins on top of a couple of scoops of the ginger and yoghurt ice cream. Drizzle with a little of the mandarin syrup and top with crunchy pralined pistachios.

SERVES 4–6

Sticky Date ... Salty, Tangy Butterscotch ... V. Good

This obscenely decadent butterscotch sauce has its sweetness reined in by the judicious use of a little salt and vinegar, making it the perfect partner to sticky date pudding or even just vanilla ice cream.

Please note that, even without the vinegar and the salt (which is a very old-school tweak), this wonderful, original butterscotch sauce (that's another beautiful recipe stolen from the recipe folder next to my friend Jen's Aga stove) has inspired weak-willed men to drink it straight from the jug at the dinner table and even propose marriage.

Preheat the oven to 180°C. Butter and flour a 6-cup muffin tray.

Place the dates, tea and bicarb soda into a bowl and set aside for 10 minutes.

Combine the flour and baking powder and add a pinch of salt.

Cream the butter and sugar in a food processor or electric mixer until light and fluffy.

Add the eggs one at a time and combine well.

Now the dates are softened, mash them into the tea with the back of a fork and fold in the flour. Now add this to the creamed butter and eggs and combine.

Divide the mixture between the muffin cups and bake for 20 minutes. Test with a skewer to make sure they are cooked and remove from the oven.

While the puddings are in the oven make the tangy butterscotch sauce. Place the butter, cream, sugar and salt into a small saucepan and bring to the boil while stirring to combine. Simmer for about 5 minutes while gently stirring, letting the sauce thicken, and then remove from the heat and add a splash of vinegar and extra salt to taste. Serve hot over the puddings when they come out of the oven.

SERVES 6

180 g dates, chopped
180 ml black tea
¼ teaspoon bicarbonate of soda
160 g flour
½ teaspoon baking powder
salt flakes
60 g butter
120 g brown sugar
2 eggs

BUTTERSCOTCH SAUCE
150 g butter
150 ml cream
150 g brown sugar
pinch of salt
splash of white vinegar, to taste

LA VINA BURNT BUT CREAMY, CREAMY CHEESECAKE

In the northern Basque country of Spain they pronounce 'tx' as 'ch'. This is important to know if you are heading to the area's epicurean epicentre of San Sebastian, which is called Donostia by many of the locals. Yes, I know, it IS already confusing.

One of the main reasons to head there – other than *kokotxas* (hake throats, pronounced 'kokotchas'), *txacoli* (pronounced 'tchakoli'), Real Sociedad and the culinary trinity of Arzak, Subihana and Aduriz – is for *pintxos*. There we go again – that's 'pinchtoz', phonetically.

The narrow alleys of the old town are lined with dark, crowded bars groaning with this local take on tapas and the raucous crowds devouring them. La Vina is perhaps neon-brighter than most and unusual as it is famous for dessert rather than something singing with the seafood or salt that roars through much of the offerings of this fishing port town.

The thing is that La Vina's cheesecake – or should that be 'Txeesecake' – is so good that you need to get there first or else it's gone. It is unlike any cheesecake I've had anywhere else in the world; the surface is the glossy dark of a moonlit quarry lake in deepest night and the inside as creamy-soft as the inner upper arm of your first love.

Owner Santiago Rivera is a generous man and gave me the recipe. But, try as I might, I could never get close to the ethereal brilliance of his original. Time to call in my personal 'cake whisperer' and before you can say, 'Make mine a *kalimotxo*', she's knocked up this so-easy recipe that uses everyday supermarket ingredients to replicate La Vina's brilliant original! Nice work, Kate.

---

600 g cream cheese

4 large eggs

300 ml double cream

260 g sugar

¾ tablespoon flour

▶ BAD INFLUENCE ◀

Serve with *kalimotxo* – the drink of Spain's young and urban poor. Mix 500 ml chilled Coca Cola with 500 ml chilled cheap red wine. Serve with ice. Marvel at the way the sweetness of the cola mellows the rough acidity and tannic pucker of the plonk.
Be concerned at the way the sugar and alcohol combine in your system after a litre or so! Careful or else you'll end up '*muturrez aurrera*' – flat on your face.

Preheat your oven to 220°C. Line a 23 cm cake pan with baking paper, making sure the paper is at least 3 cm above the tin, as the cake will rise like a soufflé during cooking.

Beat the cream cheese in the bowl of your electric mixer until it's smooth and creamy. Add the eggs one at a time, ensuring that each is fully incorporated before adding the next.

In a separate bowl combine the cream, sugar and flour. When all the eggs have been added to the cream cheese, add the cream mixture and beat until your mixture is smooth and lump free.

Pour the mixture into your lined cake pan and bake in the preheated oven for 35–40 minutes. The cake will still be wobbly in the middle but if a skewer inserted through the middle comes out clean the cake is ready. Your cheesecake should have an authentic, glossy brown Basque crust on top but be careful not to let it burn.

Remove from the oven and leave to cool before removing from the cake pan.

This cake is best eaten within hours of making.

SERVES 10–12

EASY PUFF PASTRY APPLE TART

Who says you've got no time to make dessert? If you have five minutes, you do!

2 sheets puff pastry

3 small Golden Delicious or Fuji apples, peeled, cored and cut into quarters

40 g butter

60 g sugar

Preheat your oven to 180°C. Line a baking tray with baking paper.

Cut out four circles of pastry 15 cm in diameter. You can get two circles from one sheet by cutting out one circle then cutting the remaining piece in half and joining them together to make a square, from which you can cut your second circle.

Place the circles on the baking tray and prick the pastry with a fork.

Slice the apple quarters lengthways into very fine slices about 1.5 mm thick. You could use a mandoline for this.

Melt the butter and brush each of the pastry circles, then sprinkle with a little sugar.

Place the apple slices around the outside of the pastry in a circle, one slice on top of another, leaving 1 cm clear around the edge. Then make another circle in the middle of each, until all the slices are used up.

Brush a little more butter over the tarts.

Sprinkle evenly with the remaining sugar and bake in the oven for about 20–25 minutes. The tart is ready when the pastry is golden and the apples cooked through.

Serve hot with a scoop of good vanilla ice cream.

SERVES 4

CHOCOLATE MOUSSE *with* SALTED PEANUT CARAMEL

First, the myth. Inspired by an African dancer who he drew pirouetting lightly in Achille's Bar in 1896, syphilitic absinthe drinker and keen cook Henrie de Toulouse-Lautrec mixed chocolate with whipped cream and eggs to create 'chocolate mousse' sometime shortly before his death in 1901. The only trouble was that the diminutive artist of France's Belle Époque decided a good name for his invention would be 'mayonnaise de chocolate'. Eeewww!

Now, the truth. Lovely though this story is – and the word 'mousse' does have French origins – there are records of chocolate mousse being eaten in Boston in 1897 and in New York in 1892, which rather blows this romantic story out of the water.

It seems far more likely that the idea of combining chocolate with whipped eggs and cream popped up in France in the mid-1800s. Chocolate was introduced to Europe from Central America in 1585, but for the next 200 years it was famous only as a drink. It wasn't until new milling processes were invented in the eighteenth century that it was possible to make the first solid chocolate bars (rather than hard, bitter cakes) and these cocoa buttery bars only reached popularity by the 1820s. Thus those dates for the invention of chocolate mousse in the mid-1800s seem increasingly plausible. The fact that the French have always had a penchant for plain or bitter chocolate mousse is further evidence to support this timing. Milk chocolate was only invented in 1875 (by the Swiss) and the dark stuff must have already had time to take hold in this new mousse world!

Here, though, I'm inspired by my favourite US chocolate bar, the Snickers. This has already been the culinary inspiration for far more illustrious people, such as US superchef Thomas Keller and Melbourne pastry whiz Philippa Sibley. In fact, I suspect that their desserts started the whole salty caramel craze. The recipe was worked up by my good friend and esteemed colleague at *Taste* magazine, Michelle Southam. Respect!

200 g dark cooking chocolate, finely chopped

30 g butter

250 ml (1 cup) cream

3 eggs, separated, at room temperature

double cream, to serve

100 g milk chocolate, grated, to serve

PEANUT CARAMEL

155 g (¾ cup) caster sugar

125 ml (½ cup) water

150 ml double cream

80 g (½ cup) salted roasted peanuts, coarsely chopped

To make the peanut caramel, stir the sugar and water in a saucepan over low heat for 5 minutes or until the sugar dissolves. Increase the heat to high and bring to the boil. Boil, without stirring, but brushing down the side of the pan occasionally with a wet pastry brush, for 8–10 minutes or until golden (if you get any dry sugar on the sides of the pan it can ruin the caramel at the last minute by re-crystallising). Remove from the heat. Stir in the cream until well combined. Stir in the peanuts. Spoon into six 250 ml (1 cup) glasses. Place in the fridge for 30 minutes to set.

Meanwhile, melt the chocolate, butter and 60 ml of the cream in a heatproof bowl over a saucepan of simmering water. Set aside for 5 minutes to cool slightly. Use a metal spoon to stir in the egg yolks until almost combined. If the chocolate splits you can bring it back to a smooth consistency by adding water – 4 to 5 tablespoons whipped in should do it.

Whip the remaining cream to soft peaks and fold into the chocolate. Use an electric beater to beat the egg whites in a dry, clean bowl until soft peaks form. Fold half the egg whites into the chocolate mixture. Fold in the remaining egg whites. Spoon into the glasses. Cover. Place in the fridge for 3 hours to set. Serve topped with double cream and grated chocolate.

SERVES 6

TIPS

1. You can make the mousse and caramel the day before. Just cover with plastic wrap and keep in the fridge.

2. To make curly chocolate shavings, pull a vegetable peeler down the long side of a chocolate block.

CHOCOLATE CUPS FOR FRUIT OR ICE CREAM

HACK

The last year has been taken up with much debate with Messrs Mehigan and Calombaris about balloons in the kitchen. Not for parties, but because they are the perfect shape and thickness to use as a mould or a 'form'. Oooh, it's just so cool to say form. The easiest way to play in this space is to make these chocolate cups, in which you can serve fruit or ice cream. This is a cool thing to do with the kids.

12 water balloons
400 g good-quality chocolate
1 pin

Blow up the balloons. Line 1 or 2 baking trays with baking paper.

Melt the chocolate in a small bowl in the microwave or over simmering water (don't let the hot water touch the bowl, or the chocolate will get too hot).

When the chocolate is melted, dunk the base of each balloon into the chocolate.

Spoon a puddle of chocolate on the baking tray and position the balloon so its chocolatey end sits in the puddle.

Repeat with all the balloons and leave to set in a cold place.

Pop the balloons with the pin and remove them.

Expect a 25 per cent failure rate, so make more cups than you need. The failed chocolate cups can be fed to the kids.

Carefully ease the puddle (which is now a base) off the baking paper and fill the cups as you like. We used vanilla ice cream topped with smashed peppermint crisp and teeny M&Ms.

MAKES 12

TIP

Water balloons are a good size but a bit fragile. Large balloons are the most robust but lead to big cups. Small balloons are a good alternative, provided you don't blow them up too big.

MANGO TARTE TARTIN

Mangoes are one of the kings of the fruit world. We grow about 60,000 tonnes of them here every year and they are as Aussie as a stubby holder, thongs and a straggly bush beard. Mangoes are in season from September through to April and they are totally ace eaten at the beach – so you have millions of gallons of water close to hand to wash away all the juice that will run and drip everywhere. The rather fine website Foodpairing.com talks about the happy marriage between cardamom and mango, but I think that the even more successful partnership is with green peppercorns. That is the great thing about food – it's not monogamous!

Don't be tempted to use extra peppercorns. It is a weird thing that your palate needs to reset itself with non-peppery mouthfuls to ensure that the occasional peppery spoonful really sparks brightly as it hits your mouth.

80 g sugar

½ teaspoon green peppercorns

3 large mangoes, peeled and cut into slices

40 g butter

375 g store-bought puff pastry

Preheat the oven to 190°C.

Place a large cast-iron frying pan or heavy-based, stainless steel ovenproof pan over a high heat. Scatter the sugar evenly over the base of the pan and cook until the sugar begins to caramelise. It will start to go liquid around the edges. Give the sugar a swirl to even out the cooking, but don't stir too much. Watch closely that it doesn't burn. When the sugar is a nice dark golden brown remove the pan from the heat immediately.

Scatter the peppercorns over the base of the pan, then place the mango slices around the pan, making sure to cover the whole base. Roll out your pastry and trim to a circle slightly larger than the base of your pan. Place it over the mangoes like a blanket, tucking the edges in and around the mangoes so that everything is covered. Use the tip of the handle of a wooden spoon to do this, *not* your fingers. This caramel is hot.

Bake in the oven for 25 minutes, or until the pastry is a lovely golden colour. Remove from the oven and wait a few minutes. Carefully place your hand on top of the pastry, avoiding the caramel. Gently rotate the pastry a little bit. Place a large serving platter over the pan and turn it upside down. Please avoid having scalding hot caramel drip up your sleeve in the process!

SERVES 6

TIP

Do try adding some toasted pine nuts on top for extra crunch and also because Heston Blumenthal (ker-lunk … hear that name-drop?) told me they go very well with mango and green peppercorns.

POSH RHUBARB *and* CUSTARD

If I had been smart I'd have sold the naming rights to this recipe to Sydney's retail and digital marketing specialists, Rhubarb and Custard of 27 Pyrmont St, Pyrmont, Sydney 2009, +612 8524 1500. And I would have made the name so seamlessly part of the page that the advertising would have been of the most effective subliminal kind. That number again is +612 8524 1500, and ask for Helen.

Preheat the oven to 160°C.

Put the honey, vanilla pod and seeds, orange and lemon juice, orange zest and cinnamon into a baking dish. Add the rhubarb pieces and toss to coat.

Cover with a lid of aluminium foil. Bake until the rhubarb is soft but still holding its shape – about 20 minutes.

WORLD'S BEST CUSTARD

Put the vanilla pod, milk and cream in a heavy-based saucepan over a low heat.

Put the eggs and sugar into a large mixing bowl and place it onto damp cloth, so you can whisk without the bowl moving around. Whisk until the mixture is very pale and frothy.

When the creamy milk has come to the boil remove from the heat and pour slowly over the eggs while whisking continuously. As soon as all the milk has been incorporated pour the mixture quickly back into the pan and return to a low heat. Continue to stir with a wooden spoon until the mixture begins to thicken, but be careful not to bring it to the boil as this may make the custard curdle. When you can run your finger down the back of the spoon and leave a clean line the custard is ready. Remove from the heat and serve.

SERVES 4

TIP

When buying rhubarb, choose it the same way you'd choose a retail and digital marketing specialist. Look for brightly coloured, firm and upright stalks and don't eat the toxic leaves!

3 tablespoons honey

1 vanilla pod, split and seeds scraped

zest of 1 small orange and juice of ½ the orange

juice of ½ lemon

½ teaspoon ground cinnamon

1 large bunch rhubarb, trimmed, cut into 10 cm lengths

WORLD'S BEST CUSTARD

1 vanilla pod, split and seeds scraped

300 ml milk

300 ml cream

6 egg yolks

100 g sugar

LEMON MERINGUE PIE *with* ITALIAN MERINGUE *and* THE WORLD'S BEST LEMON BUTTER, WHICH IS A WEE BIT TIME CONSUMING

I have nothing to add.

LEMON CREAM FILLING

100 ml lemon juice

zest of 4 lemons

200 g caster sugar

200 g (about 4 large) eggs

250 g butter, cut into small cubes

PASTRY CASE

butter, for greasing

store-bought sweet pastry (ready to roll or in sheets) for 1 tart case

1 egg, whisked with 1 teaspoon water

ITALIAN MERINGUE

300 g caster sugar

100 ml water

150 g egg whites (about 5 egg whites)

pure icing sugar, to dust the meringue

Whisk the lemon juice and zest with the sugar and eggs and place into a large saucepan or frying pan. Cook over a medium heat, whisking continuously until the mixture begins to thicken. At this point you must cook for another 4–5 minutes, stirring constantly.

Remove from the heat and press through a sieve to remove the zest. Pour into a food processor and, while blending, drop the butter in piece by piece, until completely combined. Pour into a bowl, cover and store in the refrigerator overnight.

Preheat your oven to 180°C. Butter a 24 cm-wide × 3.5 cm-high fluted tart pan.

Roll out the pastry to 2–3 mm thickness (or use pastry sheets) and line the prepared tart pan with the pastry. Over the pastry, line the base and sides with non-stick baking paper or foil and fill with dried beans, rice or baking beads. Bake blind for 15 minutes. Take the tart case out of the oven, remove the weights and the paper, fill any cracks with leftover pastry, and lightly brush the pastry with egg wash. Bake the entire surface for another 5 minutes until golden.

Remove from the oven and, when cool, fill the pastry case with the lemon cream and place in the refrigerator.

To make the Italian meringue, place the sugar in a small saucepan, pour the water around the edge of the sugar, begin to cook over a high heat and bring to the boil. Be careful not to allow the sugar crystals to touch the sides of the pan.

Place the egg whites in the bowl of your electric mixer. Using a sugar thermometer, test the temperature of the sugar syrup and when it reaches 115°C begin to whip the egg whites on full speed. When the sugar has reached 118°C turn off the heat, then slowly pour the hot sugar over the beating egg whites, being careful not to pour it onto the beaters or the side of the bowl. Continue to whip the egg whites until the bowl is cool to touch – this can take up to 15 minutes. The meringue is now ready.

Preheat the oven to 220°C.

Pipe or spoon the meringue on top of the lemon cream and dust it with the icing sugar. Place the pie in the preheated oven or under a grill for 1–2 minutes only, just to brown the meringue. Remove from the oven and leave in the pan to cool completely before slicing and plating.

SERVES 8–10

RASPBERRY JELLY

This is one of those must-have recipes because once you've mastered it, you can use any fruit to make the jelly by applying the same method. You can also use any juice you like, for example, cranberry, grape or pineapple. Oh, and you don't need a special mould – any cup, glass or bowl will be fine.

500 ml (2 cups) clear apple juice
2½ tablespoons caster sugar
300 g raspberries, fresh or frozen
6 gold-strength gelatine leaves
fresh berries to decorate (optional)

Gently heat the apple juice, sugar and berries in saucepan over a low heat. When the sugar is dissolved, increase the heat and simmer for 2 minutes.

Dissolve the gelatine leaves in cold water for 2–3 minutes. Wring the excess water out of the gelatine.

Take the saucepan with the raspberries off the heat, add the gelatine and stir through.

Strain the liquid through a fine sieve to get a clear liquid. Pour the jelly into your moulds or cups and place in the fridge for about 3–4 hours. Decorate with fresh berries (if using) and serve.

SERVES 4

TIP

Back dog No.3 in the 4th at Wentworth Park.
Say no more.

A Recipe to Make Coconuts Wobble

I strongly believe that if you have to make a pilgrimage to go and buy something, you need to be using it for more than just one recipe. Our cupboards are full of the pomegranate molasses, farro, coconut vinegar or *trassi* that we got to make a recipe which then sit like wallflowers in the cupboard waiting to be asked to dance again. That's why there are several recipes that use pomegranate molasses in this book, and loads that use sheet gelatine. Here it brings a voluptuous Italian set to a dessert that is all about the flavours of South-East Asia – kind of like putting Monica Belluci or Federica Ridolfi in a *sabai* and a *sin*. These are Thai dresses, not my fervent hopes.

To make the panna cotta, soften the gelatine leaves in the cold water and set aside.

Heat the milk with the kaffir lime leaves and bring to a simmer, then add the sugar and stir until dissolved. Remove the pan from the heat and leave to infuse for 15 minutes.

Reheat until just before boiling point. Stir in the coconut cream on the heat until combined.

Squeeze out the gelatine and remove it from the water. Add the gelatine to the milk and dissolve completely.

Now strain through a sieve to remove the kaffir lime leaves. Pour into dariole moulds, or small ramekins or cups, and leave in the refrigerator to set for about 3 hours.

To make the chilli caramel, boil a little water (enough to cover the sliced chilli), drop the chilli in and leave for 1 minute. Drain and set the chilli aside.

Place the sugar in a small saucepan and pour 50 ml of water around the sides. Bring to the boil and give a little swirl to dissolve the sugar, but try not to let any of the sugar touch the sides of the pan.

Leave to simmer until the sugar reaches a golden amber colour, about 5–8 minutes.

Remove from the heat and carefully add another 50 ml of hot water a little at a time. This will splatter and boil up so hold it away from you.

Add the reserved sliced chilli and set aside to cool.

To serve, dunk the dariole moulds in hot water for a count of three and tip onto serving plates. Pour over some of the caramel chilli sauce and garnish with some lime zest.

SERVES 6

TIP

If you want your chilli caramel to be a little spicier, leave the veins and ribs of the chilli in – these are the hot bits.

3½ gold-strength gelatine leaves (or 9 g powdered gelatin)

1 cup cold water

400 ml milk

4 kaffir lime leaves, bruised and finely sliced

90 g palm sugar or caster sugar

450 ml coconut cream

zest of ½ lime, to serve

CHILLI CARAMEL

1 red chilli, deseeded and finely sliced

100 g sugar

A SQUEEZE *and* A KISS ...
APPLE PIE *with* CHEDDAR CHEESE CRUST

Manchego and chorizo, brie and redcurrant jelly, blue cheese and ripe pears, figs with white castello, good parmesan or young goat's cheese with honey, cheddar cheese with apples. Every cheese has the perfect foil. Even my couldn't-cook grandmother knew this. She used to enjoy her shop-bought apple pie that came in a box with a few slices of cheddar cheese and I wanted to pay homage to this instinctive culinary wisdom. If she was a character in a English comedy she'd have also said, in between every bite, 'Apple pie without cheese is like a kiss without a squeeze', and then cackled a bit. Thankfully she wasn't that much of a cliché.

After much searching by myself, pastry whiz Kate and my colleague Michelle, we tried the cheese on the pie and in the crust. Finally, Angela Boggiano's inspirational book *Pie* set us off in the right direction and we put cheese *in* the pastry itself. Our version is slightly different and, I think, richer. But the best thing about both is that the savoury, salty cheese warmth comes through after all the sweet pastry and apple flavours dissipate.

vanilla ice cream, to serve

PASTRY

320 g plain flour

80 g icing sugar

150 g butter

60 g cheddar cheese

2 egg yolks

2 tablespoons iced water

FILLING

5 Golden Delicious apples, peeled and cored

4 Granny Smith apples, peeled and cored

1 tablespoon butter

100 g caster sugar, plus extra, for dusting

1 teaspoon ground cinnamon

To make your pastry, place the flour, icing sugar and butter in a food processor and blitz until you have a mixture that resembles coarse breadcrumbs. Add the cheese and blitz. Now add the egg yolks and blitz again. Take a small piece of dough and press it between your fingers to test. If the dough is too dry to come together, add the water, just 1 teaspoon at a time, until the mixture sticks together and you can form a ball with your dough. Wrap the dough in plastic wrap and refrigerate until needed.

Now to prepare your filling, slice the Golden Delicious apples into half-moons about 4 mm thick and roughly chop the Granny Smiths into 1.5 cm pieces.

Melt the butter in a large saucepan over a medium heat and add the apples, sugar and cinnamon and cook for about 15 minutes. You will notice that the apples will leach a lot of water and you will want to cook that out. Leave to cool completely.

Preheat your oven to 180°C and butter a 23 cm pie dish.

Cut two-thirds of your dough and roll out to a circle big enough to line your pie dish so that the dough hangs over the sides. Roll out the remaining dough to a circle large enough to cover the pie. Place the apples inside and brush a little water around the rim. Cover with the lid and trim the edges. Pinch the sides of the dough to seal the pie. Use a knife to punch some holes in the centre to let out the steam while baking.

Use the trimmed dough to create some shapes and arrange on top. Sprinkle the top with caster sugar and bake for 25 minutes until the top of the pie is golden brown. Preferably serve hot with vanilla ice cream.

SERVES 8

4 ways with SPIKED SHAKES, SPIDERS AND SLUSHIES

1. LIFFEY LIFESAVER

2 cans Guinness, chilled
tub of coffee ice cream

Split the Guinness across four glasses. Drop in a couple of scoops of coffee ice cream and serve.

SERVES 4

2. PINEAPPLE SPLICE SPIDER

750 ml (3 cups) pineapple juice
250 ml (1 cup) Malibu
250 ml (1 cup) white rum
8 scoops lemon sorbet
1 can 7-Up
250 ml (1 cup) cream, whipped

LIME SYRUP
zest (green only, no pith) and juice of 1 lime
15 ml tequila
3 tablespoons caster sugar

First make the lime syrup. Mix the lime zest, juice and tequila together and measure – you should get about 3 tablespoons in total. Pour into a small pan and put on the heat with the same volume of caster sugar. Bring to the boil and cook for a few minutes until syrupy but not thick (the syrup will thicken as it cools) and the lime zest has given up some of its flavoursome oil. Reserve and cool.

Split the pineapple juice and the spirits across four tall glasses. Dollop 2 neat scoops of lemon sorbet into each glass. Top with a layer of whipped cream. Drizzle each glass with a little of the wonderfully tart lime syrup. Devour with a straw and a long spoon

SERVES 4

3. WHITE CHOCOLATE CHRISTMAS SHAKE

2 cups vanilla ice cream

125 ml (½ cup) Kahlua

125 ml (½ cup) crème de cacao

4 scoops top-quality chocolate ice cream

12 white marshmallows

100 g (about ½ block) white chocolate, grated (if you hate white choc use milk choc instead)

Blend the vanilla ice cream with the Kahlua and crème de cacao.

Split the shake across four large, cold tumblers. Pop in a scoop of the best chocolate ice cream you can find (I use Connoisseur chocolate chip.) Don't over-fill. You need to leave a couple of centimetres of leeway at the top of the glass for the marshmallow fluff.

Place half the marshmallows in a microwave-safe bowl and zap them in the microwave for 10 seconds or until they fluff up. Carefully scoop the flurry of warm marshmallow onto the first two glasses. Now zap the remaining marshmallows and scoop onto the last two glasses. Top with grated chocolate. Eat immediately.

SERVES 4

TIPS

1. To supercharge this shake add a couple of shots of frozen vodka to make it a take on the White Russian shake.

2. For a more adult twist, feel free to substitute a little grate of nutmeg for the marshmallows and grate on some really good dark chocolate.

4. DARK AND STORMY SLUSHIE

2 × 375 ml cans ginger beer

1 large knob ginger

1 tablespoon caster sugar

250 ml (1 cup) Bundy or other dark rum

Pour the ginger beer into a plastic container and freeze it.

Grate the ginger finely and squeeze out the ginger juice. Warm the ginger juice with the sugar until it dissolves. Freeze the sweetened juice.

Place the frozen ginger beer into a liquidiser with half the rum and blitz to make a slushie slurry. Smash up the frozen ginger juice into little icy chunks. Split the ginger slushie across four glasses. Pour the remaining dark rum into the glasses so it marbles the ice. Top with a sprinkling of the ginger ice. This will add the occasional disconcerting burst of ginger heat to the slushie.

SERVES 4

BEYOĞLU ROASTED QUINCES *with* CRÈME FRAÎCHE AND HALVA

For me quinces are the sexiest of fruit; all downy, nuzzle-able skin, soft curves and heavy in the hand. On the surface they are hard to get to know, but underneath you'll discover a soft pinkness that is fresh like apple and fragranced like rose (I always seem to get like this when I talk about quinces!). This dessert is inspired by the soft but dense and almost jellied quinces they sell at Sakarya Tatlicisi in Beyoğlu in Istanbul. Halva adds texture and a different, but complementary, sweetness.

Preheat the oven to 140°C.

Peel the quinces, reserving the peelings. Slice a fat cheek of flesh from either side of the fruit. This will leave a central slice about 1 cm thick with the core and seeds in it.

Carefully zest 1 lemon and then juice it. Place the quince cheeks in a bowl of cold water with half this lemon juice.

Warm two-thirds of the wine (a little under 2 cups or about 500 ml) with 2 cups of the sugar. Do this over a gentle heat so the sugar melts.

Arrange the quince cheeks face-down in an ovenproof casserole or baking pan that will hold them snugly. Pour over the warm wine and top up with cold water so the quinces are just covered, and cover the pan tightly with aluminium foil. Place in the oven and bake for 3–4 hours, until they slice like soft butter.

Meanwhile, chop the remaining cores of the quinces and put these chunks into a saucepan with all the peelings, the cloves, and the remaining juice of the first lemon. It's the seeds, cores and peelings that hold much of a quince's prodigious pectin content. Pectin is the stuff that turns fruit sugars and water into jellies. Lemon helps this gellification. Lesson over.

Cover the chunks and peelings with the remaining wine and enough water to cover. Bring to the boil. Then simmer gently for 90 minutes.

Gently strain the liquid into a bowl through a fine sieve or piece of muslin/new Chux cloth. Do not try and press the juice out – just let gravity do its work. Throw all the trimmings and cloves away.

After 3 hours check the quinces in the oven again. Are they soft enough so a skewer can pierce them easily? Are they a wonderful rich, ruby-red colour? If the answer is 'yes' and 'yes' then it's time to make the quince glaze. While you do this, pop the quinces back in the oven to cook for the remaining hour.

Pour the quince liquor into a saucepan. Add a cup of sugar for every cup of liquor, the lemon zest, and the juice of half the second lemon. Bring to the boil and simmer for 10 minutes. Remove from the heat then leave in the fridge to cool.

When the quinces are cooked, drain them and very gently lift and turn them so they are face-up. Spoon over some of the boiled quince glaze so it covers the quinces thickly. Leave to cool.

Serve each person with two cheeks of quince, loads of the extra quince glaze and a plume of the crème fraîche. Then crumble on about 25 g of halva for each plate. Add a sprinkle of mint leaves and pistachios.

SERVES 4

4 quinces, downy grey fluff gently rubbed off or washed away

2 lemons

750 ml (1 bottle) decent red wine (I find chianti gives the best colour)

about 1 kg (4–5 cups) caster sugar

4 cloves

200 g crème fraîche

100 g plain or vanilla halva

12 teeny mint leaves and 28 of the greenest pistachios, to garnish

Blackberry Fool

There's no fool like an old fool and recipes for this smooth, creamy dessert and its close relations, possets and syllabubs, date back 500 years or so. When I was a boy – which wasn't 500 years ago but sometimes feels like it – we'd scour the lanes and woods for ripe blackberries. Most went into my grandmother's legendary bramble jelly, the rest into our gobs. We never made fool because blackberry season was autumn and fool is very much a summer thing, usually made with gooseberries or the first flush of raspberries. Here in Oz, the autumns are warmer than an English summer, so a blackberry fool makes perfect sense.

600 g blackberries, fresh or frozen

juice of 1 orange

60 g (½ cup) lightly packed brown sugar

300 ml cream

500 ml thick custard (you can make your own, but premium shop-bought is fine)

6 savoiardi (Italian sponge finger or lady finger) biscuits, to serve

PINE NUT PRALINE

100 g (²/₃ cup) pine nuts

100 g sugar

Put the blackberries in a heavy-based pan with a lid. Pour in the orange juice. Stir. Place on a low heat and cook, stirring occasionally to ensure the berries don't stick. As the berries cook they will release their juice. When this happens, after about 2 or 3 minutes, stir in the brown sugar. Continue cooking for another 3 minutes until you have a jam-like consistency. Strain through a fine sieve, discard the seeds and set the liquid aside to cool.

To make the praline, toast the pine nuts in a dry pan over low heat for 4–5 minutes until golden brown. Set aside.

In a small pan melt the sugar over low heat – allow it to dissolve without stirring. Cook until it is a golden caramel, then mix in the toasted pine nuts. Working quickly, spread out the pine nut praline on a non-stick baking tray or silicon mat to cool. When the praline is cool, crack into thin shards.

Whip the cream until it's stiff. Fold in the cooled blackberry liquid, then fold in the cold custard. The fool should be marbled with blackberries and custard. Serve in glasses with shards of pine nut praline and a savoiardi biscuit with each glass for dunking.

SERVES 4–6

TIP

You could add orange blossom water or rosewater for a more exotic flourish.

'BISCUITS, CAKES AND SWEETMEATS ARE ALSO AN ACCOMPANIMENT ... IN THE TIME OF RABELAIS A TARTLETTE OR CAKE CALLED DARIOLES WAS EATEN; THERE WERE ALSO FRIANDISES CALLED RATONS, AND CASSEMUSEAUX, AND PETIT CHOUX. THE FIRST AND LAST WORDS HAVE SINCE BEEN ADOPTED AS TERMS OF ENDEARMENT AMONG LOVERS, AND FROM NURSES AND NURSERY MAIDS TO CHILDREN.'

Andrew Valentine Kirwan, 1864

TIME
for TEA

A BUNDT CAKE STOLEN FOR THE WOODIES

I'd like to call it reverse engineering. Taking flavour pairings from high-end restaurant dishes and re-configuring them for home cooking. Most successful has been this unlikely but eye-poppingly delicious combination of grassy olive oil and fresh passionfruit pulp. Daniel Patterson from San Francisco's Coi paired them with a coconut curd at his guest chef dinner at Melbourne's Attica and I was amazed at how well they went.

My take is way simpler – make an olive oil bundt cake and then douse it with more fresh olive oil and some fresh passionfruit. It sounds like such an innocuous partnership but, like the legendary Aussie doubles pairing of the Woodies, it is devastatingly good. And just like on the court, Todd is the vibrant passionfruit and Mark is the smooth and soothing olive oil, both coming together as one impressive unit.

butter and flour, for the cake pans

3 eggs

160 ml fruity olive oil

50 ml dessert wine

140 ml Passiona (passionfruit soft drink)

290 g plain flour

170 g sugar

¼ teaspoon salt flakes

2 teaspoons baking powder

¼ teaspoon baking soda

PASSIONFRUIT GLAZE

150 g pure icing sugar

2 tablespoons warm water

3 passionfruit, plus extra for serving

3 tablespoons best olive oil, plus extra for drizzling

Preheat your oven to 170°C.

Butter and flour 6 mini bundt cake pans. To do this, grease the pans with butter then spoon a small amount of flour into each one. Tip, rotate and tap the pan around until the flour coats the pan.

In the bowl of an electric cake mixer with the whisk attached, beat the eggs until light and fluffy. Turn down the speed and gradually add the olive oil, wine and Passiona.

Combine the dry ingredients. Add the egg mixture to the dry ingredients in three batches until completely incorporated. Pour the mixture into the prepared cake pans and bake for 20 minutes.

While the cakes are baking, prepare the glaze. Sift the icing sugar into a small bowl just large enough to dip your cakes into. Add the warm water, then scrape the pulp of your 3 passionfruits into the bowl and add the oil. Stir until combined. When the cakes are cooked, remove from the oven and, one by one, dip them into the bowl of glaze while still hot. Turn them back upright onto a cooling rack and allow the glaze to seep into the cake. When all the cakes are done, spoon the remaining glaze evenly over the cakes. Allow to cool.

Serve with a generous extra glug of your best olive oil around the edge and a spoonful of passionfruit pulp in the middle.

SERVES 6

SHOCK

These cakes are rubbish with cream.

Carol's Perfect Cupcakes

Moments of true perfection often arrive unannounced. A slice of sponge tasted in Betty Croxford's parlour. A peach on the veranda at Cliffy Booth's as the shadows were lengthening. And now this …

I was mucking around with some of the good women of the Victorian CWA at their annual fair when a small, golden cupcake crossed my path. This had a good, tanned crust but was completely free of any icing or decoration. I tore a bit off without thinking too much about it … Well, if all cupcakes needed a role model to look up to then here it was. Supremely light, wonderfully and gently fragrant, and with a little rough crunch around its leading edges.

Now while I know that there is a strange and almost mystical bond between some cooks and some recipes, there is certainly something divine going on in Carol Clay's mixing bowl or her fingers to make such a notable cupcake with just the usual ingredients.

For me, a cupcake is all about the cake and Carol's is supremely light and delicate, but with a good crust from the sneaky addition of cornflour. Her other secret is in the paleness of the batter, a sign of the amount of air incorporated into it, and in leaving enough headspace in the patty pan to let the batter rise.

Or maybe it is just that no cupcake has the temerity to disobey an ex-president of the Victorian CWA – especially one who set out to successfully challenge the old image of the CWA as being only about old women, craft and scones.

1½ cups self-raising flour

1 tablespoon cornflour

230 g (1 cup) caster sugar

125 g butter, softened

2 eggs

125 ml (½ cup) milk

1 teaspoon vanilla extract

CHOCOLATE BUTTERCREAM ICING

230 g butter

1½ tablespoons milk

220 g dark chocolate (70% cocoa solids)

170 g icing sugar

Preheat the oven to 190°C.

Sift the dry ingredients. Add the remaining ingredients and beat for 3–5 minutes until the mixture is really pale and almost foamy. Don't put your beaters on too high a speed, though. Carol used a double-beater hand whisk on a stand to do this. As the whisk was turning, Carol rotated the bowl counter-clockwise to help get the whisks into the edges of the bowl.

Pour the mixture directly into fancy patty pans, but only two-thirds full as the cupcakes will rise.

Place in the oven and bake for 15–20 minutes until a skewer inserted in the middle comes out clean.

Leave to cool on a cake rack and then ice.

MAKES 10–12

CHOCOLATE BUTTERCREAM ICING

In the cleaned bowl of your electric mixer beat the butter until it is light and fluffy, about 3 minutes. Add the milk and beat again until fully incorporated. Melt the chocolate in a bowl over a saucepan of boiling water then add to the butter and combine. Gradually add the sugar and beat until creamy.

ROCK STAR BANANA BREAD

Here's a secret. I made this recipe on *MasterChef*'s MasterClass. That's hardly the secret – 600,000 people were watching. Neither is the fact that this recipe came from lovely Aunty Sandy down in Ocean Grove, who actually mentored me (and I think George AND Gary too) before my first *MasterChef* audition.

No, the secret was that the *MasterChef* food team made all the 'here's one I made earlier' banana breads and muffins for the show with double the butter, due what I'd like to call a 'totally understandable administrative bungle'. They probably called it a 'talent balls-up'. I was just impressed that this recipe is so robust and forgiving in nature that it still worked! You've got to love a bulletproof recipe like this – or should that be butter-proof.

Preheat the oven to 180°C. Lightly grease and line a 1-litre loaf pan with baking paper.

Using a hand beater, cream the butter and sugar until thick and pale.

Add the eggs and bananas and mix until combined, then add the flour, bicarbonate of soda and salt, and mix until just combined.

Pour the mixture into the loaf pan and bake for 55 minutes or until a skewer inserted in the middle comes out clean.

Set the banana bread aside in the pan for 10 minutes before turning out onto a cooling rack to cool completely.

Toast the pecans in a dry pan over medium heat, tossing them for a couple of minutes. Add 40 ml of maple syrup and the salt. Continue to toss the nuts for a minute or so to coat them in the syrup, which will bubble away to nothing. Tip onto a lined baking tray and set aside to cool completely.

To make the maple butter, beat the butter and icing sugar until thick and pale, and the sugar has completely dissolved.

Now slow down your beater and add the vanilla extract. Then add 1 tablespoon of maple syrup at a time; allow the syrup to incorporate before adding another tablespoon. This is a tricky skill, so go slow and don't overload the butter.

Serve the banana bread warm from the oven, with oozy, melted maple butter and a side of toasted pecans.

SERVES 8–10

TIP

You can freeze your banana bread for up to 2 months. Wrap it well in plastic wrap. It also toasts well.

125 g unsalted butter, at room temperature, plus extra, for greasing

230 g (1 cup) caster sugar

2 eggs

3 over-ripe bananas (black is good)

260 g (1¾ cups) plain flour

1 teaspoon bicarbonate of soda

pinch of salt flakes

PECANS

½ cup toasted pecans

40 ml (2 tablespoons) maple syrup

a good pinch of salt flakes

MAPLE BUTTER

100 g butter, at room temperature

110 g icing sugar

½ teaspoon vanilla extract

60 ml (3 tablespoons) maple syrup

DAZZLER'S CARAMATT TART

I love nothing better than when I meet others who are willing to share my obsessions. Pastry chef and *MasterChef* regular, Darren Purchese, is one such fellow obsessive. I let it slip that I was keen to work up a tart that aped the flavour of the favourite chocolate bar of my youth, the Caramac, and he immediately offered his assistance. Five recipes and too many tarts to mention later, Darren called to say he'd perfected it. Thanks, Daz! Even better, it's super-simple and uses very trendy caramelised, roasted white chocolate.

200 g white chocolate, in buttons or small pieces

60 g unsalted butter

pinch of salt flakes, plus more to dress

185 g cream

6 individual blind-baked tart cases (shop-bought or use your favourite sweet pastry recipe)

200 g sour cream or crème fraîche

Preheat the oven to 120°C.

Place the chocolate into the base of a small, shallow baking tray. Pop it in the preheated oven and bake for 20–25 minutes. The chocolate will soften – the buttons slightly losing their shape – but colour only slightly on the surface, while bizarrely it will brown up inside. No, we can't work out why either!

As soon as the baked chocolate has come out of the oven, smear it and move it around using a flat-bladed implement like a spatula. You'll see a lovely caramel colour quickly start to appear in the chocolate. As the chocolate cools, smooth it out and remember the hot pan is continuing to cook it so move quickly.

You will now have 180 g of roasted white chocolate.

Place the roasted white chocolate, butter and salt into a warmed bowl. Boil the cream and pour over the chocolate. Leave to sit for a minute or so to allow the chocolate and butter to melt.

Stir with a dry metal whisk to emulsify the ingredients.

When smooth and combined, pour into your baked tart cases.

Leave to set in a cool spot. You can use the fridge if it's a warm day but note that this will impact on the pastry slightly and give you a firmer set.

Dress with a few flakes of salt and a dollop of sour cream. These will help mellow the intense sweet richness of the tart.

SERVES 6

TIP

This is a decadently gooey tart. Use wider, shallower individual tart cases for more of a set.

Mary's Kourabiethes

Mary Calombaris has become Gary's and my 'Melbourne mum'. I sit behind her at the soccer and she's always got these delicious almond shortbreads that are impossible to eat without getting your Melbourne Victory shirt covered in a fine white dust of icing sugar. 'Hey, Scarface!' is not what I want to hear echoing round the stands.

I've always loved Mary's kourabiethes, but at a recent impromptu kourabiethes taste-off, after a big dinner with Greek mates, her shortbreads blitzed the other *yiayias'* sterling efforts.

Better yet, these biscuits will keep for a month in an airtight biscuit tin lined with baking paper. That's important as this recipe makes 20 biscuits.

250 g unsalted butter (room temperature and slightly squidgy)

25 g vanilla sugar

¼ cup caster sugar

1 cup slivered almonds

pinch of salt flakes

1 cup plain flour

1½ cups self-raising flour

500 g icing sugar, for dusting (You won't use it all but it's easier to dust these biscuits with loads of icing sugar in the bowl.)

Preheat your oven to 250°C, or as hot as it will go! Position an oven rack in the lower middle section of the oven.

Wash your hands and use them to mix together the butter, the sugars, almonds and salt. Do this for about 3 minutes to cream. Mary refuses to use the Mixmaster because she believes it breaks the butter down and makes it watery. Your hands won't.

Add the plain flour and 1 cup of the self-raising flour to the creamed mixture. Using your hands, mix in these ingredients too. Stop when just combined. Work into a bound dough. Add more self-raising flour until the dough is no longer sticking to your hands but is still soft. We used pretty much all of the extra ½ cup the last time I made these with Mary.

Place a piece of plastic wrap on your kitchen scales and measure out the dough in 40 g balls. Shape these balls as you like – crescents are traditional but just leaving them as balls is fine.

Lay on a baking tray with space between them. Put any remaining biscuits on a second tray and throw these in the oven after the first batch is cooked.

Wash and dry your hands.

Reduce the oven temperature to 200°C. Place the tray in the middle of the oven. Make the sign of the cross over them three times, which always makes them turn out good. That's Mary's tip!

When cooked (about 20 minutes), place the hot biscuits on a wire rack to cool.

Pour the icing sugar into a bowl. One by one, press the icing sugar onto each biscuit, using your hands to really pack it on until the icing sugar makes a sort of white crust. Place them on a plate and dust with more icing sugar.

Repeat with the second tray when they are ready. Eat with a little καφέ! That's a Greek coffee if you haven't been to Greek school!

MAKES 20

TIP

You can roast your almonds, but let them cool before using.

CLASSIC PINEAPPLE *and* CARROT CAKE *for* DOROTHY

Where we shoot the pictures for our books is almost as important as who shoots them*. Each year we've got closer and closer to finding the right spiritual home. This year we found it.

There was something very right about shooting this book in the craft hall at the back of the beautiful 1875 Italianate villa that houses the CWA's Victorian headquarters. There was something calming about the view out over the Edna Walling–style gardens (in the rare moment when I let the kitchen skivvies take a break), and something right about using their almost Downton-like kitchens, which have been celebrating the best country cooking for 66 years.

For the three weeks we were there, State President Dorothy Coombe looked after us. It's the least we could do to name one of the dishes after her and this carrot cake, that sings with the sweet, juicy acidity of pineapple, is another country favourite that we all love. Thanks, Dorothy, and all our new CWA chums.

* Again, that's wonder photographer Mark Roper, who is really, really, really important and takes the very best pictures.

Preheat your oven to 170°C. Line a 23 cm springform cake pan with baking paper.

Sift together the flour, baking powder, bicarb soda, cinnamon and nutmeg and set aside.

Melt the coconut oil until just liquefied.

Whip the eggs and sugar together until light and fluffy, then turn down the speed and add the oil until just combined.

Add the pressed pineapple and the grated carrot to the eggs and stir to combine.

Add the sifted flour and mix through until just combined.

Pour the mixture into the prepared cake pan and bake in the preheated oven for 35–40 minutes.

Test for doneness by inserting a skewer into the centre of the cake. When it comes out clean the cake is ready.

Remove the cake from the oven and leave it to cool completely before icing.

Whip the cream cheese and butter together in your electric mixer until soft and smooth.

Add the vanilla extract, then add the icing sugar gradually to the cream cheese and whip until very smooth. You can use the icing to ice just the top of the cake or all over. Dollop a large portion on top of the cake and, using a spatula, gently push the icing towards the edges. Thick is good.

SERVES 8–10

250 g plain flour

2 teaspoons baking powder

½ teaspoon bicarbonate of soda

2 teaspoons ground cinnamon

1 teaspoon ground nutmeg

140 g cold-pressed coconut oil

4 eggs

200 g dark brown sugar

1 × 440 g can crushed pineapple, drained and pressed to remove juice

200 g coarsely grated carrot (about 4 carrots)

CREAM CHEESE ICING

250 g cream cheese, room temperature

50 g butter, room temperature

1 tablespoon vanilla extract

500 g pure icing sugar, sifted

THE WORLD'S SIMPLEST BREAD *and* BUTTER

This bread recipe, which was given to me by my friend Kareen in Perth, is brilliant because it takes minimal time, requires no kneading and gives you the sort of result that draws murmurs of approval from all who taste it. Pure genius! Make it and be amazed.

WELL BREAD

1 kg bread flour, plus extra to dust (Sshh – don't tell anyone but it works with bog standard plain flour as well)

1 tablespoon dry yeast

1½ tablespoons salt flakes

950 ml lukewarm water

NICE BUTTER

300 ml cream

300 ml sour cream

iced water

salt flakes, to taste

In a large bowl, combine the flour and yeast. Then mix in the salt and water until well combined. Cover with plastic wrap, then refrigerate overnight. Note: this is a really wet dough.

Remove the bowl from the fridge 1 hour prior to cooking and leave it to come to room temperature.

Preheat the oven to 220°C.

Line 2 baking trays with baking paper, and generously dust them with flour. On one tray, shape half the dough into a rough 30 cm log shape and place in the oven for 1 hour or so until it looks golden, and the inside sounds hollow when you knock on the base with your knuckles.

Make 6 small rolls with the remaining dough. You'll note that the form actually has a profound impact on openness of the crumb. The larger loaf is denser and has a crumb that is a lot less elastic than the ciabatta-like openness of the rolls. The larger, heavier loaf does, however, make exceptionally good toast.

Bake this next batch of rolls in the oven for about 40 minutes, or until they are golden. They're good when they sound hollow inside when you tap them. (It's such a pity this tapping approach doesn't also work on men. It could save people so much time!)

MAKES 1 LARGE LOAF AND 6 ROLLS

NICE BUTTER

Place the cream and sour cream into the bowl of an electric mixer.

Whisk until the butter fat starts to coagulate and the mixture splits. You know this is happening when you see the yellow fat separating out from the blue–white buttermilk.

Pour off the buttermilk into a separate container. Use that buttermilk later for baking. It is especially good in scones – or for soaking chicken before crumbing it for deep-frying, Southern style.

Keep whisking and more buttermilk will appear. Drain this off too and keep going until the globules of butter fat are nuggets the size of popcorn.

Tip the nuggets into a colander placed over a bowl to catch the last of the buttermilk. Remove that bowl and next pour iced water over the butter in the colander to rinse off any excess whey. To help this happen, massage the butter under the flow of icy water. Note that the temperature is important; in warm water the butter would just melt away.

Transfer your new butter to a sheet of baking paper, season with salt and roll into a log. Keep in the fridge until needed.

Serve the butter slathered on the warm bread!

Golden Almond, Pear and Maple Cake

This is a particularly moist cake that stays that way for days. I would suggest it is one of the ten most delicious things in this book, so do yourself a favour and make it!

Preheat the oven to 190°C.

Line the bottom of a cake pan, approximately 30 × 12 cm, with baking paper. Lightly grease the sides with olive oil or oil spray.

In a large bowl combine the maple syrup, sugar, olive oil, vanilla and eggs. Stir with a wooden spoon or whisk until combined. Stir in the salt, almond meal, oat bran, baking powder and cinnamon. Dice one pear into small pieces and stir it through the batter.

Cut the other pear into small wedges and arrange on the bottom of the pan in a row. Scatter the raspberries into the cake pan and pour the batter on top.

Place in the preheated oven and bake for 35–40 minutes.

Remove your cake from the oven and leave it to cool slightly. Run a knife around the inside of the pan. Place a serving plate or board over the pan, turn it upside down and gently remove the pan. Remove the baking paper.

Serve the cake warm or cold on its own, or with cream or ice cream.

SERVES 8–10

TIP

If being gluten free is important then check that the baking powder used is also gluten free.

100 ml olive oil, plus extra for greasing

2 tablespoons maple syrup

140 g (¾ cup) brown sugar (or white)

1 teaspoon vanilla extract

2 large eggs

½ teaspoon salt flakes

100 g (1 cup) almond meal

75 g (½ cup) oat bran

2 teaspoons baking powder

½ teaspoon ground cinnamon

2 pears, poached or canned

50 g raspberries, frozen or fresh

cream or ice cream, to serve

KARINA'S RIDICULOUSLY THICK ITALIAN HOT CHOCOLATE *that you can* STAND YOUR SPOON UP IN *and* ORANGE SHERBET MARSHMALLOWS

I'm sorry, I just can't look … Please tell me that the last 15 words of this recipe's title didn't fall off the page in the printing of this book. I don't want to have to tell one of the more competitive women I've ever met, and the magnificent cook who cooked much of the food in these pages, that the recipe she gave me to share through my book is now just 'Karina's ridiculously thick'. Phew, it's OK.

MARSHMALLOWS

455 g sugar

1 tablespoon liquid glucose

340 ml water

9 gold-strength gelatine leaves

2 egg whites

1 teaspoon vanilla extract

icing sugar, for dusting

cornflour, for dusting

ORANGE SHERBET

1 teaspoon citric acid

1 teaspoon bicarbonate of soda

125 g icing sugar

zest of 1 orange

THICK, ITALIAN-STYLE HOT CHOCOLATE

115 g good-quality dark chocolate (70% cocoa solids or higher), roughly chopped

350 ml whole milk

2 tablespoons sugar

2 tablespoons cornflour

Place the sugar, glucose and 200 ml of the water in a heavy-based saucepan. Bring to the boil and continue cooking until it reaches 127°C on a sugar thermometer.

Meanwhile, soak the gelatine leaves in the remaining 140 ml of cold water.

In an electric mixer, beat the egg whites until stiff.

Once the syrup is up to temperature, place the softened gelatine sheets and water into the hot sugar syrup. Be careful as the mixture will bubble up. Pour the syrup into a metal jug.

With the mixer set at a low speed, continue to beat the egg whites while gradually pouring in the hot syrup from the jug. The mixture will become shiny and start to thicken. Add the vanilla extract and continue whisking for about 10 minutes or until the mixture has cooled. It should be thick, glossy and stiff enough to hold its shape on the whisk.

Lightly oil a shallow baking tray, 30 × 20 cm. Dust the tray with sieved icing sugar and cornflour. Spoon the mixture in and smooth it with a knife or spatula. Let the marshmallow set at room temperature for about 3 hours.

In a medium-sized bowl, mix all the sherbet ingredients together, rubbing between fingertips, then set aside.

When your marshmallow is set, dust a work surface with more icing sugar and cornflour. Loosen the marshmallow around the sides of the tray with a knife, and then turn it out onto the dusted surface. Cut the marshmallow into squares and roll in the sherbet mixture.

THICK, ITALIAN-STYLE HOT CHOCOLATE

Place all the ingredients into a medium-sized saucepan. Gently heat over medium heat, stirring constantly. Continue stirring until the chocolate melts and the mixture becomes thick, smooth and oozy. Serve alongside the marshmallow squares.

Dip the heavenly pieces of fluffy marshmallow into the lush, dark, thick hot chocolate. Finish by licking the sherbet off your fingertips. I challenge you to do it without cracking into a smile. It's impossible.

SERVES 4

STOLEN APPLE, PRUNE, WALNUT and ALMOND CAKE

'No, officer, I don't know where it came from ...'

'Yes, I do have an alibi, officer. I was with Marnie, Kate, Karina, Caroline, Clare, Mark and Richard shooting the pictures on the previous pages ...'

'If you are going to dust the cake for fingerprints, then please use my icing sugar rather than your aluminum powder.'

125 g butter, at room temperature, plus extra, for greasing

170 g sugar

2 eggs

120 g ground almonds

80 g self-raising flour

125 ml (½ cup) milk

1 teaspoon vanilla essence

1 tablespoon boiling water

½ teaspoon baking powder

cream or ice cream, to serve

TOPPING
14 pitted prunes

100 g chopped walnut pieces

2 sour green apples such as Granny Smith, peeled and thinly sliced

2 tablespoons raw sugar

FURTHER TOPPING
2–3 tablespoons raw sugar

50–60 g butter

1 teaspoon ground cinnamon

Preheat the oven to 180°C. Lightly grease a 22 cm springform cake pan and line with baking paper.

Place all the cake batter ingredients in a food processor and blitz for 20–30 seconds. Pour into your prepared cake pan.

Arrange the topping ingredients on top of the batter and sprinkle over the sugar.

Place in the oven and bake for 40 minutes.

Remove the cake from the oven and, while it is still warm, sprinkle over another 3 tablespoons of raw sugar, some little knobs of butter and a dusting of cinnamon. Now pop it back into the oven and bake for a further 20–25 minutes.

Remove from the oven and serve warm or cold with ice cream, cream or both.

SERVES 8–10

PRETTY LITTLE RASPBERRY TARTS *with* ROSEWATER MASCARPONE CREAM *and* MINT SUGAR

So pretty, so delicate, so easy. These little dainties are the perfect dessert or decadent teatime treat when you are feeling so lazy that even the prospect of whipping cream seems like too much work!

Preheat the oven to 170°C. Butter and flour six 9 cm fluted tart cases and place in the refrigerator.

Make sure the pastry is very cold when you roll it out so it is easier to work with. Roll to about 3 mm thick and line each case separately. You can keep the remaining pastry in the refrigerator while you work to keep everything cold.

Line each pastry case with foil and put them back in the refrigerator for 10 minutes.

Now blind bake the cases. Fill with dried beans (or rice) and bake the cases for about 12 minutes. Remove the foil and beans (or rice) and pop them back in the oven for a couple of minutes to slightly brown the insides. Be careful not to burn them! Allow to cool completely.

To make the mint sugar, place all the ingredients in a small food processor and blitz to combine.

To make the filling, beat the egg and sugar together until very light and creamy. Add the mascarpone and rosewater and beat again to combine. Spoon into the cooled tart cases and top with the fresh raspberries. Sprinkle each with a little of the mint sugar and serve.

MAKES 6

butter, for greasing

flour, for dusting

1 × 435 g packet sweet shortcrust pastry sheets

1 egg

90 g caster sugar

250 g mascarpone

½ teaspoon rosewater

2 punnets fresh raspberries

MINT SUGAR

5 mint leaves

2 tablespoons caster sugar

zest of 1 lime

PAT'S SLICE

I have always found that pleasure leaves its scars. In the case of Pat's slice, it's likely to leave you catatonic in a sugar coma with a beatific smile frozen on your face. That is why is it essential to never eat this slice without a nice pot of tea or coffee, which is the perfect panacea.

Preheat the oven to 180°C.

Grease and line a 20 × 30 cm pan or a 24 cm × 24 cm pan.

Melt the butter and pour it evenly into the cake pan over the baking paper.

Cover with a layer of chocolate biscuits and fill in the gaps with broken pieces.

Sprinkle over the coconut, chocolate drops and almonds in that order.

Pour over the condensed milk and bake in the preheated oven for about 20 minutes.

When the slice is cool, cut it into small squares.

SERVES 10+

90 g butter, plus extra for greasing

15–20 Chocolate Ripple biscuits

90 g (1 cup) desiccated or shredded coconut

250 g milk chocolate drops

125 g flaked almonds

1 × 395 g can sweetened condensed milk

Butternut Snap Tarts

HACK

Do as I have done and make an effort to visit the great biscuit factories of the world and you will discover one key thing: that biscuits that are crisp in the packet are seldom crisp on the production line. And if knowledge is power, here's a 1000 kW idea. When you heat up some of these biscuits, like Anzacs or butternut snaps, they will become pliable again and you can turn them into little cups that will crisp up as they cool. Then you can fill them with anything from chocolate ganache to a little mascarpone cream topped with fresh fruit. We've gone with caramel here, but that's just a starting point. Add sliced banana, whipped cream and grated chocolate and you've got mini banoffee pies; add a little sprinkle of salt flakes and peanuts to the caramel, then top with melted chocolate and you've got a sort of giant Snickers pod.

250 g (1 packet) butternut snap biscuits

1 × 395 g can sweetened condensed milk

250 ml cream

Preheat your oven to 175°C.

Place the biscuits over the holes of a round-bottomed patty pan tray and place in the oven for 6–7 minutes. Open the oven door and, using a clean oven glove, push the now soft biscuits down into the cups.

Remove from the oven and allow to cool. Repeat until you have softened all of the biscuits.

Store in an airtight container until needed (the biscuits are better slightly soft so you don't have to use them straight away and they can be made a day or two ahead of time).

Place the can of condensed milk in a large saucepan full of water, enough to completely cover it by about two inches. Bring the water to the boil and leave bubbling away for about 2 hours and 40 minutes, topping up with water from time to time to keep it covered. Remove the tin from the pot and leave to cool completely.

When ready to serve, take one of the biscuits and fill with the caramel from the tin. Repeat until the caramel has been used up. Top each biscuit with a dollop of freshly whipped cream and serve immediately.

MAKES 21

CHOCOLATE CAKE

Same same but different. Serve this as a birthday cake for the kids with the drippy raspberry icing or, for adults, go the chocolate ganache route and serve it glazed with some brandy-poached orange segments or fresh raspberries on the side.

butter or oil, for greasing

100 g good-quality dark chocolate, chopped into pieces

260 g plain flour

60 g Dutch processed cocoa powder

1½ teaspoons baking powder

1 teaspoon bicarbonate of soda

pinch of salt flakes

160 g butter, soft

250 g light brown sugar

100 g caster sugar

2 eggs

300 ml buttermilk

FOR A CHILD'S BIRTHDAY CAKE

juice from ½ cup of squashed frozen or fresh raspberries

300 g icing sugar

300 ml cream

1 punnet strawberries, hulled and quartered

1 punnet raspberries, to decorate

ADULTS-ONLY CHOCOLATE GANACHE CAKE

600 ml cream

600 g dark chocolate, broken or chopped into small pieces

6 tablespoons caster sugar

Preheat the oven to 160°C. Lightly grease and line two 20 cm round cake pans with baking paper.

Melt the chocolate over a double boiler and leave it to cool.

Sift together the flour, cocoa powder, baking powder, bicarb soda and salt into a bowl and set aside.

Cream the butter and both sugars in the bowl of your electric mixer with the paddle attachment until very light and fluffy. Add the eggs one by one, making sure that each one is fully incorporated before adding the next. Pour in the chocolate and continue beating to combine. Add the buttermilk and combine. Turn the mixer down to the lowest speed and add the sifted flour mixture and continue beating until fully incorporated.

Divide the mixture evenly between the two prepared cake pans and bake in the oven for about 30–35 minutes until done. Leave to cool, and then turn out upside down onto a wire rack. When the cakes are completely cool you can begin to ice.

FOR A CHILD'S BIRTHDAY CAKE

Mash the raspberries with the back of a spoon in a strainer over a bowl to catch the juices. Discard the pulp. Beat the icing sugar and raspberry juice until smooth. Whip the thickened cream until soft and billowy and spread over one layer of the cake. Push some of the strawberries into into the cream. Place the second cake upside down on top of the cream and carefully pour the raspberry icing on top. Decorate with fresh raspberries, or anything you fancy.

ADULTS-ONLY CHOCOLATE GANACHE CAKE

For a more adult version, divide the cake mixture between three prepared cake pans and bake for 20 minutes or until done.

Make a chocolate ganache by heating the cream until just before boiling. Place the chocolate pieces and sugar in a heatproof bowl, pour over the hot cream and leave it to melt. When the chocolate has melted, stir from the centre until the chocolate has amalgamated with the cream and you have a thick, glossy ganache. If the chocolate separates during this process add a couple of tablespoons of water and stir again. You can also add liqueur for flavour. Allow to completely cool before spreading between the layers of the cake and drizzling over the top. Leave in the refrigerator to set, but remove an hour before eating.

SERVES 8–10

CARDAMOM CUPCAKES
with ROSE BUTTERCREAM ICING

I am a huge believer in the power of flowers, but there are rules:

1. Always give a ridiculously large bunch of cheap flowers like daffodils instead of a meagre bunch of posher blooms.

2. Never give flowers when they are expected. Flowers should always be a surprise.

3. If you do want to give flowers for a birthday or Valentine's Day, give a plant instead. The line approved for use here by the Florida Association of Smooth Talkers is, 'I hate the idea that those flowers are already dying, I want this plant to grow and flourish like our love; I want it to be a constant symbol to remind us, in good times and bad, of why we are together.' They'll either throw up or fall into your arms at this point.

4. Never give flowers as an apology. It is disrespectful to the flowers.

5. When you want an excuse to bail from the relationship, it is not acceptable to poison your love plant (see point No.3 above) and claim that this is a divine sign.

6. Never buy flowers from a garage, even if they look good. This tells people that there is something inherently thoughtless about you.

So anyway, here is a sweet bunch of roses for you! My favourite spice pops up in the cake batter, adding some extra exotica to these pistachio beauties and it's the perfect foil for the rosewater icing.

Preheat your oven to 170°C.

Sift the flour, baking powder and bicarb of soda together, add the ground cardamom, and set aside.

Cream the butter and sugar until light and fluffy.

Add the eggs one at a time, incorporating each one before adding the next.

Add the pistachios to the butter and eggs.

Turn down the speed of your machine and add the sifted flour mixture a little at a time, alternating with the crème fraîche and ending with the flour.

Divide the mixture between 12 patty pans and bake in the preheated oven for 15–20 minutes. Allow to cool before icing.

To make the rose buttercream icing, cream the butter in your electric mixer until white then slowly add half of the icing sugar and continue beating.

Beat in the rosewater and milk and then the rest of the icing sugar.

Add some pink food colouring to make a light pink and continue to beat until your icing is smooth and ready to pipe.

Fill a piping bag with your nozzle of choice or use a palette knife to ice the cupcakes.

MAKES 12

180 g plain flour

½ teaspoon baking powder

¼ teaspoon bicarbonate of soda

½ teaspoon ground cardamom

120 g butter

200 g raw caster sugar

2 eggs

45 g finely ground pistachios

100 g crème fraîche

ROSE BUTTERCREAM ICING

120 g butter

500 g icing sugar

2 teaspoons rosewater

2 tablespoons milk

pink food colouring

CHOCOLATE GANACHE BISCUITS

It is remarkable how something as simple as these biscuits can be quite so very good. Bake 'em and let the good times roll!

120 g plain flour

60 g Dutch processed cocoa powder

¼ teaspoon baking soda

⅛ teaspoon baking powder

pinch of salt flakes

90 g unsalted butter, very soft

40 g ganache (see below)

150 g sugar

1 tablespoon milk

GANACHE

200 g dark chocolate, chopped into small pieces

200 ml double cream

20 g caster sugar

80 g liquid glucose

First, make the ganache. Place the chocolate in a clean mixing bowl.

Pour the cream into a saucepan with the sugar and the glucose and bring to the boil. When the cream is ready, pour it over the chocolate and let it sit for about a minute to allow the chocolate to melt. Using a whisk, begin to stir your chocolate and cream mixture, making small circles in the centre until the chocolate begins to meld with the cream, slowly widening your whisk to incorporate all of the chocolate. Place in the refrigerator until cold and thick.

Preheat the oven to 170°C. Line two baking trays with baking paper.

Sift together the flour, cocoa powder, baking soda, baking powder and salt. Set aside.

In the bowl of your electric mixer, using the flat beater attachment, combine the butter, 40 g of the ganache, and the sugar and beat until smooth. Turn the speed to low and slowly add the sifted dry ingredients and the milk until you have a soft, dark chocolate dough.

Take about 15 g of dough (about a tablespoon) at a time and roll quickly into balls, placing them 4 or 5 cm apart on the baking trays. Bake one tray at a time on the middle shelf for about 12 minutes, then remove and leave the biscuits on the tray to cool completely. Repeat.

Spoon the rest of the ganache into a piping bag. Pipe some of the ganache onto one biscuit and sandwich together with another. Repeat until all of the biscuits are filled.

MAKES 16

Thank You

We'd need a much bigger book if we had to put the heads of all the people on the cover who deserve to be there. This book has been a collaborative process and would not be possible without the professionalism, enthusiasm and support of a huge ensemble cast.

Mary Small is so much more than the publisher of this book. She's the inspiration and the sounding board that always rings true. She's also very, very brave! She and the rather talented editor Clare Marshall are responsible for all the good bits of the book that you love. The ideas you think are rubbish will undoubtedly be mine! Huge thanks to them for making this book so beautiful, and to designer Kirby Armstrong, typesetter Pauline Haas, editor Margaret Barca and proofreader Lucy Malouf for helping make my words look a lot more approachable than they were. Oh, and everyone else at Pan Macmillan, including Publicity Director Tracey Cheetham and Managing Director Ross Gibb who have been so supportive of this project.

The photos are by Mark Roper, who is still the most talented, unflappable and happy photographer ever put on this planet. I am sure his assistant Rich MacDonald has something to do with that! The images were styled by the eagle-eyed superstar Caroline Velik, who worked the miracle of making my food pretty. Karina Duncan cooked much of it for the shoot and provided some wonderful ideas for improving recipes. That's her marshmallow and hot choc recipe on page 336 too. Caitlin Bell, Kelly Eastwood, Ben Sisley and Emma Warren also helped out massively. Huge thanks to State President Dorothy Coombe and all at the Country Women's Association of Victoria for providing us with the perfect location and the utmost hospitality while shooting this book. And a special word of thanks to Gary at Gary's Meats for all the advice and the magnificence of his meat!

There are, however, two people who deserve the lion's share of the praise for this book. This is the second year I've worked with Marnie Rowe and Kate Quincerot. They are my muses, my mates and my professional better halves. This year they have taken wonderful ownership of this book and it is much the better for it. I value their skills, their palates, their inspirational ideas, their precision at testing and improving recipes, and their brilliance at turning my ideas into something even more delicious than I could imagine. They question and they push and I love them for that! You'll find their names throughout this book but their fingerprints are all over it.

Along my decade-long road of recipe writing I've had many mentors and guides, but I'd especially like to thank the amazing Danielle Opperman, Valli Little and her team at *delicious.* magazine, along with the influential Jana Frawley, Simon Wilkinson and the teams who put together the magnificent Taste section of the News Limited metro papers. My life was made all the sweeter this year by having new collaborators like Michelle Southam and Brodee Myers-Cooke at *Taste* magazine, who seem to have the same appreciation for the twisting up of old ideas as I do! Then there are those leaders who have supported me over the years and pushed me when needed; people like Fiona Nilsson, Nicole Sheffield, Trudi Jenkins, Kylie Walker, Sarah Nicholson, the late (and greatly lamented) Caroline Roessler and my other great photographic collaborator, Catherine Sutherland.

Inspiration and wisdom doesn't just come from those I work with and so I'd also like to acknowledge the dizzying amount of light-bulb moments and knowledge shared by so many chefs and cooks, both here and overseas. Some like Maggie Beer, Massimo Bottura, Marco Pierre White, Heston Blumenthal, Nigella Lawson, Nobu Matsuhisa, Jale Balci, Andoni Aduriz, Tessa Kiros, Riccardo Momesso, Daniel Patterson, Darren Purchese, Gontran Cherrier, Mary Calombaris, my mother-in-law Judy Bennison, Ben Shewry, Paul Wilson, Frank Camorra, Mat Follas, Jen Clarke and Sat Bains are represented in this book, not that they're likely to spot their high level inspiration in my bargain basement recipes.

A special mention also to all at *MasterChef*, especially the contestants, who constantly surprise and inspire in the kitchen, and to the team behind it all – David McDonald, Margie Bashfield, Keely Sonntag, Michael Venables, Maurzi McCarthy, Charmaine de Pasquale, Ingrid Beilharz, DJ Deadly and Sandy Paterson – who make it the best job in the world. Oh, and not forgetting the unfailing weather vanes and living, breathing brains trust that are Gary and George. Thank you boys, for everything! I've said it before but it is still true: food is both a dialogue and a journey, and I have been lucky enough to share both of these with you. Of course the show wouldn't happen without the team at Ten, so big props to Hamish, Beverly, Russell, Rick and Anthony, who have allowed *MasterChef* to once again become a force for good food in this country and around the world.

Huge thanks are also due to my beautiful, intelligent and soulful wife, Emma, and to our three children, Jono, Will and Sadie. You are the reason I do all of this. Thank you for giving me the freedom to do what I do and for being kinder and wiser in your criticism this year. (This isn't to say there aren't a number of recipes again this year that didn't make the book due to their disapproval, but I think it might just be because there were so many more that they loved!)

Finally, a huge thank you to my other family, the beautiful and extremely smart Henrie Stride, who puts up with most of my unacceptable behaviour with a charm and professionalism that confirms what a special person she is. She is wise where I am foolish – although neither of us are virgins. OK, if you haven't had a Sunday school upbringing that is going to sound REALLY weird! Then there are David Vodicka and Yasmin Naghavi, who are so much more that my legal eagles but also confidantes, friends and the wisest of counsel; Aaron Hurle, who keeps me solvent and honest; and the dynamic duo of Charlotte James and Aleesha De Mel-Tucker, who have keep me social since the very start. By the way, you can join the 200 K+ who follow me on Facebook or on Twitter at @mattscravat. They'd like me to say that!

And do send me your shots of anything you've cooked from this book. I'd love to see them! Twitter, Instagram or Facebook are all good!

Love, Matt

INDEX

* SOME RECIPES IN THIS BOOK CONTAIN RAW EGG. CONSUMING RAW EGGS MAY INCREASE YOUR RISK OF FOOD-BORNE ILLNESS, AND SHOULD BE AVOIDED IF YOU ARE PREGNANT OR HAVE A MEDICAL CONDITION.

A PLUM BOOK
First published in 2014 by
Pan Macmillan Australia Pty Limited
Level 25, 1 Market Street,
Sydney, NSW 2000, Australia

Level 1, 15–19 Claremont Street,
South Yarra, Victoria 3141, Australia

Text copyright © Matt Preston 2014
Photographs copyright © Mark Roper 2014

The moral right of the author has been asserted.

All rights reserved. No part of this book may be
reproduced or transmitted by any person or entity
(including Google, Amazon or similar organisations), in
any form or means, electronic or mechanical, including
photocopying, recording, scanning or by any information
storage and retrieval system, without prior permission in
writing from the publisher.

A CIP catalogue record for this book is available from the
National Library of Australia.

Design by Kirby Armstrong
Edited by Margaret Barca
Index by Jo Rudd
Photography by Mark Roper
Prop and food styling by Caroline Velik
Cover prop and food styling by Karina Duncan
Food preparation by Caitlin Bell, Karina Duncan, Kelly Eastwood,
Kate Quincerot, Marnie Rowe, Ben Sisley and Emma Warren
Typeset by Pauline Haas
Colour reproduction by Splitting Image Colour Studio
Printed and bound in China by 1010 Printing International Limited

Some of the material in this book has been adapted from articles
previously published by taste.com.au, delicious. magazine or in
episodes of MasterChef Australia. At the time of writing, recipes
on the following pages have appeared on taste.com.au: 42, 77, 86,
176, 218–221, 238, 297, 310, 312, 313, 315 and 322; in delicious.
magazine: 292 and 315; and on MasterChef Australia: 256, 276,
280, 325 and 332.

The publisher would like to thank the following for their generosity in
providing props for the book: Market Import, Mud Australia, the Orient
Express, Potier and The Works.

10 9 8 7 6 5 4 3 2 1